David Lloyd George

Makers
of the
Modern
World

David Lloyd George
Great Britain
Alan Sharp

HH
HAUS HISTORIES

First published in Great Britain in 2008 by
Haus Publishing Ltd
26 Cadogan Court
Draycott Avenue
London SW3 3BX
www.hauspublishing.com

Copyright © Alan Sharp, 2008

The moral right of the author has been asserted

A CIP catalogue record for this book
is available from the British Library

ISBN 978-1-905791-61-3

Series design by Susan Buchanan
Typeset in Sabon by MacGuru Ltd
Printed in Dubai by Oriental Press
Maps by Martin Lubikowski, ML Design, London

Contents

For Jen

Acknowledgements

I would like to thank Barbara Schwepcke of Haus Publishing for the courage and vision of her original idea for these studies and for inviting me to become the series editor. Jaqueline Mitchell has been unfailingly helpful throughout as the commissioning editor and it has been a pleasure to work with them both. I am very grateful to two good friends, Professors Tony Lentin and David Eastwood, for reading my drafts and saving me from errors of fact, interpretation and punctuation. The responsibility for any remaining mistakes is entirely my own. Cheryl Cunningham has mastered new computing skills to bring all the various pieces together whilst simultaneously dispensing tea, coffee and good humour. The University of Ulster remains a congenial and supportive environment in which to work. As always my principal debt is to the tolerance and kindness of my wife, Jen, who has had to live with Lloyd George for the last few months (indeed the last 40 years). I am still not sure how to answer her perceptive question –'But do you admire him?'

Alan Sharp
University of Ulster

Lloyd George after the presentation of the Treaty of Versailles to the German delegation, 7 May 1919.

Prelude: Paris 1919

The Council of Four is debating a complex issue concerning shipping in the Adriatic and Lloyd George is eloquently arguing the British case on which he has been briefed that morning by two of his officials, Dudley Ward and John Maynard Keynes. To their horror, over lunch, they agree that they have primed the Prime Minister to propose something contrary to British interests. They rush to the meeting – too late, he is already speaking. As a forlorn hope Keynes passes him a note advising him to reverse the British demands and provides him with some points on which to base this new case. Even so, given the complexity of the problems, it must surely be beyond his capacity to do so. Spellbound they listen as gradually Lloyd George introduces a new line of argument, at first mere hints and indications, then a full flood of rhetoric which totally reverses his original position. He carries the day, persuading Clemenceau, Orlando and Wilson of the virtues of the British policy, using Keynes' suggestions and adding a telling point of his own. The Welsh Wizard is at his brilliant best, the quickness of his wit and the magic of his silver tongue in the intimate setting of the Four has once more triumphed in the pursuit of British interests.

Paris marked the zenith of the extraordinary career of David Lloyd George, the 'Welsh Wizard'. It provided him with a stage on which to exercise his considerable powers of persuasion, charm and deception, and an opportunity to shape a new world order. He was in his element, conjuring agreement from apparently impossibly opposed positions, reconciling the irreconcilable and smoothing the passage of the negotiations, always with an eye to British aims and ambitions as he interpreted them. He would remain Prime Minister for a further three years, years not without significant achievements though not on the grand scale of Paris. Then at the age of 59, relatively young for a politician, he left high office for ever, though he cast a long shadow over the domestic and international politics of the next two decades.

Lloyd George on his appointment as Chancellor of the Exchequer in Asquith's Liberal government, April 1909.

I

The Life and the Land

1

The Rising Star

William Orpen's Peace Conference portrait of David Lloyd George shows a vibrant, genial, smiling figure, with a bristling moustache and a shock of white hair. It conveys much of the wit, energy, vitality and sheer exuberance of a man who was revelling in the excitement of the largest and most significant peace conference of the 20th century. The premiership of his country, a major – perhaps the leading – role in the Paris negotiations at the end of a war that he was credited with winning, were hardly predictable as the fate of someone born in relatively humble circumstances in Chorlton-on-Medlock near Manchester on 17 January 1863. His schoolmaster father, William George, died in 1864, leaving his mother, Elizabeth, pregnant with his brother William, his elder sister, Mary Ellen, and 18-month-old David. They moved to Llanystumdwy, near Caernarvon, North Wales, finding a home with Elizabeth's brother, Richard Lloyd, a shoemaker and pastor in the nearby Baptist chapel in Criccieth.

Uncle Lloyd was a huge figure in David's life even beyond his death in February 1917. *All that is best in life's struggle I owe to him first* he told his wife, Maggie. He gave him his name and steeped him in Welsh identity and language, education, non-conformist religion, oratory, Liberalism and radical politics, and provided him with a moral compass. *Yes – how often have I kept straight from the very thought of the grief I might give him*. Perhaps it would be unwise to over-state this aspect. Many of those who came into contact with him later might have found it ironic that Davy Lloyd's first public appearance was singing 'Cofia, blentyn, ddwed y gwir' ('Remember, child, to speak the truth'). David provided evidence of all these influences, organising, at 12, a strike of his schoolmates, who refused to recite the Anglican catechism for visiting local gentry. The strike lasted until brother William cracked. From that time onwards David had an enduring dislike of the predominantly English rural landowners in Wales and sympathy for their estate workers.

Uncle Lloyd had belief in his nephew's ability: *It has often struck me how remarkable his confidence has been in my some time or other doing great things*. He determined that David should follow the law.[1] Articled in 1877 to the firm of Breeze, Jones and Casson in Portmadoc, he qualified as a solicitor in 1884 – though his third class honours suggested no enthusiasm for things academic. He opened a practice in Criccieth that year and, in January 1888, after a courtship in which his radical, Baptist background was not entirely acceptable to his prospective in-laws, he married Margaret Owen, a local farmer's daughter. Maggie can have had few illusions about his determination to succeed in politics. Even before their marriage he told her: *My supreme idea is to get on ... I am prepared to thrust even love itself under the wheels of my Juggernaut, if it obstructs the way*. Those ambitions were not modest. He visited the House of Commons in 1881, declaring: *I will not say but that I eyed the assembly in a spirit similar to*

*that in which William the Conqueror eyed England at his visit
to Edward the Confessor, as the region of his future domain.
Oh vanity!* [2]

He approached his goal in a systematic way, honing his oratorical skills, getting his name well-known in the local press both in terms of his legal practice, particularly in his defence of poachers, and his involvement in political controversies. Never one to avoid confrontations with the Establishment, whether the Anglican church or the local squires, his success in the Llanfrothen burial case in 1888 came at a particularly opportune time, helping him to be nominated as the Liberal candidate for the constituency of Caernarvon Boroughs.

In 1889 he was elected as an alderman on the new Caernarvon county council, but his major breakthrough came in April 1890, when, at the age of 27, following the death of the Conservative MP, he won the ensuing by-election by 18 votes. He would defend the seat 13 times, somewhat precariously in the early years, and remain continuously as the MP for Caernarvon Boroughs until, perhaps rather sadly, he took a peerage in January 1945. It had been offered kindly by the Prime Minister, his old friend Winston Churchill, to spare Lloyd George another electoral campaign, which was not guaranteed to be successful. He accepted, not from love of titles, which he

The 1880 Burials Act permitted Nonconformists to conduct burials in parish graveyards, using their own rites. The rector of Llanfrothen persuaded the donor of additional land for the graveyard to stipulate that only Anglican burials would be permitted. Robert Roberts wished to be buried beside his daughter, with a Methodist service. The rector refused permission. Lloyd George advised the family to break into the graveyard, conduct their service and bury Roberts. The rector sued them for trespass. Lloyd George persuaded the jury to find for his clients, but the judge, misinterpreting the verdict, found for the rector. The appeal to the High Court was successful, gaining the young lawyer much publicity.

despised and cheerfully bestowed or sold as Prime Minister, but because he hoped to influence the second Paris Peace Conference as a distinguished elder statesman. Churchill himself would not follow the same path, preferring to remain the great commoner and, in the event, Lloyd George's death in March would have spared him a new election.

The young radical

Lord Salisbury was the Conservative Prime Minister when the youngest MP in the House began his career on the opposition back benches. A colleague described him as being 'of small stature, slight figure and primitive raiment, his personal appearance ... not impressive; his early speeches in the House of Commons were, with a thin thread of argument, incoherent declamations ...'.[3] He was often dubbed 'the little man', usually, though not universally, with affection. His height (about five foot six) was perhaps perceived to be less because of his broad shoulders and large head. No matter what his male colleagues thought of his appearance, his attraction to women was both obvious and potentially dangerous (his less affectionate nickname was 'the Goat'). If Maggie had not reluctantly appeared by his side in court in 1909 when, following insinuations that he was about to be cited in a divorce case, he successfully sued the *People* newspaper for libel (possibly perjuring himself in the process), his career might have been over.[4]

In 1892 Gladstone won the general election and became Prime Minister for the fourth, and final, time and Lloyd George became a vociferous campaigner for Welsh causes. When it became clear that these, particularly the disestablishment of the Anglican church in Wales, were not the main priority of Lord Rosebery, who replaced Gladstone as Prime

Minister in 1894, Lloyd George resigned, temporarily, the party whip and, although not the main cause of the Liberal defeat in the 1895 general election, he did not endear himself to the party leadership.

Another former Liberal maverick, Joseph Chamberlain, now Colonial Secretary in Salisbury's new government, believed 'Lloyd George is a very able man and will go far. It is a pity however that he is so pro-vincial in his views.'[5] There was a real danger that he would become typecast as a Welsh nationalist and radical rebel without much interest in the wider social, impe-rial and defence issues that were becoming increasingly important at the turn of the century. His record in the ten years of Conservative rule from 1895 to 1905, however, indicated a growing maturity of attitude and broadening of his awareness of questions beyond Wales and rural affairs. He became an accomplished speaker in the House, attacking the government effectively on its 1896 Agri-cultural Land Rating Bill and its 1897 Education Bill (which was withdrawn) but, significantly, he also spoke in some debates on foreign affairs and imperial questions, whilst his membership of a Commons select committee on old age pen-sions whetted his interest in social problems.

His rough reception by Liberals in Newport, South Wales, in January 1896 revealed their resentment about domination by North Wales with its aspirations for the Welsh language and identity and helped to convince him that his political future should be on a British rather than a purely Welsh stage. He did not neglect Wales, however, and his championing of the striking workers in a protracted industrial dispute in the

> 'Lloyd George is a very able man and will go far. It is a pity however that he is so provincial in his views.'
> JOSEPH CHAMBERLAIN

Penrhyn slate quarries linked his Welsh roots with new interests in labour relations and social welfare. He further widened
his horizons, travelling in Europe and South America.

Domestic tensions

The new MP, Maggie and their growing family – they had
four children, Richard born in 1889, Mair in 1890, Olwen in
1892, and Gwilym in 1894 – moved to a succession of flats and
houses in London but Maggie preferred Criccieth and Lloyd
George found himself often alone. Being cited as the father
of Mrs Catherine Edwards' illegitimate child in 1897 cannot
have helped their marriage, even though the court found
him innocent of any blame. In August 1897 he complained
to Maggie: *I have more than once gone without breakfast.
I have scores of times come home in the dead of night to a
cold, dark and comfortless flat without a soul to greet me. I
am not the nature either physically or morally that I ought to
have been left like this ... You have been a good mother. You
have not – and I say this now not in anger – not always been
a good wife.* Their marriage survived, in name at least, until
her death in 1941, and their drift apart was gradual, indeed
Kenneth Morgan suggests that the family was at its closest
in the early years of the new century. Another child, Megan,
was born in 1902 but the death of their eldest daughter, Mair,
in 1907 from peritonitis after an emergency operation for
appendicitis, accelerated their growing estrangement. Lloyd
George blamed Maggie for allowing Mair's operation to be
performed at home and himself because he believed she had
hidden her illness to avoid disappointing his expectations
of success in her matriculation examination. He later told
Frances Stevenson that they *each had their poignant grief but
could not go to each other for sympathy and understanding.*[6]

Maggie rarely smiles in their later family photographs and Lloyd George sought comfort elsewhere.

A recent study suggests cautiously that 'it seems quite likely that he was a serial adulterer'. His son, Richard, admittedly not a friendly witness, was less coy: 'He carried on, adventure following adventure, with many hair's breadth escapes. For years he remained unscathed, protected by his wife from the consequences of his excesses.' There were, however, two really important women in his life, Maggie, the mother of his five children and nursemaid to his constituency, and Frances Stevenson, who came first as a summer companion and tutor for Megan in 1911 and then, in 1912 became his private secretary, knowing that this also meant becoming his lover. In 1911 Frances was a 23-year-old graduate in French from Royal Holloway College, teaching at Allenswood School in Wimbledon, where the girls nicknamed her 'Pussy'. Coincidentally she had been a friend of Mair's at school and, when Maggie wrote to their old headmistress seeking a recommendation for a temporary governess for the summer of 1911, she contacted Frances. Given what would follow, Maggie's part in introducing Frances into the equation was ironic.[7]

For over 30 years Lloyd George and Frances lived, as discreetly as possible, in a parallel marriage. This could be complicated, sometimes producing scenes from a French farce with people being shuffled about the house to avoid unwanted meetings. In 1936 he holidayed with Frances and her (their?) daughter Jennifer in Jamaica.[8] Maggie and Megan sailed to join him. At church, the minister prayed for their safe arrival and the congregation sang 'For those in peril on the sea'. Frances, preparing to leave, was understandably ambivalent, much to his amusement – *You ought to have seen your face.* In October 1943, she became his second wife. As she herself recorded 'Our real marriage had taken place thirty years before.'[9]

The Boer War

The Second Boer War, fought between October 1899 and May 1902, changed Lloyd George's career and the development of the United Kingdom. He became much better known – at some risk to himself when his condemnation of the war and sympathy for the Boers, coupled with the fact that he was attacking Chamberlain in his own fiefdom, led to him fleeing a public meeting in Birmingham in December 1901 disguised as a policeman. Lloyd George was not opposed to the British Empire, indeed he claimed in 1901: *I also am an imperialist. I believe in Empire* but his definition of empire was one based on consent, self-government for the colonies, and involved British responsibilities.[10]

He opposed the war in South Africa as the immoral, expensive and unnecessary result of Chamberlain's bungled diplomacy. Yet, demonstrating a facility that typified much of his career, he developed political friendships with Liberal Imperialists like Rosebery and Edward Grey and repaired his relationship with Herbert Asquith, at the same time as he was building links with the radical editors like C P Scott of the *Manchester Guardian* or A G Gardiner of the *Daily News* and attracting approaches from Keir Hardie's socialists. His ability to rub along with colleagues of widely differing views was one of his great strengths.

Salisbury won the 'khaki' election of 1900 but the longer term effects of the war harmed him and his party. Many volunteered for military service, but what this unintended census of the population revealed were striking deficiencies in health and education. Almost half the potential recruits were rejected on medical grounds, highlighting both the consequences of industrialisation and urbanisation and the need for drastic reform. Equally, Britain's diplomatic isolation and the inadequate performance of its armies undermined the confident, perhaps complacent, pragmatic approach of Salisbury to foreign policy and ushered in a new era of men like Chamberlain, who believed that more dynamic methods were required, involving more formal commitments. They wanted Britain to join the Triple Alliance of Germany, Austria-Hungary and Italy. When, in the course of alliance negotiations in 1898 and 1901, Germany overplayed its hand and demanded too much too soon from Britain in terms of European commitment, Britain drifted away. Eventually, the 1904 Anglo-French and 1907 Anglo-Russian ententes moved it closer to the orbit of the rival Franco-Russian Dual Alliance.

Salisbury's government concluded the Boer War with a generous peace in 1902, but its high costs – in soldiers' lives, nearly 6,000 killed and 16,000 dead of disease, in financial terms, over £222 million, and morally, with the scandal of 20,000 Boer deaths from disease in the concentration camps into which families had been forced in order to counter the Boers' guerrilla tactics – all undermined its support. Subsequent difficulties, such as controversy over the cheap indentured Chinese labour introduced into South Africa, attacked by Lloyd George as equivalent to slavery, added to the government's unpopularity.

Balfour's contentious 1902 Education Bill, which offended Nonconformists by the subsidies offered to Anglican and Catholic schools, allowed Lloyd George not only to become a major opposition spokesman, but also to demonstrate his ingenuity by his clever policy under which the Welsh counties agreed to assist the church schools – but only if the government repaired their buildings to a proper standard. He was again ready to engage with opponents in the hope of finding compromises, establishing a good personal relationship with Bishop Edwards of St Asaph, the *bête noire* of many Welsh liberals.

When Chamberlain split the Conservatives in 1903 by proposing to end free trade and create a system of tariffs and imperial preference, Lloyd George was among the leading defenders of a Liberal article of faith, though his subsequent career demonstrated that he was no true believer. All this, and his attacks on the government's 1904 Licensing Bill, helped to promote Lloyd George as an outstanding figure amongst the younger generation of Liberal politicians. When, in December 1905, Arthur Balfour, who had succeeded his uncle Robert Salisbury as premier in 1902 (whence the expression 'Bob's your uncle') unexpectedly resigned, the new Liberal Prime Minister, Henry Campbell-Bannerman, offered Lloyd George a cabinet post as President of the Board of Trade. He would not relinquish cabinet rank for almost 17 years until his resignation as Prime Minister in October 1922.

The old order changes

Britain, in late 1905, faced increasing challenges to its trading, industrial and naval pre-eminence. France and Russia were old rivals, Germany and the United States were important new competitors, whilst Japan's unforeseen victory over Russia in the war of 1904–5 announced its presence as a major regional player. The world power balance was becoming ever more complex and patterns of cooperation and competition were increasingly fluid. Britain's traditional imperial rivalry with France seemed to be undergoing a transformation as a result of the entente concluded in 1904, but this process had not yet been extended to France's ally, Russia, Britain's opponent in the Great Game, played out on the frontiers of India, for the control of expanses of Asia.

As with most European states, Britain's population had increased enormously in the 19th century, with the 15 million of 1815 now approaching 45 million. Unlike most of Europe, however, the majority of Britain's population lived in cities, employed in industry rather than agriculture. Britain had pioneered industrialisation, but it now faced the inevitable problems of the first in the field, as later competitors equipped themselves with more modern plant, employing more scientific methodologies and more efficient techniques. The first industrial revolution based on coal, iron and cotton, led by Britain, gave way to the second wave, based on developments in chemistry, electrical power, steel and oil. Germany and the United States dominated these areas at the same time as they overtook Britain in coal and steel production – which, along with demography, constituted crude indices of power in the new century. The old order was changing.

Germany had made massive strides since its unification. The predominantly rural and agricultural country of 1871 was now an industrial giant, with the majority of its population living in cities. That population had increased from 49 to 66 million by 1913, with a proportionate emphasis on its youth and vigour. Its annual coal production rose from 89 to 277 million tons, only marginally behind Britain's 292 million tons. Its annual steel production of 17.6 million tons in 1913 was greater than the combined totals of Britain, France and Russia, yet in 1870 Britain had produced twice as much steel and three and a half times as much coal as Germany.

Britain itself still enjoyed enormous wealth, much of it earned by its invisible exports in banking, insurance and merchant shipping and, whether or not in a fit of absence of mind, had, by the end of Queen Victoria's long reign, acquired an empire of 12 million square miles inhabited by a quarter of the world's population. The question marks raised by the Boer War, however, had undoubtedly dented the confidence that marked Victoria's era.

Yet, despite Kaiser Wilhelm II's bluster, Germany had not intervened during that war because it could not defend its shores and shipping from the Royal Navy. In common with the United States and Japan, anxious to use the technological masterpiece of the modern battleship as symbols of their industrial and economic might, and enticed by the idea that control of the oceans was the key to world power, Germany now planned a fleet to challenge Britain's dominance at sea.

Britain based its security on maintaining a fleet larger than the combined strengths of the next two most powerful navies, but this 'two-power standard' reflected an age in which there were very few naval powers and when the pace of technological change was much slower. At the battle of Trafalgar in 1805 both Nelson and his flagship *Victory* were 48 years old. No ship in the line of battle at Jutland in 1916 was even ten years of age. Ships now had to be replaced at more frequent intervals and at greater and greater cost.

Two further developments had a profound impact on subsequent events, one relatively short-term, the other reflecting a broader revolution which remains an element of enormous significance in our present and future affairs. The first was the British decision to build HMS *Dreadnought*. In theory (and disregarding grave deficiencies in British naval gunnery at the time) *Dreadnought*, the first all-big-gun battleship, launched in 1906, could, with its ten 12in guns, sink almost any vessel afloat before it came in range to return fire, whilst its steam-turbine engines made it faster than any of its competitors. The Royal Navy, under the dynamic leadership of Admiral Sir John ('Jackie') Fisher, believed it could not allow another navy to develop such a ship before it did so itself, but, at a stroke, this wiped out Britain's enormous advantage in 'conventional' battleships (pre-dreadnoughts) and made it much easier for new competitors like Germany to mount a credible challenge. Its short-term effect was a rapid escalation of a naval arms race and a worsening of Anglo-German relations.

The other development was Churchill's decision that the 1912 *Queen Elizabeth* class dreadnoughts would be oil-fired. Britain had plentiful and secure reserves of the coal previously used to power its main line of defence but (to the best of its contemporary knowledge) no oil. Ensuring the security of an adequate oil supply now became a new strategic objective which would have far-reaching consequences for the post-war settlement and beyond. Lloyd George played a major role in these matters, both before the war and during the Peace Conference.

The United States, with its population now approaching 100 million and its industrial production dwarfing that of the rest of the world, clearly had the potential, should it so wish, to become a major international presence, not just economically and commercially but also militarily. There were signs, at the turn of the century, that America intended to increase its naval strength, but its army remained appropriately small for a state with no serious enemies. Nonetheless it was clear that, although the world now might be dominated by Europe, this might well change in future and this potential need to readjust the international power balance, both within and beyond Europe, could pose major problems for the existing structure of international relations. Lloyd George was certainly living in interesting times as he began his ministerial career.

The Board of Trade

His record at the Board of Trade was impressive both for the volume of legislation that he steered through Parliament and for his skilful handling of a number of industrial disputes. When Churchill succeeded him in 1908 he believed it was a 'gleaned field' and – on another occasion (not to mix his metaphors) – he complained that 'Lloyd George has taken all the plums'.[11] The Merchant Shipping Act in 1906, the Patent and Designs Act of 1907, the Companies Act of 1908 and, in conjunction with Churchill, the Port of London Authority Act of 1908, represented a considerable legislative achievement. He was also credited with averting a national railway strike in 1907, with a *Punch* cartoon of 'Lloyd the Lubricator' depicting him as a cherub applying olive-branch oil to a set of signals set at deadlock.[12]

Chancellor of the Exchequer

His reward, when Asquith took over from the dying Campbell-Bannerman in April 1908, was to become Chancellor of the Exchequer – a potentially poisoned chalice at a time when the pressing needs for domestic reform, particularly the provision of old age and sickness pensions, were vying for finite government funding with defence requirements, especially the perceived need to outbuild Germany in dreadnoughts. But it was also a huge opportunity and he scored an early triumph by providing a modest old age pension of five shillings a week for 70-year-olds.

His interest in social reform was strengthened by a visit to Germany in 1908 and a developing political partnership

with Winston Churchill with whom he constituted a powerful force on the radical wing of the party. The major fruit of
their collaboration was the National Insurance Act of 1911
which provided insurance against unemployment and ill-
health. Lloyd George conducted the bulk of the negotiations
with the various interested parties, handling trade unions,
employers, friendly societies, commercial insurers and the
British Medical Association with his usual dexterity. Among
his great strengths were his ability to listen and his knack of
spotting deal clinchers – in this case promising payment of
MPs to encourage reluctant Labour members to support the
bill. He also demonstrated his mastery of the Commons by
the way in which he steered this complex legislation on to the
statute book.

The People's Budget and a constitutional crisis

The expansion of the Liberal social programme was mainly
financed by economies in military and naval expenditure. In
1906 and 1907 the dreadnought building programme was
cut from seven to five and Admiral Tirpitz in Germany saw
an opportunity to reduce Britain's lead by laying down more
ships. In early 1909 this provoked the popular press-driven
demand in Britain of 'We want eight and we won't wait'.
Lloyd George was torn between the need to satisfy the voters
and to keep naval expenditure under control. Once again his
skill in negotiation came into play and he was an important
contributor to the compromise that four ships would be built
immediately with provision made to build four more rapidly
should the need arise.

Nonetheless he still had to increase the government's
income to pay for all these ambitious schemes which threatened a deficit of £16 million. The result was the 'People's

Budget' of 1909 which taxed alcohol, tobacco, motor cars, raised death duties, introduced a 'super tax' of sixpence (2.5p) in the pound on incomes over £5,000 a year and – most controversially – threatened to tax the profits of landowners by first introducing a new land tax, but, more significantly, instituting a land valuation scheme to provide a benchmark for measuring increases in value. Here was a typical piece of Lloyd George sleight of hand – a land valuation scheme would not pass the House of Lords as an independent measure, but he bundled it up into the Budget, with which, by long-standing parliamentary convention, the Lords did not tamper. This time they did, causing a long-drawn out constitutional crisis rich in consequences both intended and unintended.

There is no doubt that, whether or not the original intention was to provoke a test of strength with the Lords, Lloyd George delighted in the opportunity offered by their opposition, laying into his traditional foe, the landlords, in a violent speech at Limehouse in July and mocking peers in another in Newcastle in October. *A fully equipped duke costs as much to keep up as two 'dreadnoughts' and they are just as great a terror* he suggested, whilst he defined the Lords, famously, as *five hundred men, ordinary men, chosen accidentally from among the unemployed … on the principle of first of the litter.*[13]

When, in November, peers rejected the Budget Lloyd George was a central figure in the ensuing confrontations with the Conservatives about the power of the Lords, which were not resolved by two general elections in January and December 1910. Both resulted in a virtual tie between Liberals and Conservatives, with the Irish nationalists, the Irish Parliamentary Party (IPP), led by John Redmond holding the balance.[14] Asquith convinced the new king, George V, to force the issue in August 1911, by promising, if necessary, to create enough new peers to pass the Parliament Bill. It limited the power of the upper house in a number of important ways, one of which was to reduce its power of veto, a development that was crucial in the unfolding of another highly controversial question, that of Irish Home Rule.

Redmond's price for maintaining the Liberals in power was the re-opening of the enormously divisive Irish question which had played havoc with British politics for generations. This was indeed an unintended consequence of the 1909 Budget, raising once again all the emotive questions of nationalism, religion and the perennial problem of whether Ulster, with its predominantly Protestant and Unionist population, should be excluded from any measure creating an Irish government in Dublin. As both Unionists and nationalists armed and drilled, civil war was a distinct possibility, and tensions ran high both in Ireland and Westminster. Asquith's government persisted and the Home Rule Act of 1914 was passed, only to be suspended for the duration of the First World War.

A coalition?

Lloyd George illustrated throughout his career that he was never dominated by party or ideology. His record during and after the war, when he was anxious to engage non-politicians with appropriate expertise to undertake important tasks, indicated a disregard for convention and a pragmatic determination to get the job done. The idea of government based on a consensus of intelligent leaders, regardless of party affiliation, appealed to him and he was ideally suited to become the leader of a coalition government between 1916 and 1922. It is typical that, in the midst of an enormous constitutional struggle, he should make a secret approach to the Conservative leadership, suggesting that they should unite to tackle social reform at home and the defence of Britain's interests abroad. *No party has a monopoly of able and efficient men, nor has it a monopoly of duffers. No party commands the services of more that half a dozen first-rate men ... It is therefore necessary to any scheme of national reorganisation that the best men that the nation provides should be secured as heads during the period of reconstruction. This can only be achieved by drawing upon the resources of both Parties in the State.*[15]

This early example of what would re-emerge after the war as the politics of Fusion foundered, as would the later scheme, because Lloyd George did not appreciate the deep-rooted nature of party politics in Britain.

The Marconi Affair

His own career also nearly foundered on the Marconi scandal of 1912. Most commentators agree that Lloyd George was careless in money matters but not corrupt, although the failed Patagonian mining venture of the 1890s, the Marconi affair, the sale of honours and the notorious Lloyd George Fund did little to establish his record of financial probity, even if, in all these cases, there was nothing technically wrong (or, in terms of selling political honours, nothing very new) in what he did. As he himself pleaded in the Commons debate on the affair: *If you will, I acted thoughtlessly, I acted carelessly, I acted mistakenly, but I acted innocently, I acted openly and I acted honestly.*[16] The problem was that the collective effect, taken in conjunction with his reputation for economy with the truth and general deviousness, was cumulative, confirming for many that he was not entirely reliable or trustworthy.

The Marconi affair was more one of confusion and then inept explanation than anything else. In the spring of 1912 the British government commissioned the Marconi company to build a network of wireless stations to link the Empire. The Attorney-General, Rufus Isaacs, bought shares from his brother Godfrey, Marconi's managing director, kept some himself and sold others to Lloyd George and Alec Murray, the Master of Elibank. It appeared that they had taken advantage of ministerial and family knowledge, but, whereas the British government's contract was with Marconi's British company, their shares were in Marconi's independent American company which had no part in the contract. It is illustrative of his lack of financial acumen that Lloyd George actually lost money on his dealings.

Neither had done anything wrong, but, when Isaacs stated in the House of Commons that October that neither he, nor Lloyd George, had bought shares in 'that company', he did not make it plain that he meant the British Marconi Company and it thus appeared, when news of their dealings in the American company emerged, that he had mislead the House. Both offered to resign but Asquith stood by them. Subsequently, following misleading articles in the press, two prominent Conservative lawyers, Edward Carson and F E Smith, appeared in a successful libel action against *Le Matin* on behalf of Isaacs and Herbert Samuel (the minister responsible for awarding the contract) and were able to bring out the distinction between the two companies and clarify the share ownership issues and the matter seemed to be fading away. Then it emerged that Elibank had also purchased shares for the Liberal Party and it required the majority report of a Liberal-dominated select committee and a virtuoso performance in the Commons from Lloyd George, which had members in tears, together with Asquith's firm support, to save the government and his position.

Stumbling into the abyss

Lloyd George's fortunes declined in 1913 and 1914. He suffered a series of setbacks to his new land campaign and plans
for public housing. He threatened to resign after losing a
battle about the naval estimates with Churchill, now, as First
Lord of the Admiralty, enthusiastic to expand the British
fleet. He ran into procedural difficulties when the Speaker
ruled that his ambitious 1914 budget was not, in the terms
of the 1911 Parliament Act, a money bill, thus frustrating his
plans to by-pass the Lords. He did make an important contribution to the Home Rule negotiations, revealing himself
as a supporter of Ulster's exclusion for at least a number of
years and he remained an important ally for Asquith, but
he seemed rather isolated in the cabinet and no longer the
unstoppable force he had once been.

As with so many other lives, his would be irreversibly
changed when Europe hurtled to war after the assassinations
of Archduke Franz Ferdinand, heir to the Austro-Hungarian
empire, and his wife in Sarajevo on 28 June 1914. The Austrians were determined to use this outrage as an excuse to deal
with Serbia, whether or not there was substantial evidence
linking it to the plot. Serbia was an independent Slav nation
whose existence was perceived to pose a growing threat to
a multi-national empire feeling the increasing pressures of
national demands for autonomy similar to that granted to
the Germans and Magyars in the *Ausgleich* (compromise) of
1867. They knew that an attack on Serbia could well trigger
a Russian response, not least because Russia's claims to be
the protector of the Slav states in the Balkans had taken a
severe dent as a result of the Austrian annexation of Bosnia
and Herzegovina in 1908–9 and its ineffectual role during the
Balkan wars of 1912–13. A crucial factor in 1914 would be

the various states' perceptions of the unsuccessful outcomes of earlier crises and of the need to avoid further humiliations or loss of prestige.

The Austrian emperor, Franz Josef, thus sought assurance from Kaiser Wilhelm that, notwithstanding the defensive nature of their alliance, which compelled them to support each other only if they were attacked, he could count on Germany's backing even if Austria provoked the war. The German response – the famous 'blank cheque' – of 5 July 1914 undertook to support its one remaining reliable friend. Unleashed, Austria issued an impossible ultimatum to Serbia on 23 July and then declared war on 28 July, provoking Russia to begin mobilisation.

Germany, which had evolved the Schlieffen Plan to tackle its nightmare of a two-front war against Russia in the east and France in the west, now feared that Russian mobilisation would undermine its strict timetable for a rapid strike against France, to be conquered in the six weeks the Germans calculated it would take the Russians to mobilise. Russia could then be defeated in six months. Germany therefore declared war on Russia on 1 August but now found itself driven to declare war on France on 3 August in order to implement the Schlieffen Plan, thus precipitating the two-front war it sought to avoid. Worse would follow: in order to maintain the speed of its advance and to by-pass France's fortifications on the traditional invasion routes, on 3 August Germany violated Belgian neutrality, guaranteed by all the major powers in the 1839 Treaty of London, but denounced by the German Chancellor Bethmann-Hollweg as a 'scrap of paper'.

Where did this leave Britain? Asquith had a difficult task during the July Crisis of 1914. His party did not command an automatic parliamentary majority and its leadership was deeply divided over British intervention in a continental war. He knew he had the support of the Conservative opposition, but he did not want to destroy his own party's unity. The government found itself facing a crisis which was both unexpected and posed fundamental questions about Britain's role in Europe.

A number of factors came into play. On the one hand there was a tradition of non-commitment that permitted Britain to make up its mind on individual issues – the idea of 'the free hand' – which had a strong connection to Lord Palmerston's concept of a permanent British national interest and the need for flexibility to preserve a balance of power in Europe. On the other was the growing trend for long-term alliances and the growth of blocs – the Triple Alliance of Germany, Austria-Hungary and Italy opposed to the Dual Alliance of France and Russia. In 1902 Britain made its only modern pre-war alliance (an undertaking to go to war on behalf of an ally in prescribed circumstances). This was in the Far East, with Japan, but it also reached accommodations with its two traditional rivals, France and Russia.

The ententes of 1904 and 1907 were, as befitted states with many long-standing imperial disagreements, settlements of colonial disputes and compromises over spheres of influence. Neither had any overt reference to cooperation in the wider field of international relations and there was no question of Britain joining the Dual Alliance. However, Asquith, his Foreign Secretary Sir Edward Grey and other influential members of the cabinet like Lord Haldane, took the view that, although there was no written commitment, the perception of other nations was that Britain was a supporter of France and, unless it lived up to those expectations, it would be seen as an unreliable international friend and left isolated.

German attempts to loosen Anglo-French links did much to strengthen them. At the heart of the 1904 Anglo-French entente was what amounted to a swap – Britain could have Egypt and, in return, France should take Morocco. When Germany made the legitimate point that its interests deserved consideration, it did so in such a clumsy and bullying fashion that it provoked an international crisis in 1905, finding itself isolated at the ensuing Algeçiras conference, with only Austria in support. Britain and France commenced military planning, apparently of an hypothetical nature, as to how Britain's army might best be utilised in support of France, in the case of a possible future war in which Britain might possibly become involved. Similarly, the 1911 Agadir crisis encouraged further military and naval cooperation, none of which involved a commitment to an alliance, but which helped create an expectation of British involvement and commitment.

How far all members of the cabinet knew of these Anglo-French arrangements became a matter of controversy. Lloyd George displayed one of his less attractive traits when he tried to distance himself from responsibility in such matters. His *War Memoirs*, written in the 1930s, were less than honest, trying to pin blame exclusively on Grey: *A Cabinet which was compelled by political and economic exigencies to concentrate its energies on domestic problems left the whole field of foreign affairs to Sir Edward Grey. Anyone reading with care and impartiality the record of the way in which he missed his opportunities must come to the conclusion that he lacked the knowledge of foreign countries and the vision, imagination, breadth of mind and that high courage, bordering on audacity which his immense task demanded.*[17]

Yet he was aware of much more than he cared to admit and his general attitude in 1914 was supportive of Grey. He had a good grasp of the issues – the balance of power, the threat to British security and the importance of Belgium both strategically and as a symbol. Following the assassinations in Sarajevo, Lloyd George hoped to avoid British entanglement, but, at the same time, he believed that there might come a point at which a realistic judgement of Britain's interests would compel it to intervene. He was perceived to be part of the group in the cabinet opposed to war, and, whilst the reality may have been more complicated, he certainly hoped to avoid it if possible. As he wrote to Maggie on 28 July 1914: *War trembling in the balance. No one can tell what will or will not happen. I still believe peace will be preserved.*[18]

He was also aware that, in a deeply split cabinet, his role could be crucial for the fate of the government, whilst there was also the personal consideration that any decision he took could have the most profound effect on his political career. Asquith sensed his dilemma and praised his attitude in contrast to cabinet members like John Morley and John Simon who were determined to keep Britain neutral, writing on 31 July: 'Lloyd George – all for peace – is more sensible and statesmanlike for keeping the position open.'[19]

The general public would have recognised Lloyd George as an advocate of peace, partly perhaps because of two misconceptions. The first, encouraged obviously by his stance during the Boer War, was that he was a pacifist. The other was that he was pro-German. Whilst he admired Germany, particularly for its social policies, he made it clear, in what was seen as both a surprising and important speech at the Mansion House on 21 July 1911 during the Agadir crisis, that: *I would make great sacrifices to preserve peace. I can conceive of nothing that could justify disturbance of international goodwill except questions of the greatest national moment, but if a situation were to be forced upon us, in which peace could only be preserved by the surrender of the great and beneficial position which Britain has won by centuries of heroism and achievement, by allowing Britain to be treated, where her interests are vitally affected, as if she were of no account in the Cabinet of Nations, then I say emphatically that peace at that price would be a humiliation intolerable for a great country like ours to endure.*[20]

This was generally interpreted as a warning to Germany and provoked a furious reaction there, with calls for his dismissal, but he had spoken the government's mind. Nonetheless his general reputation remained that of someone who sought a peaceful resolution of disputes.

Throughout the crisis Lloyd George remained cautious, seeming to resist those members of the cabinet, including Grey and Asquith, who believed that Britain should support France. Yet he understood that Britain's interests might force it to fight and neither faction in the government was entirely sure where he stood. The German invasion of Belgium was a crucial determinant for many members of a wavering British cabinet – and, apparently, persuaded Lloyd George himself. On 3 August he wrote to Maggie: *I am moving through a nightmare world these days. I have fought hard for peace and have succeeded so far in keeping the Cabinet out of it but I am driven to the conclusion that if the small nationality of Belgium is attacked by Germany all my traditions and even prejudices will be engaged on the side of war.*[21]

Frances, reflecting years later, was not convinced: 'My own opinion is that L.G.'s mind was made up from the first, that he knew we would have to go in, and that the invasion of Belgium was, to be cynical, a heaven-sent excuse for supporting a declaration of war.'[22] Whatever the truth, after 3 August

Lloyd George's mind was set and he accepted, however reluctantly, that war was inevitable. The invasion of Belgium also helped to maintain Liberal unity, with only two resignations from the cabinet – Morley and John Burns. Thus it was still Asquith's Liberal government that led Britain during the early part of the war.

At midnight on 4 August Britain went to war when its ultimatum to Germany to withdraw its forces from Belgium expired unanswered. Lloyd George's historical judgement was that *the nations slithered over the brink into the boiling cauldron of war* and he was less than generous in his assessment of Grey's handling of the July Crisis: *They tell their own tale of a pilot whose hand trembled in the palsy of apprehension, unable to grip the levers and manipulate them with a firm and clear purpose.*[23] Neither verdict was entirely accurate or fair, but the destiny of Europe, the world and Lloyd George himself would be determined by the conduct and outcomes of the struggle upon which they had embarked.

2

The Man Who Won the War

Lloyd George went to war with his customary energy. He restored confidence after an early financial panic in the City of London. The issue of £1 and 10/- (50p) paper banknotes ('Bradburies', so called because they bore the signature of John Bradbury, the Permanent Secretary to the Treasury) overcame worries about the money supply. *What are they made of? Rags. What are they worth? The whole credit of the British Empire.* The *flapping penguins* (city financiers) restored to calm, Lloyd George's reputation for sound finance was boosted by his 1914 war budget, whilst his vigorous September recruiting speech attack on Germany as *the road hog of Europe* dispelled doubts about his commitment to the war, going down well with Conservatives,

> It will be a terrible war. But in the end we shall march through terror to triumph.
>
> LLOYD GEORGE

but did raise concerns amongst Liberal supporters about this new-found enthusiasm for conflict. He predicted: *It will be a terrible war. But in the end we shall march through terror to triumph.*[1]

Setbacks and concerns

The war went badly from the outset. The British Expeditionary Force, a highly trained professional army of 100,000 volunteers, was tiny in comparison with the European conscript armies, and the Kaiser's description of it as 'contemptibly small' was not unjustified. It was largely destroyed in the early battles in 1914 on the Western Front in France and Belgium. Britain had to recruit, equip and train new and larger armies to reinforce and replace it. Spring offensives in France in 1915 failed, with questions raised about an inadequate preparatory barrage because the artillery had insufficient shells. Lloyd George's concern about this, whether genuine or manufactured, became part of a long battle with Lord Kitchener, the iconic War Minister, who resented interference in the affairs of his department, despite its obvious shortcomings.

The Summer Time Act of 17 May 1916 put forward clocks an hour in summer to make better use of natural light in the evening. William Willett (1856–1915) proposed this in a 1907 pamphlet 'The Waste of Daylight' as a way to increase the nation's health and leisure time. A number of belligerents adopted it as a wartime measure to increase efficiency and save fuel. There is a memorial sundial to Willett in Petts Wood, on the southern outskirts of London.

Lloyd George attributed the shell shortage in part to the excessive drinking of the munitions workers. One of the longest lasting legacies of the First World War, apart from British summer time, would be Britain's strange licensing laws designed to limit drinking hours, which were only comprehensively reformed in 2003. He also persuaded George V to abstain from alcohol for the duration of the war. Kitchener proved the only cabinet minister prepared to follow him. When he drowned in 1916, the King was the sole abstainer. He, like his grandmother, was not amused, and did take the occasional nip of spirits to aid his recovery after suffering serious injury in a fall from his horse.

The obstacles to ensuring adequate munition supplies contributed to Lloyd George's mounting frustration with Asquith's leadership. Britain could produce mass armies numbering millions, but would need both time and fundamental shifts in policies and attitudes. Gearing the country for total war required government to take responsibility for matters in which it had never before intervened. 'Business as usual' was a cheerful but misleading concept; new thinking was necessary. He increasingly despaired of it coming from Asquith, whose watchword of 'wait and see' no longer seemed appropriate or adequate.

In contrast, faced with a need for increased production and a competition between industry and the armed forces for fit young men, Lloyd George's skilful negotiations with the trade unions instituted radical changes to established labour relations practices. The unions agreed to suspend strikes and to permit the employment of unskilled workers (including women) in positions previously reserved for skilled men.

Lloyd George sought ways to defeat Germany that did not involve major manpower losses. From the outset he argued *that any attempt to force the carefully prepared German lines in the west would end in failure and appalling loss of life.* He preferred a strategy of *knocking the props* from under Germany by seeking a less direct route to Berlin – either through the Balkans or the Middle East.[2] He supported Churchill's Gallipoli campaign to force the Dardanelles, knock Turkey out of the war and open easier supply routes to Russia.

The Gallipoli landings on 25 April 1915 were, quite literally, a shambles. The image of bloodstained water would haunt

Churchill for the rest of his life. Troops from Dublin, Lancashire, Australia, New Zealand and elsewhere were slaughtered as they established a toe-hold on the peninsula and, despite all their efforts, they made little further progress. The only remarkable Allied success of the whole campaign was the skilful two-stage evacuation in December. This adventure threatened to destroy Churchill's career, though it established the reputation of Mustafa Kemal, the young Turkish general who masterminded the defence.

The new coalition government

Gallipoli did not, of itself, bring down Asquith's Liberal government but it was part of a series of events, not all connected, that made continuing Conservative support impossible. The shell shortage, publicised in Colonel Repington's famous *Times* article of 14 May, 'Jackie' Fisher's resignation as First Sea Lord on 15 May, the failures in France and a general sense of malaise that not enough was being done to prosecute the war with real determination, created the political crisis of 17 to 24 May 1915 that ended with Asquith leading a Liberal-Conservative coalition national government.

Lloyd George's exact role in the demise of Britain's last Liberal government is not clear. Churchill recollected him threatening resignation unless a coalition was formed. Lloyd George denied this, but the necessity of his support for Asquith's survival gave him immense leverage in the negotiations about positions in the new administration. Churchill, demoted to the Duchy of Lancaster, and Haldane, unjustly thought to be pro-German after a pre-war remark about Germany being his 'spiritual home', were the major casualties, but the great political gamble for Lloyd George was to give up the Exchequer (though not his Downing Street address) to become Minister of Munitions. He now had to solve the shortages he had highlighted and his future depended on his success.

The early signs were not auspicious – when Lloyd George and Frances arrived at the new ministry in 6 Whitehall Gardens they found only two tables and a chair, themselves about to be removed. When he left in July 1916 he had quadrupled the supply of medium guns, quintupled that of machine guns and raised heavy gun production by 1,200 per cent. He improved conditions for the workers in government factories, instituting a welfare department under Seebohm Rowntree, which did much for his standing with the trade unions.

Edward Grey summed it up well: 'Critics said that he made chaos, but out of it came a department and the Munitions, and but for Lloyd George the country would not have been organized as soon as it was for the work of making munitions.'[3] His methods were unorthodox: he brought in *men of push and go* from industry and elsewhere to drive through his programmes. He also retrieved skilled men from the army. There were inevitable complications and he perhaps took credit for developments already in the pipeline, but he delivered the goods.

The new government enjoyed no more success than the last, but there was now no credible alternative. Asquith, distressed by his eldest son's death on the Somme, seemed less and less in touch with the task of winning the war as he manoeuvred to keep the ministry together and his wits in place. He had certainly not signed the pledge. *We are all at sixes and sevens* Lloyd George had complained to C P Scott in October 1915: *If it were only a conflict between those who are for an energetic conduct of the war and those who aren't … then the matter would be comparatively simple. But it isn't like that:*

there are all sorts of cross-currents and the result is hopeless confusion.[4]

His disillusion with Asquith increased but his own political position was isolated. Liberals were concerned that, in his ruthless pursuit of victory, he had abandoned many of the values and institutions they held dear. His conversion to the necessity for conscription – anathema to Liberals – was not sufficient to dispel Conservative anxieties about his reliability and his relations with their leaders remained correct, but not cordial. He was still vital to the government however, and his threats of resignation forced Asquith first to skirt the issue in October 1915 by instituting Lord Derby's scheme to save the voluntary recruiting system by encouraging eligible men to 'attest' their willingness to serve and then, reluctantly, to accept in December conscription of unmarried men between 18 and 45. Finally, in April 1916, married men also were included, though conscription was never implemented in Ireland.

Catastrophe piled on catastrophe in 1915 and 1916 – Gallipoli, Loos, Arras, rebellion in Ireland, the 420,000 casualties of the battle of the Somme (with 20,000 dead and 40,000 wounded on the first day) and the disappointment of the inconclusive Battle of Jutland for a people used to striking naval successes. At Verdun the French were being bled dry and, in the east, Russia's troops, inadequately supplied and poorly led, fell to defeat upon defeat. Discontent with Asquith grew, as did conspiratorial conversations amongst his exasperated colleagues. Lloyd George hinted at resignation several times. On 6 June Kitchener drowned when HMS *Hampshire* struck a mine and sank. Lloyd George replaced him at the War Office in July in a reshuffled government. Mrs Asquith read the runes: 'We are out,' she wrote in her diary, 'it is only a question of time when we shall have to leave Downing Street.'[5]

It took another five months. Lloyd George might proclaim, for the benefit of the American press, *Britain has only begun to fight ... The fight must be to the finish – to a knock-out blow* but, to Maurice Hankey, secretary of the War Committee, he confided in November, *We are going to lose this War.*[6] Drastic change was required. In his *War Memoirs* he wrote *I neither sought nor desired the Premiership.*[7] This may have been true – he was willing to retain Asquith or to serve under Balfour or Bonar Law – but he wanted the power to direct the war. The Conservatives' leader, Andrew Bonar Law, preferred keeping Asquith as premier, but his backbenchers demanded change. On 1 December he and Lloyd George proposed a war-directing executive committee of three, excluding Asquith, who would remain as Prime Minister. Asquith refused, but accepted a new scheme on 3 December only to reject it the next day. Lloyd George and Bonar Law resigned, leaving Asquith with no option: refusing to serve under anyone else he resigned on 5 December. George V asked Bonar Law, as leader of the largest parliamentary party, to form a new government. After consultations with Asquith and Balfour he declined, and advised the King to send for Lloyd George. On 6 December Davy Lloyd from Llanystumdwy kissed hands and became Prime Minister of the United Kingdom.

The premiership

Football supporters often taunt their rivals 'You only sing when you're winning'. Leadership is easy when things are going well, leadership in adversity is the real test. Lloyd George, like Churchill in the next war, was at his best in bad times. Lord Swinton compared them: 'I was with Lloyd

George every day when the Germans broke through in March 1918 and nearly separated the British and French armies. I was with Churchill for hours on the first night of Dunkirk. Both were alike – courageous, imperturbable, unshakeable and never doubting victory, however hopeless the odds seemed. I remember both using almost the same language, expressing not just the belief but the certainty that we should win through.'[8]

Lloyd George faced many crises – the U-boat threat, the Russian revolution, and agonies over the slaughter of Passchendaele in 1917, the German onslaught in March 1918 – yet he asked *Why should we not sing during the War? The blinds of Britain are not down yet, nor are they likely to be. The honour of Britain is not dead, her might is not broken, her destiny is not fulfilled, her ideals are not shattered by her enemies ... why should we not sing?*[9]

Lloyd George's exact contribution to the policies that helped first to stave off defeat and then drive to victory is the subject of many historical debates – what were the roles and significance of his executive War Cabinet and the Imperial War Cabinet he created in 1917? Was he the main instigator of the convoy system that thwarted the U-boat menace? Why did he allow General Nivelle to persuade him to back the disaster of the Battle of Chemin des Dames (to which French soldiers went baaing, knowing they were like sheep to the slaughter, before regiment after regiment mutinied)? Could he have resisted more firmly Douglas Haig's plans for the Flanders campaign of 1917 which he was convinced could not succeed? Could more have been done to help Russia? Should he have forced Haig to accept unity of Allied command on the Western Front before the prospect of defeat in the field in March 1918 finally persuaded him? Could he have overcome the weight of political intrigue and royal influence and dismissed Haig altogether? Did he deliberately mislead Parliament over manpower statistics in the Maurice debate? All are important and interesting questions, but it is the overall effect that is the key. For many of his close associates, and certainly for the British public – even for Adolf Hitler – Lloyd George was 'the man who won the war'.

A *Punch* cartoon of 20 December 1916 showed 'The New Conductor', baton raised, bristling with determination, poised, ready to direct the 'opening of the 1917 overture' with huge vigour.[10] It was this image of an unquenchable spirit, of driving energy, above all of a sense of purpose and direction, that constituted his great contribution. Sometimes he bullied, sometimes he cajoled, sometimes he charmed, sometimes he lied, but he persuaded a potentially unstable parliamentary coalition to support his ministry, reluctant admirals and generals to rethink, industrialists and trade unionists to compromise and a beleaguered British public to believe in victory. He was astute and flexible, backing able men to get on with their tasks, assembling an effective team from erstwhile opponents with strongly held convictions and diverse talents. He was visible – either in person in factories and at the Front, or in the cinema newsreels. He personified a determination to win.

Lloyd George's Statement on British War Aims

Such a determination was essential because 1917 was a disastrous year for the Allies, despite America's declarations of war against Germany in April, and Austria-Hungary in December. Allied morale was sapped by the French army mutinies, the muddy and bloody nightmare of Passchendaele, the Italian rout at Caporetto, the revolutions in Russia and growing industrial unrest at home, peace negotiations between Germany and the new Bolshevik rulers of Russia, Trotsky's publication of embarrassing inter-Allied imperial agreements, and the third year of a war that should have finished by Christmas 1914, and to which no end was in sight. In November a respected former Conservative foreign secretary, Lord Lansdowne, called for a compromise peace, which Lloyd George rejected because the Allies were too weak to negotiate. But if Britain's citizens, whether in uniform or in the vital industries, were to continue to support the war effort, they needed a clear and uplifting statement to justify their sacrifices. The Austrians were also sniffing at the possibility of a separate peace and wanted to know Britain's terms. The bland generalities of earlier years would not do.

On 5 January 1918, significantly speaking in person to the leaders of organised labour, the Trades Union Congress, but figuratively to the whole nation, Lloyd George set out his war aims. He had previously consulted Arthur Henderson and George Barnes, the leaders of the Labour Party, Asquith and Grey of the Liberal opposition, Redmond of the IPP and various Dominion statesmen. Britain, he said, had no wish to destroy Germany, Austria-Hungary or to deprive Turkey of its Turkish lands or its capital, though it should relinquish its Middle Eastern possessions. Germany's form of government was a matter for the Germans – democracy was preferable, but they must choose. The rest of Europe had a right to justice and stability based on government by the consent of the governed. In calling for the full restoration, in every sense – economic, political, territorial – of Belgium, Serbia, Montenegro, France, Italy and Romania, he denied any demand for punitive costs, but reparation was essential. He backed the French wish for a reconsideration of the Alsace-Lorraine question. He acknowledged Russia's great sacrifices but he repudiated responsibility for the actions of the Bolsheviks. *Russia can only be saved by its own people.*

He backed independence for Poland, and autonomy of the national groupings in the Austro-Hungarian Empire. Germany's colonies had the right to self-determination, which he partially defined as being placed under an acceptable (presumably Allied) administration. Breaches of international law, especially those at sea, should be punished. He hinted at continuing inter-Allied economic cooperation after the war, when raw materials would be in short supply. To free men and women from conscription, the weight of great armaments and waste of resources, *a great attempt must be made to establish by some international organisation an alternative to war as a means of settling international disputes.*

His was a three-point programme: *First, the sanctity of treaties must be re-established; secondly, a territorial settlement must be secured based on the right of self-determination or the consent of the governed; and, lastly, we must seek by the creation of some international organisation to limit the burden of armaments and diminish the probability of war.*[11]

It was very close to, but independent from, President Woodrow Wilson's more famous Fourteen Points speech three days later. Both were liberal clarion calls designed to revitalize a flagging Allied cause, to re-inspire both domestic and international audiences and to reach across the battle lines to sympathetic spirits in the enemy camps. Indeed, recorded Edward House, his friend and confidant: 'When George's speech came out in Washington Saturday afternoon, the President thought the terms which Lloyd George had given were so nearly akin to those he had worked out that it would be impossible for him to make the contemplated address before Congress.'

PRESIDENT WILSON'S FOURTEEN POINTS, 8 JANUARY 1918

The program of the world's peace, therefore, is our program; and that program, the only possible program, as we see it, is this:

I. Open covenants of peace, openly arrived at, after which there shall be no private international understandings of any kind but diplomacy shall proceed always frankly and in the public view.

II. Absolute freedom of navigation upon the seas, outside territorial waters, alike in peace and in war, except as the seas may be closed in whole or in part by international action for the enforcement of international covenants.

III. The removal, so far as possible, of all economic barriers and the establishment of an equality of trade conditions among all the nations consenting to the peace and associating themselves for its maintenance.

IV. Adequate guarantees given and taken that national armaments will be reduced to the lowest point consistent with domestic safety.

V. A free, open-minded, and absolutely impartial adjustment of all colonial claims, based upon a strict observance of the principle that in determining all such questions of sovereignty the interests of the populations concerned must have equal weight with the equitable claims of the government whose title is to be determined.

VI. The evacuation of all Russian territory and such a settlement of all questions affecting Russia as will secure the best and freest cooperation of the other nations of the world in obtaining for her an unhampered and unembarrassed opportunity for the independent determination of her own political development and national policy and assure her of a sincere welcome into the society of free nations under institutions of her own choosing; and, more than a welcome, assistance also of every kind that she may need and may herself desire. The treatment accorded Russia by her sister nations in the months to come will be the acid test of their good will, of their comprehension of her needs as distinguished from their own interests, and of their intelligent and unselfish sympathy.

VII. Belgium, the whole world will agree, must be evacuated and restored, without any attempt to limit the sovereignty which she enjoys in common with all other free nations. No other single act will serve as this will serve to restore confidence among the nations in the laws which they have themselves set and determined for the government of their relations with one another. Without this healing act the whole structure and validity of international law is forever impaired.

VIII. All French territory should be freed and the invaded portions restored, and the wrong done to France by Prussia in 1871 in the matter of Alsace-Lorraine, which has unsettled the peace of the world for nearly fifty years, should be righted, in order that peace may once more be made secure in the interest of all.

IX. A readjustment of the frontiers of Italy should be effected along clearly recognizable lines of nationality.

X. The peoples of Austria-Hungary, whose place among the nations we wish to see safeguarded and assured, should be accorded the freest opportunity to autonomous development.

XI. Rumania, Serbia, and Montenegro should be evacuated; occupied territories restored; Serbia accorded free and secure access to the sea; and the relations of the several Balkan states to one another determined by friendly counsel along historically established lines of allegiance and nationality; and international guarantees of the political and economic independence and territorial integrity of the several Balkan states should be entered into.

XII. The Turkish portion of the present Ottoman Empire should be assured a secure sovereignty, but the other nationalities which are now under Turkish rule should be assured an undoubted security of life and an absolutely unmolested opportunity of autonomous development, and the Dardanelles should be permanently opened as a free passage to the ships and commerce of all nations under international guarantees.

XIII. An independent Polish state should be erected which should include the territories inhabited by indisputably Polish populations, which should be assured a free and secure access to the sea, and whose political and economic independence and territorial integrity should be guaranteed by international covenant.

XIV. A general association of nations must be formed under specific covenants for the purpose of affording mutual guarantees of political independence and territorial integrity to great and small states alike.

House persuaded him to proceed and, despite their similarities in tone and content, it would be Wilson's speech that captured the imagination of the world and later historians. This should not disguise the shared values and objectives of the two men. In most, though not all, of the key questions in Paris, their common Gladstonian liberal heritage meant that there was close Anglo-American cooperation, even when two strong personalities found themselves at loggerheads. There were however, in both speeches, a number of hostages to fortune, mainly in the form of expectations raised beyond the possibility of delivery and of undertakings at odds with reality.[12]

THOMAS WOODROW WILSON (1856–1924)
A Democrat elected twenty-eighth President of the United States in 1912, and re-elected in 1916. An academic, who was previously President of Princeton University, and Governor of New Jersey. Winner of the 1919 Nobel Peace Prize.

Victory

In November 1918 a year that had begun with the terror of a near German breakthrough in the west – as late as June the French government considered evacuating Paris – ended in triumph as the Central Powers collapsed. In September Austria-Hungary asked about peace terms. On 29 September Bulgaria quit, opening the gates to Turkey, which requested an armistice on 14 October and accepted abject conditions on 30 October. On 3 November Austria-Hungary agreed an armistice, the last act of an imploding empire. But the key was Germany. On 4 October the Germans sent a telegram to Woodrow Wilson, via Switzerland, requesting him to negotiate a settlement based on his Fourteen Points.

Not until 8 October did Wilson convey to his European friends the German request and his reply. This stipulated that

President Wilson's most famous speech was that of 8 January 1918, the Fourteen Points, but he insisted to the Germans that the peace must also be based on three other of his 1918 speeches.

On 11 February he defined his Four Principles as:

- That every part of the settlement must be based on justice and contribute to a permanent peace.
- That 'peoples and provinces are not to be bartered about from sovereignty to sovereignty'.
- That 'every territorial settlement involved in this war must be made in the interest and for the benefit of the populations concerned'.
- That 'all well defined national aspirations shall be accorded the utmost satisfaction'.

On 4 July he delivered his Four Ends speech. These were:

- The destruction or weakening of every arbitrary power that threatens peace.
- The free acceptance by the people involved of the territorial, political and economic arrangements of the settlement.
- The need for modern civilized states to behave with the same codes of conduct and honour and respect for the law as is expected of their citizens.
- The establishment of a new international organization to deal with disputes between states.

He summed up the Four Ends as 'What we seek is the reign of law, based upon the consent of the governed and sustained by the organized opinion of mankind'

The Five Particulars of 27 September were:

- The need for impartial justice for all the parties in the war
- Fair treatment, without special privileges, for all.
- No special groupings or alliances within the family of the League of Nations.
- No special selfish economic arrangements within the League.
- The open publication of all treaties and international agreements.

Reflecting on Wilson's twenty-seven 1918 'points', the cynical Clemenceau remarked that 'the good Lord Himself required only ten points.'

his other major speeches – the 'Four Principles' (11 February), the 'Four Ends' (4 July) and the 'Five Particulars' (27 September) – must also form the basis of the peace and demanded a responsible German government with which to negotiate.[13] The Allies already knew, having instantly intercepted and decoded the Swiss telegram. Their resentment that Germany had ignored them was matched by fear that Wilson would be duped into allowing the Germans a respite in which to regroup and rejoin the fight. But the Germans were not feigning (indeed Eric Geddes later lamented 'Had we known how bad things were in Germany, we might have got stiffer terms'). They accepted Wilson's conditions on 12 October. He then responded, stressing that the military terms of the armistice would be settled by the Allied experts and would ensure their superiority. He required the cessation of the destruction of evacuated territory and submarine warfare and additional assurances of political change in Germany. Only when the Germans agreed to all this on 20 October did Wilson recommend that the Allies consider an armistice.

The military terms drawn up by the French Allied supreme commander, Marshal Ferdinand Foch, were so tough that Lloyd George expected the Germans to refuse. They amounted to a military surrender – something which was confirmed in June 1919 when the German generals admitted that these terms crippled any possibility of renewing the fighting, no matter how unpalatable the treaty terms. Unlike 1945 however, this was not an unconditional surrender. Germany had requested that Wilson's 1918 speeches should be the foundation of the peace. The Allies agreed in American Secretary of State, Robert Lansing's note of 5 November, though with some caveats, of which more later. To that rather flimsy extent it was a negotiated armistice and the German representatives came to Compiègne, in Northern France, to receive the conditions, which they signed at 5 a.m. on 11 November.

The British general election

After the armistice the British government immediately called an election. There were compelling constitutional reasons for this – the existing Parliament had far exceeded the maximum of five years between elections stipulated by the 1911 Parliament Act that it had been elected to pass in 1910. In a total electorate of 21 million the electoral reforms of 1918 created some 13 million new voters – more than any previous or subsequent legislation – enfranchising women aged over 30, many men previously excluded from what claimed to be 'manhood suffrage', and, for this election only, servicemen between 18 and the normal qualifying age of 21. The government needed a mandate from them to make peace. Equally compelling was the coalition leaders' wish to exploit their victory in war. In particular Lloyd George needed to use his popularity to create a more secure political base than the currently constituted parliamentary Liberal Party, divided as it was between his supporters and Asquith's. Bonar Law was also keen to exploit the Prime Minister's standing to maintain and boost the electoral standing of the Conservatives.

They had discussed a joint election programme since July 1918. When Lloyd George's efforts to bring Asquith and his followers into the Coalition failed in September, they agreed an electoral deal allowing their supporters an unopposed run in most constituencies. The two leaders issued short letters of endorsement, which Asquith disparagingly dismissed as 'coupons', to their chosen candidates – 159 Lloyd George Liberals, 364 Conservatives and 18 National Democrats.

Their initial programme concentrated on domestic issues – tariff reform, home rule for Ireland, social reform and the disestablishment of the Anglican church in Wales. Lloyd George was clear: *Let us have no vengeance, no trampling down of a fallen foe,* but the electoral agents around the country reported a lack of enthusiasm – except for the punishment of Germany. Anti-German feeling played well, fuelled by anger at the mistreatment of prisoners of war, the sinking of merchant ships – most recently, on 10 October 1918, the Irish mail packet *Leinster* with the loss of 431 lives – the executions of Edith Cavell and Captain Fryatt, atrocity stories, not all of which were the fabrication of a lively British black propaganda, and the efforts of the Northcliffe press, including *The Times* and *Daily Mail*. On 11 December the Coalition's last manifesto had four priorities: punish the Kaiser; make Germany pay; get the troops home; create better housing and social conditions.

The folk memory of the election was of one in which Sir Eric Geddes, the First Lord of the Admiralty, promised that 'the Germans ... are going to pay every penny; they are going to be squeezed as a lemon is squeezed – until the pips squeak' and George Barnes declared 'I am for hanging the Kaiser'. Some candidates were careful to dampen expectations and Lloyd George was more cautious and ambiguous in his statements, but he did not repudiate Geddes or Barnes and he encouraged the voters of Bristol and Newcastle to have optimism in Germany's capacity to pay and his determination to pursue this *to the uttermost farthing*. The result was an overwhelming coalition victory, 334 Conservatives, 127 Lloyd George Liberals and a number of other friendly independents giving an official Commons majority of 237 but, in the absence of 72 Sinn Feiners who never took their seats, this understated the reality. Asquith, Simon, Henderson and Ramsay MacDonald were among the prominent casualties.

Perhaps because there were many new MPs – almost half the Conservatives for example – who may have been naïve about the relationship between electoral promises and the pragmatism of power, or perhaps because they were, in Stanley Baldwin's memorable phrase 'a lot of hard-faced men who look as if they had done very well out of the war', the new House expected Lloyd George to deliver.[14] In the euphoria of electoral triumph Bonar Law declared: 'He can be Prime Minister for life if he likes' but, by March 1919, Conservatives

> 'George thinks he won the election. Well he didn't. It was the Tories that won the election, and he will soon begin to find that out.'
>
> WALTER LONG

like Walter Long took a different line: 'George thinks he won the election. Well, he didn't. It was the Tories that won the election, *and he will soon begin to find that out.*'[15] The next month over 200 MPs sent a telegram to Paris demanding that he fulfil his electoral pledges, present the bill in full to Germany and make it pay. Three years later the Conservatives would consign him to the political wilderness.

Preparing for peace

On the morning of 11 November 1918 Harold Nicolson, a young British diplomat, chanced to look from the Foreign Office towards Downing Street: 'It was 10.55 a.m. Suddenly the front door opened. Mr Lloyd George, his white hair fluttering on the wind, appeared upon the front doorstep. He waved his arms outwards. I opened the window hurriedly. He was shouting the same sentence over and over again. I caught his words. "At eleven o'clock this morning the war will be over."'

Nicolson went back to his study of a potential peace conference problem, 'When I again emerged the whole of London had gone mad.'[16]

It was significant that Nicolson was preparing for peacemaking. That process had already begun, even though the war ended more swiftly than expected. The jubilation of the crowds implied an expectation that the peace would reflect their victory. The forthcoming negotiations would be much influenced by wartime expedients, promises, statements and policies as well as by peacetime political developments. Lloyd George's premiership encompassed many of these, most notably in terms of his statement of war aims in January 1918, but also the conflicting undertakings given to various parties concerning the Ottoman Empire and the Middle East, and the British general election in late 1918.

Wartime developments in the Middle East

The Entente's declarations of war on the Ottoman Empire in November 1914 encouraged an assumption of its imminent collapse. The Allies divided the carcass in advance. In March and April 1915 Britain and France acceded to Russian demands for post-war control of Constantinople and the Straits, overturning Britain's consistent 19th-century policy of denying the Russians access to the Mediterranean from the Black Sea. The Jingoes would be turning in their graves.

The Jingoes were originally Russophobes, taking their name from a popular music hall song by G W Hunt from the 1877–8 Balkan crisis: 'We don't want to fight, but by jingo if we do, we've got the ships, we've got the men, we've got the money too. We've fought the Bear before, and while we're Britons true, the Russians shall not have Constantinople.' The term took on a more general meaning of bellicose super-patriots.

The Treaty of London, signed in April 1915, promised the

Italians not only acquisitions from Austria-Hungary but also a share of the Ottoman Empire, whilst in May 1916 the agreement between Sir Mark Sykes and Georges Picot, representing Britain and France respectively, proposed to divide that empire amongst Britain, France and Russia, making some provision for an independent Arab state or confederation of states, with international control over Palestine. The Treaty of St Jean de Maurienne in April 1917 added the Italians to the deal, but the revolutions in Russia meant this treaty was never ratified. Much more significantly, the collapse of Russia left Britain and France as the only two serious players in the region. Lord Milner's comment, originally directed at the colonial distribution in Africa, was equally apposite here: 'Ultimately, I presume, Italy will have to be satisfied with what France and Great Britain are prepared to give up.' It would not be a lot.[17]

Anglo-French rivalry dominated Middle Eastern affairs, but Britain also engaged in a complex series of manoeuvres with other parties, partly to recoup what came to be seen as excessive concessions to France, particularly in the Sykes-Picot agreement which George Curzon said was 'hanging like a millstone around our necks'. Russia's elimination had destroyed France's value to Britain as a buffer between the British and Russian spheres of influence.

In Europe, only with great reluctance did Britain play the potentially suicidal card of encouraging nationalist discontents in the Central Powers (which might set a dangerous example to Irishmen, Indians and others). Not so in the Ottoman Empire. As early as October 1914, even before hostilities began, Lord Cromer suggested that 'a few officers who could speak Arabic, if sent into Arabia, could raise the whole country against the Turks'. Failure in Gallipoli and humiliation at Kut, when Asquith had tried – and failed – to ransom a defeated British force, made the idea of internal disruption even more attractive and Britain opened negotiations with a number of Arab leaders, of whom, in the short term at least, Sherif Hussein of Mecca, was the most important.[18]

Hussein's correspondence in 1915 and 1916 with Sir Henry MacMahon, the British High Commissioner in Egypt, secured some ambiguous British indications of support for a large independent Arab kingdom, provided the Arabs mounted a successful revolt against the Turks. From this sprang the campaigns in the desert associated with T E Lawrence – Lawrence of Arabia – and a complicated wrangle about whether the British had included Palestine in the proposed new Arab state. The probability is that the careless use of an ambiguous word, *vilayet*, which could mean either a district or a province, did ascribe Palestine to the Arabs, but this was not a formal treaty, only an exchange of letters, though Hussein might be forgiven for believing it to be more.

If the promised land of Palestine had been gifted to the Arabs or divided with the French and Russians in 1916, it became the 'twice- or thrice-promised land' in November 1917 when the British government approved the Balfour Declaration which stated that 'His Majesty's Government view with favour the establishment in Palestine of a National home for the Jewish people'.[19]

The government made this pledge for several reasons. It hoped to encourage Jews in Russia to continue to support the war, at a time when Russian resolve was wavering, but this came too late to do any good. It hoped to impress an important Jewish lobby in the United States. Crucially, even though the logic was somewhat obscure, it hoped a Jewish settlement in Palestine, sympathetic to Britain, might undo some of the perceived disadvantages of the Sykes-Picot pact. It was not,

THE BALFOUR DECLARATION
Foreign Office, November 2nd, 1917.
Dear Lord Rothschild,
    I have much pleasure in conveying to you, on behalf of His Majesty's
Government, the following declaration of sympathy with Jewish Zionist
aspirations which has been submitted to, and approved by, the Cabinet:
'His Majesty's Government view with favour the establishment in
Palestine of a national home for the Jewish people, and will use their
best endeavours to facilitate the achievement of this object, it being
clearly understood that nothing shall be done which may prejudice the
civil and religious rights of existing non-Jewish communities in
Palestine, or the rights and political status enjoyed by Jews in any
other country'.
    I should be grateful if you would bring this declaration to the
knowledge of the Zionist Federation.
    Yours sincerely
    Arthur James Balfour

as Lloyd George later claimed, given in gratitude for the scientific acumen of Chaim Weizmann, a Russian-born Zionist and chemistry don at Manchester University, whose contribution to the mass production of acetone had been important to the British war effort. For Lloyd George, the pragmatic prospect of a British land bridge from Europe to India and Asia was complemented by the less tangible factor of his fascination with the Holy Land.

He was a committed Zionist – someone who believed that the Jews, driven by the Romans from Palestine in the second century AD, should be permitted to reconstitute a Jewish state and reassemble there such descendants of the Jewish diaspora as wished to return. Although alternatives such as Cyprus or Uganda were suggested, Palestine was the preferred option. He may have lost his belief in God as a young man, but his Zionism sprang in part from his Nonconformist roots. His Calvinism was not necessarily conventional, but it was a powerful presence in his psyche.

He became the British legal representative for Theodore Herzl's Zionist movement in 1902, sharing his commitment to their cause with some of his closest associates, including C P Scott of the *Manchester Guardian* and Lord Milner, a member of his War Cabinet and leader of the influential imperial *Round Table* ginger group, of which Philip Kerr, his private secretary, was an important member. Lloyd George always disputed the General Staff's claim that the war could only be won on the Western Front. He was an 'Easterner' – someone who sought less direct ways to assault the Central Powers. By 1917 he believed Britain should direct its main efforts against Turkey and he was committed to bringing much of the Middle East under British control. This represented yet another happy Lloyd Georgian coincidence of principle and practical advantage.

The Declaration raised concerns in the cabinet. Edwin Montagu, the Secretary of State for India, spoke for many non-Zionist Jews when he asked whether the promise of a Jewish home in Palestine might undermine their rights as citizens of their present countries. Curzon raised other questions, repeated many times: Could the territory support a greater population? How was it possible to allow the immigration of Jews into Palestine without disturbing the native culture and life style? Would this not inevitably lead both to an eventual Jewish take-over and provoke political unrest? 'What is to become of the people of the country?' he asked. 'They profess the Mohammedan faith. They will not be content either to be expropriated for Jewish immigrants or to act merely as hewers of wood and drawers of water to the latter.'[20] The wording of the Declaration tried to counter both sets of fears by claiming that the national home did not affect the rights of Jews in their present states and that Jewish immigration would not be allowed to prejudice the rights of the non-Jewish communities in Palestine. It did not indicate how this latter tall order, in particular, would be accomplished.

Given that even the 'secret' arrangements between the Allies were fairly common knowledge, it is difficult to believe that the Arabs were much impressed by the Anglo-French declaration of 7 November 1918 that they were fighting for 'the complete and definite emancipation of the peoples so long oppressed by the Turks and the establishment of national governments and administrations deriving their authority from the initiative and free choice of the indigenous populations'. Any faith remaining would have been further eroded had they known Milner's definition of Arab independence: 'what we mean by it is that Arabia while being independent herself should be kept out of the sphere of European political intrigue and within the British sphere of influence: in other words that her independent native rulers should have no foreign treaties except with us.'[21]

As Balfour pointed out, in March 1919, Britain had committed itself to a number of contradictory undertakings: the McMahon-Hussein correspondence; Sykes-Picot Pact; the Anglo-French declaration of November 1918; the Covenant of the League of Nations: '... so far as I can see, none of them have wholly lost their validity or can be treated in all respects as of merely historic interest. Each can be quoted by Frenchmen, Englishmen, Americans and Arabs when it happens to suit their purposes. Doubtless each will so be quoted before we come to a final arrangement about the Middle East.'

He had omitted his own Declaration and the added complication of the Jews from his list. This would not be an easy tangle to unravel at the Peace Conference.[22]

'The Distractions of an Indispensable': *Punch* cartoon of 26 March 1919 (see page 76).

II
The Paris Peace Conference

3
Paris

The Paris Peace Conference marked the peak of Lloyd George's career. He represented the British Empire at the fullest height of its power: its air force and navy the largest in the world; its armies victorious in the Middle East and responsible for the final defeat of the German army in the west; Germany's submarines were rusting in Harwich and its High Seas Fleet was interned at Scapa Flow. He had just won a crushing electoral victory. He could now stride the world stage and reveal the complete range of his diplomatic ability and statesmanlike qualities.

He revelled in the cut-and-thrust of negotiations at the conference and returned from Paris believing: *It has been a wonderful time.* His ability to find solutions to insoluble questions and to reach compromises where none seemed possible, above all his skill in persuading his colleagues by the eloquence and ingenuity of his arguments, meant that he could tell Frances on 5 April 1919: *We are making headway, which means that I am getting my own way!*[1]

All this was in the future when he arrived in Paris on 11 January 1919 taking up residence in an opulent flat in the Rue

Nitôt. Maggie and Megan accompanied him for the first few weeks before Maggie returned home. Sadly, the splendid story that, asked if he intended to take Mrs Lloyd George to the Conference, he replied, *you don't take a sandwich to a feast,* cannot be entirely true. Megan, who had not yet worked out his relationship with his secretary, moved to share Frances's accommodation at the Majestic, until she was sent to finishing school, allowing Frances to spend more time at the Rue Nitôt. One floor above them, frequently entertained by the Prime Minister's love of Welsh hymns and Negro spirituals, though not always so well informed about his intentions, was Arthur Balfour, the Foreign Secretary, viewing 'events with the detachment of a choir-boy at a funeral service'.[2]

Organising the delegation

Accommodation for the other members of the British delegation was less settled, and one of Lloyd George's first tasks was to try and resolve a growing crisis as more and more people, from Britain and its Dominions, flooded into Paris, expecting to find somewhere to work and sleep. Even before the Conference began, Lord Derby, the British ambassador to France, complained in November 1918 that: 'There is not a day that telegrams do not arrive asking me to secure accommodation for Tom, Dick or Harry.'[3]

That month Derby assisted the Foreign Office (after the obligatory face-off with the Treasury) to hire the Hotels Majestic and Astoria in the Avenue Kléber, and a site for a printing press at the Auteuil race course (much to the chagrin of a Parisian public looking forward to a resumption of horse-racing). Maurice Hankey and the British secretariat were housed in the Villa Majestic, across the street from the hotel. The Astoria was where the delegation worked. The

Majestic, with its 430 bedrooms, was where the senior staff slept though, as the Dominions sent more delegates than expected, this proved inadequate.

More accommodation was soon needed for servants and the Treasury agreed to hire the Hotel La Perouse – 'might do but fear too luxurious' – and then, as the numbers of typists, Girl Guides, chauffeurs, charwomen, caterers and waiters continued to swell, the Hotels Baltimore and d'Albe, 51 Avenue d' Iéna, 55 Bois de Boulogne, 46 Rue la Perouse and accommodation for 120 printers near Auteuil. The Girl Guides, who were hired as messengers, required chaperoned accommodation and recreational facilities. The youngest, Jessie Spencer, was 13. In February Balfour banned any further personnel from arriving. At its height there were well over 1,000 people in the British Empire Delegation in Paris, while others commuted to and from London as required, some by air, including Churchill who, as a qualified though eccentric pilot, occasionally flew himself.

Obtaining the requisite furniture, equipment and stationery was a struggle – epic battles were waged over wardrobes, huts for the printers, baths, banking facilities, the correct bill books for the restaurant, the prompt delivery of that day's *The Times,* and uniforms for the waitresses. Gatekeepers and Foreign Office officials complained about wages and allowances – the former with greater success.

Later there were equally titanic struggles over settling the bills after the Conference: with Harrods for two unreliable Daimler cars; the Majestic for replacement linen (a staggering £14,000); and for assorted damages which Eyre Crowe, a senior Foreign Office official, thought not unreasonable given the poor quality of some of the staff. 'It was indeed a rarity to get through a meal in the restaurant or in the dining room' he wrote in November 1919, 'without one, or more frequently several, big crashes of glass and crockery, and it was currently reported at one time that, rather than wash up dirty plates and dishes, the kitchen staff deliberately broke them and threw them in the dustbin.'[4]

The British diplomat, Esme Howard, described the early atmosphere in January: 'It is amusing at meals at the Majestic Hotel and rather like the beginning of a voyage on a big Atlantic liner when one looks at all the people and wonders who they are. Little by little one meets them and makes acquaintances.' The hotel became a small British world, famous for its Saturday dances: 'Why' asked Foch, when he visited one, 'do the British have such sad faces and such cheerful bottoms?' There was a theatre in the basement and the delegation turned to amateur dramatics, under the direction of a young Foreign Office official, Robert Vansittart. In between they worked very hard, often to exhaustion, whilst many took advantage of the proximity of the battlefields to visit the graves of their relatives.[5]

The ghost of Metternich blighted the culinary expectations of the British delegation. At the Congress of Vienna he had bribed servants to bring him the contents of other delegations' waste baskets. Determined to avoid this, Alwyn Parker, the Foreign Office librarian who was in charge of the administrative arrangements, hired British staff for the Majestic. Harold Nicolson bemoaned the results: 'The food, in consequence, was of the Anglo-Swiss variety, whereas the coffee was British to the core.' He also questioned Parker's logic, because the staff in the Astoria, where all the delegation's papers were kept, were French.

Parker was also the luckless creator of a planisphere designed to show Charles Hardinge, the Permanent Under

Secretary of the Foreign Office, as the central figure in the administration of the British delegation. Nicolson records that 'Upon this reeling orrery, Prime Ministers and Dominion Delegates whirled each in his proper orbit, coloured green or red or blue. Mr Parker himself could be discerned revolving modestly as a moon attendant upon Jupiter, Lord Hardinge of Penshurst, the "Organising Ambassador" ... Mr Lloyd George on seeing it, laughed aloud.' Despite Hardinge's title (which was much resented by Derby who believed there should only be one ambassador in Paris), it was Hankey who played the principal role in terms of British coordination.[6]

Lloyd George faced another early battle when he arrived. The First World War had made a profound difference to the relationship between Britain and its Dominions. The sacrifices made by the Australians and New Zealanders at Gallipoli, the South Africans at Delville Wood, the Canadians at Vimy Ridge and the Indians in France and the Middle East all increased their sense of nationhood whilst raising doubts about what Sir Robert Borden, the Canadian premier, called the 'incompetence and blundering stupidity of the whiskey and soda British H.Q. Staff'. The Dominions demanded that Lloyd George secure them independent representation. His initial suggestion that one Dominion premier be appointed as a British delegate was rejected as inadequate, and because, as Hankey observed, 'the dominions are as jealous of each other as cats'. With no little difficulty, and amidst claims of extra votes for the British Empire, he obtained two plenipotentiaries each for Australia, Canada, India and South Africa and one for New Zealand.[7]

Organising the British case

The end of the war came much quicker than expected – most commentators predicted victory in 1919, some even in 1920 – but despite this the British delegation was well prepared when it arrived in Paris. The Historical Section of the Foreign Office produced a remarkable series of Peace Handbooks, packed with statistics and information on almost every subject that was likely to be discussed at the Conference. All were written by experts, many by members of the Political Intelligence Department (the PID), a group of academics, educationalists, journalists and others gathered together during the war to analyse public and secret information and to advise the Foreign Office on policy and propaganda.

This formidable 'Ministry of All the Talents' included in its ranks, Lewis Namier, E H Carr, Arnold Toynbee, Harold Temperley and Alfred Zimmern. Most were classical scholars, but some, like James Headlam-Morley, its effective head, had already adapted their skills to the analysis of contemporary events. Many, after their temporary service in the Foreign Office ended, would help to create the new disciplines of international relations and contemporary history, attempting thereby to make a contribution to avoiding a future calamity on the scale of the recent war. There must always be a question as to how many of the decision-makers actually found time to read these briefings, but they are witness to the thoroughness of the Foreign Office preparations.[8]

Organising (?) the conference

The conference itself was less well-ordered and did much to justify the prediction by the veteran French diplomat, Jules Cambon, at its opening on 18 January, that the outcome would be *'une improvisation'*. His brother Paul, the long-serving ambassador in London, agreed: 'No matter how hard you try, you cannot imagine the shambles, the chaos, the incoherence, the ignorance here. Nobody knows anything because everything is happening behind the scenes.' Almost all contemporary accounts emphasise the lack of structure and organisation, especially in the early days of the Conference.[9]

There were various reasons for this. First there was no agreed agenda or order of priorities. The French delegation was the only one to propose an agenda, but placing Wilson's League of Nations idea as its final item was tactless, and casting doubt on the value of the Fourteen Points as a peace programme ensured that it was consigned to oblivion by the indignant President. No-one suggested an alternative. Then it was not entirely clear what the structure or purpose of these meetings would be. Was the intention to hold a preliminary inter-Allied discussion to agree their terms, then invite the Germans and their allies to a peace conference to negotiate the questions directly at issue between them, and finally to involve them and the neutrals in a peace congress to consider a wide-ranging settlement of international issues?

This would follow the model of 1814–15 where the victors had first settled accounts with France in the Treaty of Paris and then, at the Congress of Vienna, discussed a range of international questions including those territorial claims and ambitions of the powers that did not directly involve France: the establishment of a balance of power in Europe; the settling of the protocol of diplomatic precedence; the control of international waterways; and the suppression of the slave trade. Above all, the Congress established a new international order, at first the Congress System, which then developed into the later and more long-lived, if looser, Concert of Europe, both of which were based on the idea of consultation amongst the Great Powers.

This does seem to have been the pattern that many expected to be followed, but it was not. Any idea of a sequential series of discussions in Paris was soon dropped. Instead the Allies set up simultaneous and parallel inter-Allied meetings, discussions about the wider territorial settlement and commissions to consider issues of a general international significance like the creation of an International Labor Organisation or the League of Nations. Furthermore there were precedents from 1815 of which the victors in 1919 did not care to be reminded. Then the skilful diplomacy of Talleyrand enabled him to set France's former enemies at each others' throats and to rescue a much stronger position than seemed possible.

Rapidly realising how difficult it was to create even fragile agreements amongst themselves, the Allies knew that any German delegation would not need a fraction of Talleyrand's talents to undermine any semblance of Allied unity. Thus any thought of bringing the Germans to Paris to negotiate the terms of the Treaty was, over the course of the early stages of the Conference, quietly dropped, and the Allies tacitly assumed, as the French had proposed originally, that their decisions would 'be imposed severally on the enemy without any discussion with him'.

This did incur some inconveniences, however, because much of the early work of the various commissions set to draft the Allied terms was based on the assumption that there would be negotiations. Hence they gave themselves latitude for concessions and stated their most extreme positions. When no negotiations occurred, these maximum demands became the actual terms of the Treaty. Nicolson's opinion was that: 'Had it been known from the outset that no negotiations would ever take place with the enemy, it is certain that many of the less reasonable clauses of the Treaty would never have been inserted.' There was another consideration: each of these maximum demands might, in isolation, be justifiable, but their cumulative effect would produce a mathematical impossibility, a whole greater than the sum of its parts.[10]

The peacemakers were not helped by the collapse of traditional authority throughout much of central and eastern Europe and the additional responsibility, which their predecessors at Vienna had not shared, to create order there. They were, as Margaret MacMillan has pointed out, a sort of emergency government for Europe, whilst Paris was, for the first six months of 1919, the capital of the world.[11]

Making sure the Germans knew who had won

Paris was itself a controversial choice. Lloyd George and Wilson had originally thought of a neutral city, possibly Geneva or Lausanne, but Wilson then decided that Switzerland was 'saturated with every kind of poisonous element and open to every hostile element in Europe' and, when House agreed to the French premier Georges Clemenceau's strong plea for Paris, Lloyd George was left isolated. He acquiesced with a bad grace: *I never wanted to hold the Conference in his bloody capital ... but the old man wept and protested so much that we gave way.* Only somewhere the size of Paris could accommodate the thousands of delegates who would soon flood there, but the atmosphere in a city so recently menaced by

GEORGES CLEMENCEAU (1841–1929)
A formidable French politician well-worthy of his nickname 'the Tiger'. Survivor of several duels, with a wicked sense of humour and a talent for the cutting phrase. Prime Minister of France 1917–1920, credited as 'le père la victoire' – 'Old Man Victory' in 1918.

German armies, raided by German planes, and bombarded by the terrifying 'Big Bertha' shells – one of which, hurtling through the roof of Notre Dame cathedral, killed many of those at prayer – was hardly likely to be conducive to moderation or generosity.[12]

Clemenceau did nothing to dispel such concerns. The conference opened officially on 18 January, a Saturday – an odd choice, except that it was on 18 January 1871 that Bismarck had proclaimed the German Empire in the Hall of Mirrors at Versailles, following Prussia's victory in the Franco-Prussian War. The Tiger had already produced the *wagon lit* used by Napoleon III in the 1870 campaign for the signature of the armistice, and later the Treaty would be signed in the same Hall of Mirrors, on a table that had belonged to Louis XIV, which Clemenceau had chosen personally for the occasion. He missed no opportunity to make a point. Esme Howard recorded the following scene after the opening ceremony: 'I hear that when the Delegates were putting on their hats to leave Wilson who saw Clemenceau putting on an old soft felt said "I was told I must wear a tall hat for this occasion" "So was I" retorted C. cramming his soft hat over his eyes.'[13]

> I never wanted to hold the Conference in his bloody capital ... but the old man wept and protested so much that we gave way.
>
> LLOYD GEORGE

To his embarrassment Lloyd George was late for the ceremony because of a misunderstanding of the meaning of the times on the invitation. In his apology to the French president, Raymond Poincaré he wrote: *No-one therefore was more surprised than myself to find that I was the last to enter the conference room and that the proceedings had commenced before my arrival*. It was not a good omen.[14]

'There is a Conference of the Great Powers going on in the next room'

The Conference's first plenary session, at which most of the participating states were represented, was a purely formal affair, a pattern that Clemenceau was determined to follow. In theory all states were equal; in practice they were not and Howard's diary contains a revealing entry for 24 January 1919: 'The conference is moving on. Today was the second plenary session to which small powers were also invited. Some of their representatives complained bitterly that they were not sufficiently consulted especially the Belgian Hymans who had a passage of arms with Clemenceau. The latter said that the object of the Conference was to get on with its work and too many cooks would spoil the broth or words to that effect.' Nicolson reinforced the impression: 'Clemenceau rather high handed with the smaller Powers. "Y a-t-il d'objections? Non? … Adopté." Like a machine gun.' Clemenceau was absolutely candid: 'I make no mystery of it – there is a Conference of the Great Powers going on in the next room.'[15]

RAYMOND POINCARÉ (1860–1934) A lawyer from Lorraine who was five times French Prime Minister and President of the Republic from 1913–20. A hard-liner in terms of Treaty enforcement, he was responsible for the occupation of the Ruhr in January 1923. According to his bitter enemy, Georges Clemenceau, there were two perfectly useless things in the world, an appendix, and Poincaré.

Initially therefore it was the two main representatives of the five major powers – Britain, France, Japan, Italy and the United States – who dominated the key decision-making body, the Council of Ten, but Lloyd George, Balfour, Clemenceau, Pichon, Matsui, Chinda (later Saionji and Makino), Orlando, Sonnino, Wilson and Lansing all had advisers and the numbers involved swelled to alarming proportions – at its

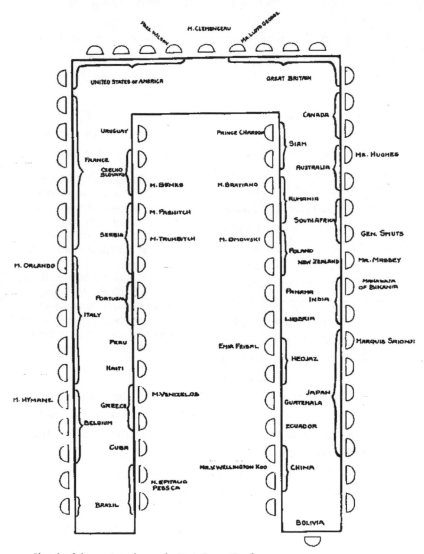

Sketch of the seating plan at the Paris Peace Conference.

last full meeting on 24 March there over 50 people in the room. Perhaps unsurprisingly it was not an effective body. At its last meeting it still had not decided an item raised at its first. It could not be faulted for its diligence, it had met 72 times, initially twice a day, latterly once, and established 58 sub-committees, many of which would provide impor-

VITTORIO ORLANDO (1860–1952)
A lawyer and academic from Sicily who became Prime Minister of Italy in 1917. He resigned on 23 June 1919, before the treaty was signed, disappointed by his failure to gain Fiume for Italy.

tant recommendations contributing towards the final treaties, but it did not decide. By late March only two things were settled – all the German colonies would be forfeit and the text of the first draft of the Covenant of the League of Nations was agreed.

Drafting the League Covenant

The failure of the existing international organisations to prevent the 1914 July crisis escalating into war encouraged calls for reform and new ideas. Grey was among the early advocates of a universal alliance for peace. He always believed he could have averted the war had he had the authority to force the major powers to a conference in July 1914. Undoubtedly the most important convert, however, was Woodrow Wilson, who, in May 1916, endorsed the idea, in a speech encapsulating many of the key concepts of the League as it emerged from the Paris conference. He called for a 'Universal association of the nations to maintain the inviolate security of the highways of the seas for the common good and unhindered use of all the nations of the world and to prevent any war begun either contrary to treaty covenants or without warning and full submission of the causes to the opinion of the world – a virtual guarantee of territorial integrity and political independence.'[16]

Wilson, perhaps surprisingly, would do little in a practical sense to investigate how this idea might be translated into reality. Instead committees were established in France in 1918, chaired by Léon Bourgeois, the French politician and jurist and, earlier, in 1917, one convened by Lloyd George in Britain, under the leadership of Sir Walter Phillimore, a high court judge. Nonetheless Wilson's advocacy was vital. Without his support it is clear that neither Clemenceau nor Lloyd George would have given the League any great prominence in their Peace Conference programmes.

Phillimore's committee produced the more significant results, highlighting many of the problems and dilemmas that would face League supporters in the future. In particular its support for the concept of automatic and obligatory collective action against an alliance member that broke its undertakings not to go to war without exhausting the alternative avenues, did raise the central choice between the demands of collective security and the paramount claims of national sovereignty.

Given that the most important decision ever taken by a sovereign state is that of going to war, it was difficult to envisage any state surrendering that decision to the actions of another power, even if one left aside the not inconsiderable issue of national constitutions, like that of the United States, under which the power to declare war was assigned, quite specifically, to the Congress. Yet, if the innocent party in such a dispute where war had occurred could not count on the automatic support of its fellow members, wherein lay the value of an insurance policy that only paid out on the whim of the individual decisions of all the other subscribers? This conflict between the concepts of collective security and national sovereignty remained at the heart of the debates over the League – and, predictably, there would only be one winner.

Lloyd George had only limited belief in the League idea but he was astute enough to understand that there was a broad constituency of people who wanted an assurance that the international system would be reformed to prevent future catastrophes on the scale of the present war. He acknowledged this in his 5 January 1918 speech, when he called for a new international organisation offering an alternative to war for the settlement of disputes between states. When Wilson echoed this demand in the concluding of his Fourteen Points three days later, it was clear that the League would be a central part of any Anglo-American liberal response to the challenges of war and revolution.

Lloyd George might be uneasy about its implications, and aware that some of his advisers saw the League as 'flapdoodle', 'moonshine' or 'futile nonsense', but he knew that he had to be seen to be a League supporter. There was, however, a potential further advantage, because Wilson's obsession with the League might offer opportunities to exchange support for the President's plan for American backing on issues seen to be of more practical importance to Britain. Lloyd George appointed two known enthusiasts, Lord Robert Cecil and the South African Jan Christian Smuts, as Britain's representatives on the League Commission established on 25 January, to be chaired by Wilson. It was a good two-way bet, though Cecil, in particular, interpreted his brief in a very liberal fashion and went much further than Lloyd George wished in his quest to create a meaningful League.

The Paris negotiations on the drafting of the Covenant illustrated what could be achieved by the close and productive informal relationships at various levels between the British and American delegations. By the time they reached Paris there were several different schemes at various stages of development and Cecil, Lansing and House agreed, on 8 January, that it would be wise for them to coordinate their approach before meeting their allies. Into the melting pot went ideas from Smuts (whose December 1918 *The League of Nations: A Practical Suggestion* was the most influential of the pre-Paris proposals), Cecil, and Wilson himself. Cecil worked hard to resolve as many of the points of dispute as possible, drawing up a new composite Anglo-American draft with an American lawyer, David Hunter Miller, then holding a series of meetings with Smuts, Lloyd George, Wilson and House. Once they had reached agreement on a broad set of principles Cecil Hurst, from the Foreign Office, together with Miller, drew up the Hurst-Miller draft, which formed the basis for the discussions in the League Commission, which met for the first time on 2 February.

The Commission, which met ten times in eleven days, worked with a speed and an energy that was unmatched at this stage of the Conference. It was a striking proof of the idea that he who produces the draft, dominates the agenda, and, despite its size – there were two delegates from each of the five major powers and one from each of nine smaller powers – the commission was very much an Anglo-American affair. Wilson chaired all but its last meeting, and, working very closely with Cecil, drove through most of the key points on which they were agreed.

The League, with its permanent capital and bureaucracy in Geneva, would be governed by periodic meetings of all its members in the Assembly, with its executive body, the Council, meeting more frequently. The original plan was for the Council to consist only of the Great Powers, but the smaller powers, appealing for some gesture towards international democracy and the equality of states, insisted that, in addition to the permanent great power members, a number of smaller powers would be elected for fixed terms. The Covenant offered various methods for disputes to be settled without resort to force and provided sanctions at varying degrees of intensity to deter non-compliance with League rules.

At the heart of the League was the promise that all members made in Article 10 'to respect and preserve as against external aggression the territorial integrity and existing political independence of all Members of the League. In case of any such aggression or in case of any threat or danger of such aggression, the Council shall advise upon the means by which this obligation shall be fulfilled.'

Given the uncertain and controversial nature of many of the new frontiers that the treaties would create, even if one discounted pre-1914 territorial disputes and international quarrels, this was an undertaking of enormous proportions, but, as Wilson pointed out, without it the League would be no more than a talking shop. The crucial question, put by Cecil, was: 'Yes, but do any of us mean it?'

He might have added: 'If so, what are we going to do about it?' Phillimore, and Wilson's first draft for the League, had envisaged that any member breaking or disregarding its covenants '.. shall thereby *ipso facto* [by that very fact, i.e. automatically] become at war with all the members of the League'. In other words, it would be the actions of an aggressive covenant-breaker that would take the decision, for other League members, of whether or not they were at war. On the one hand such wording would create an effective, automatic and definite response from the international community but, on the other, it was an unprecedented, and predictably unacceptable, violation of the principle of national sovereignty. Wilson's later version, which effectively became the basis of

Article 16, stated that a covenant-breaker '... shall thereby *ipso facto* be deemed to have committed an act of war against all the members of the League'. The power to decide if, and how, to react now reverted to the individual national capitals of League members, reinforcing the paramountcy of national sovereignty at the expense of collective security.

One of Lloyd George's concerns, shared with other British representatives, was that Article 10, by guaranteeing, effectively, the *status quo*, would create dangerous inflexibilities in the international system and deny the possibility of peaceful change. To counter this they proposed Article 19, which allowed members to advise the reconsideration 'of treaties which have become inapplicable and the consideration of international conditions whose continuance might endanger the peace of the world'. This constituted another interesting ambiguity, casting further doubt on the effectiveness of collective security.

On 14 February Wilson, his hand resting on the Bible, presented the draft Covenant to a plenary session of the Conference, claiming 'a living thing is born'. He was aware that there were still a number of unresolved questions, but he had great hopes for his project, telling his wife: 'This is our first real step forward for I now realise, more than ever before, that, once established, the League can arbitrate and correct mistakes which are inevitable in the treaty we are trying to make at this time.'[17]

The Anglo-American consensus faced a number of challenges. The French were anxious that the League should have teeth, and wanted it to have its own armed forces and an international general staff. The Japanese wished to include a racial equality clause. Both these proposals were defeated, though Wilson and Cecil found, to their embarrassment, that they had to resort to dubious procedural tactics to head off the Japanese. When he returned from the United States, smarting from the criticisms and rebuffs of League opponents in the Senate, Wilson had to seek the agreement of his colleagues to changes to accommodate the special status of the Monroe Doctrine and to make provision for members to leave the League.

Lloyd George was never an enthusiast for Wilson's ambitious attempt to revolutionise international relations. He would have preferred an organisation more on the lines of the inter-Allied wartime Supreme Council, and a more effective operation of the balance of power, but his political antennae warned him that he must at least appear to believe in the League, though America's refusal to join did nothing to increase his faith. In many ways he was typical of many inter-war British leaders, who disguised their private disbelief in the League for the benefit of an electorate which was instead offered an impression of whole-hearted support. The Abyssinian crisis of 1935 would reveal, starkly, the dangerous chasm between apparent British enthusiasm for collective security and the reality of belief in the old-fashioned virtues of preserving a balance of power.

In October 1935 Mussolini's Italy invaded fellow League member, Abyssinia. Britain found itself torn between the electoral need to support the League and the consideration that Italy might be a useful counter-weight to the growing power of Hitler's Germany. At Stresa, in April 1935, Britain, France and Italy had agreed to uphold the Versailles and Locarno treaties against German revisionism. To apply sanctions against Italy for its clear act of aggression would destroy the Stresa agreement; not to apply sanctions would destroy the credibility of the League and risk defeat in the imminent general election. The outcome was a hopeless fudge of collective security and balance of power policies: inadequate sanctions were applied; the League proved toothless and collapsed; Abyssinia was defeated; Italy became Hitler's ally.

The outcome of this deceit was a disaster that destroyed both the League and the possibility of an Anglo-Italian alliance; collective security and the balance of power were both the losers.

Resolving the crisis of the conference

The League Covenant now existed, but Lloyd George was acutely aware that many other questions were unresolved: the definition of Germany's new frontiers, both in the east and west; how much it should pay in reparations; the size of its armed forces; who would inherit responsibility for its colonies; the Italian claims to Fiume; the Polish claims to Danzig and a 'corridor' to the sea; Anglo-French rivalries in the Middle East; and what to do about the looming ideological menace of Soviet Russia. The peacemakers felt themselves to be in a race between decisions and anarchy – the longer they delayed the more likely it was that Bolshevism – which they did not define with any precision, rather equating it with disorder, lawlessness, famine and mayhem – would succeed in filling the vacuum of power in eastern and central Europe. A new, more decisive, mechanism was needed – and with some urgency.

There was another reason as well. A *Punch* cartoon showed Lloyd George as a bareback circus rider, standing on two horses, 'Peace Conference' and 'Labour Unrest', whose paths were starting to diverge. The chief executives of the world's major states were in Paris, as their countries strove to come to terms with the difficult problems of demobilisation. Total war had required governments to direct and control areas where they previously had little competence or interest. Huge armies had to be dismantled, industry and shipping freed from wartime regulation, men returning from the war found jobs, and the women who had been encouraged to replace those men on the benches to free them for service in the trenches, now had to be returned to domesticity.

Just as the whole process of mobilisation for war had been a sharp learning curve, so too now was the process of demobilisation, and early indications in Britain were that the government was not getting it right. The first schemes, to release men in the army who could obtain a letter from their employer guaranteeing work, favoured those who had recently been conscripted, to the obvious detriment of the earlier volunteers. This provoked unrest and near mutiny. As democratically elected leaders the peacemakers knew that their future depended equally, if not more, on the decisions they should be taking at home, as well as those to be taken in Paris. It is thus to Lloyd George's credit that in the midst of a serious coal crisis in Britain, he wrote to Tom Jones, one of the cabinet secretariat, on 17 March: *Unfortunately if I have to choose between letting things go smash in England or go smash here I feel that my first duty must be to the Peace Conference. It is a horrible choice, but I must take it.*[18]

After two months in Europe Wilson felt he must return to America to confront growing Republican opposition to the League. Lloyd George made the shorter journey to England, whilst Clemenceau, who had the advantage of being on home soil, was attacked by a would-be assassin. On 19 February Lloyd George wrote to Philip Kerr, his private secretary, who had remained in Paris: *I was very shocked to hear the news of the attempt on Clemenceau, but I am delighted to find that nothing serious has happened. He is a gallant old boy – one of the bravest men I ever met.* Tough old bird that he was, Clemenceau was back at the Conference within a week, though he carried a bullet inside his chest for the remaining ten years of his life and Lloyd George felt he was never quite the same again: *Now he so often asks for twenty-four hours in which to make up his mind. Before, he made it up in twenty-four seconds*. For whatever reasons, each of the leaders knew that time was pressing.[19]

March proved to be crucial in a number of ways. The Council of Four – Lloyd George, Clemenceau, Vittorio Orlando, the Italian premier, and Wilson – replaced the Council of Ten as the Conference's key decision-making body. The Council of Five – the American, British, French and Italian foreign ministers, together with the Japanese representative, who retained his seat on this body (thus explaining the unarithmetical split of the Council of Ten) – were set to deal with the less controversial issues and to make preliminary recommendations on many of the frontiers that had to be adjudicated. Wilson's relationship with House was much less intimate after his return from the United States because he believed House's attempts to drive the settlement forward in his absence had compromised many of his principles and weakened the American negotiating position: 'House has given away everything I won before we left' Wilson told his wife. The offer of British and American guarantees for French security proved vitally important in enabling a log-jam of interlocked problems to be broken and Lloyd George and his main advisers produced the Fontainebleau Memorandum, a British statement of principles and policies and long-term aims and objectives for the Conference.

The Council of Four

On 7 March Lloyd George, Clemenceau and House met privately to discuss a wide range of issues, marking the beginning of the more informal style of business that would dominate the conference until the German treaty was signed. When Wilson returned from the United States and then, on 24 March, Orlando attended for the first time, the Council of Four was born. Lloyd George conveyed the sense of urgency and crisis that brought about this change in a letter of 17 March: *We have started a series of private conversations between Clemenceau, Wilson and myself for the discussion and determination of these very baffling problems, and unless we reach an agreement peace will be definitely postponed. What is still worse for all practical purposes, the alliance will cease to exist. I am hopeful of reaching complete accord and we are getting appreciably nearer.*[20]

> We have started a series of private conversations between Clemenceau, Wilson and myself ... and unless we reach an agreement peace will be definitely postponed.
>
> LLOYD GEORGE

The Council met over 200 times, mostly in Wilson's house, at first with just Professor Paul Mantoux as an interpreter. Its efficiency was transformed when Maurice Hankey became its secretary, on an *ad hoc* basis from 6 April, and permanently from 19 April. There was now a clear record of its decisions but even Hankey could not change the haphazard way in which issues reached the Four, whose agenda was often set by the order in which papers arrived from the printers. Nonetheless its great virtue was that it did decide.

Orlando's modest grasp of English put him at a disadvantage in the more informal style of business now adopted. He had to wait for Mantoux to translate for him, while his colleagues could well have moved on to discuss a fresh topic. He was also aware that Italy's credentials for a seat at the top table were not clear-cut and that Italy's interests were less wide-ranging than those of the other three powers. On 21

April, unable to convince them of Italy's claim to Fiume, he withdrew from the Conference, only to be forced to return, empty-handed and humiliated – as Wilson put it – 'fiuming', on 6 May, just in time for the handing over of the draft treaty to Germany. This episode emphasised that real power lay with America, Britain and France, but Italy's influence on the final shape of the settlement, particularly in the Near East, should not be underestimated.

The relationships between Lloyd George, Clemenceau and Wilson were fascinating. They did not necessarily like each other. Clemenceau complained that he found himself sandwiched between Wilson, who imagined himself to be Jesus Christ, and Lloyd George, who saw himself as Napoleon. He took delight at Wilson's illness in April – 'He is *worse* today!' – and nearly came to blows with Lloyd George in an incident that required Wilson's physical intervention. Lloyd George had more social contact with Wilson than Clemenceau, often eating with the President. *He thought him more sincere than he had done at first. He talks a lot of sentimental platitudes but he believes them. He is not a hypocrite.* Thrown together in close proximity for a hectic six-week spell at the crisis point of the Conference they argued and fought – 'How did you get on?' House asked Clemenceau after a meeting with Wilson, 'Splendidly, we disagreed about everything' – compromised, sought the advice of informal groups of experts and crucially reached decisions. Contemporaries were not always impressed by those decisions: 'These three ignorant men ... with a child to guide them', complained Balfour after they had settled the fate of Asia Minor with the aid of Nicolson – but at least there were now decisions.[21]

Our image of the council is dominated by the pen portraits recorded by J M Keynes in *Economic Consequences of the*

Peace – his bitter and magnificent attack on the conference and all its works: Clemenceau, the aged cynic whose love of France was matched only by his distrust of his country-men, seated by the fireplace, wearing grey gloves to disguise his eczema, intervening rarely but incisively; Lloyd George, whose skilful manipulation of words and facts sometimes disguised the poverty of his preparation, brilliant but unscrupulous and unreliable, a master of intimate diplomacy; and Wilson – for whom Keynes reserved the full measure of his vitriol because the President had so disappointed his expectations – portrayed as a bumbling 'blind and deaf Don Quixote', bamboozled by Clemenceau and Lloyd George and without the wit to embrace Lloyd George's later efforts to debamboozle him.[22]

Given the swiftness with which Lloyd George could change his position, Wilson might be forgiven this failing. One of Lloyd George's major handicaps was that, although his long-term visions were frequently commendable, and his short-term skill in negotiations was dazzling, there was often no bridge between them such that his success in obtaining agreement at the table translated into lasting fulfilment of his aims. A striking example of the breadth and strength of his grasp of British objectives is the Fontainebleau Memorandum of 25 March 1919.

The Fontainebleau Memorandum

By the middle of March Lloyd George's own anxieties about the way in which the Conference was heading were reinforced by those of close colleagues in the delegation. Hankey's note of 19 March expressed these concerns well: 'For some time past I have felt a vague and indefinite uneasiness as to whether the Peace Treaty was developing on sound lines of policy.

Mr Philip Kerr has several times pointed out to you and me that, while every exaction on Germany can be justified on its merits, the accumulation of these will put Germany in an utterly impossible position.' Hankey added that Henry Wilson also held this position very strongly.[23]

Lloyd George told Lord Riddell *I ... mean to put in the hardest forty-eight hours' thinking I have ever done. The Conference is not going well, and I must try to pull things together.* He therefore assembled some of his closest colleagues – Kerr, Hankey, Montagu and Wilson, to be joined later by Lords Cunliffe and Sumner (two of his key advisers on reparations) – for a weekend at a hotel in Fontainebleau where each was assigned various roles and asked to express the hopes, fears, views and concerns of their character or state. Hankey represented Britain, Montagu a visiting Martian to provide impartiality, Henry Wilson, full of enthusiasm for the venture, played first a German officer and then a French woman, whilst Lloyd George listened and intervened as required. Kerr was then set the task of pulling their ideas together into a paper expressing the British vision of what the final settlement should encompass. The outcome was 'Some Considerations for the Peace Conference before they finally draft their Terms' – one of the most impressive documents of the Conference, which Lloyd George delivered to Clemenceau, Orlando and Wilson on 25 March.[24]

Lloyd George said that his objective was not the comparatively easy one of piecing together a peace that would last 30 years but rather to avoid the seeds of future conflict in this

> **I ... mean to put in the hardest forty-eight hours' thinking I have ever done. The Conference is not going well, and I must try to pull things together.**
> LLOYD GEORGE

settlement. In essence he stated: *You may strip Germany of her colonies, reduce her armaments to a mere police force and her navy to that of a fifth-rate Power; all the same, in the end, if she feels that she has been unjustly treated in the peace of 1919, she will find means of exacting retribution … To achieve redress our terms may be severe, they may be stern and even ruthless, but at the same time they can be so just that the country on which they are imposed will feel in its heart that it has no right to complain. But injustice, arrogance, displayed in the hour of triumph, will never be forgotten or forgiven.*[25]

Lloyd George did not want to transfer more Germans than was absolutely necessary to the rule of other peoples. He believed *that as far as is humanly possible the different races should be allocated to their motherlands, and that this human criterion should have precedence over considerations of strategy or economics or communications.* He felt too *that the duration for the payments of reparations ought to disappear if possible with the generation which made the war* and he did point out that Germany must have access to raw materials and markets: *We cannot both cripple her and expect her to pay.*[26]

He was concerned about the alienation felt by working people generally and especially those in the defeated countries, whose situation was made worse because they did not know what fate the treaties proposed for them. *The greatest danger that I see in the present situation is that Germany may throw in her lot with Bolshevism and place her resources, her brains, her vast organising power at the disposal of the revolutionary fanatics, whose dream it is to conquer the world for Bolshevism by force of arms … . If we are wise we shall offer to Germany a peace, which, whilst just, will be preferable for all sensible men to the alternative of Bolshevism.*[27]

He also pinpointed one of the key issues of the post-Treaty world: *Finally, we must offer terms which a responsible Government in Germany can expect to be able to carry out.* The Allies were relying on democratically elected German administrations to execute the Treaty and the position of any government would become untenable if those conditions were too onerous. He wanted to see a Treaty-compliant Germany as part of the League of Nations at the earliest opportunity and he was prepared to offer France a guarantee of British support in the event of an unprovoked German attack, provided France was reasonable in its territorial demands.[28]

> If we are wise we shall offer to Germany a peace, which, whilst just, will be preferable for all sensible men to the alternative of Bolshevism.
>
> LLOYD GEORGE

The cynical Clemenceau was quick to point out that Lloyd George, by late March, was in a position to be magnanimous to Germany. None of the concessions that he was urging would impact on the striking naval, mercantile and colonial successes that Britain had enjoyed and Lloyd George was an expert at portraying decisions that favoured British interests as being universal goods. Nonetheless, the Fontainebleau document does offer interesting insights into British thinking about the settlement.

There were inevitable ambiguities and matters which, because it would be inconvenient to clarify them, were left deliberately vague – would, for example, national self-determination ever be allowed to work in Germany's favour? The reparations issue was discussed only in the most general terms and there was no thought of returning Germany's navy or colonies. Yet it was still possible to see the close parallels in the broad thinking of Wilson and Lloyd George that their January 1918 speeches had revealed and which Lloyd George now reiterated: proper restitution for damage done; a fair readjustment of frontiers; the survival of Germany, under whatever system of government it chose for itself; its speedy re-admittance to international organisations and trade; and above all, a peace of justice with prospects for long-term survival.

The draft Treaty emerges

The Memorandum also helped focus the discussions of the Four, while the offer of an Anglo-American guarantee of French security made by Lloyd George and Wilson to Clemenceau on 14 March proved crucial in creating an atmosphere of greater confidence in which the logjam of unresolved questions could gradually be freed. The problems were still tackled in a haphazard manner and issues came before the Four in a random order. On 22 April, for example, Lloyd George, Clemenceau and Wilson tackled questions relating to: Alsace-Lorraine; the withdrawal of Orlando; Syria and Palestine; arrangements for meeting the German delegates; draft clauses on the demilitarisation of the Rhineland; the draft American treaty of guarantee to France; the situation in Archangel; negotiations with the Japanese over their claims to Jiaozhou and Shandong; Italian claims in the Adriatic; and, finally, the Chinese counter-claims to Jiaozhou and Shandong.[29]

As they reached their decisions on each individual matter, those decisions were conveyed to the Allied legal advisers for drafting into treaty clauses but there was no overall coordination. No-one read the whole draft Treaty until just before it was delivered to the Germans on 7 May, thus exacerbating the problem that Nicolson pinpointed – the unintentional extra severity of the sum of the parts of a settlement which was never considered in its entirety. The effect on the British delegation was startling. Headlam-Morley, on 10 May, believed: 'that the territorial clauses are not bad, but everyone I have talked to agrees that the treaty as a whole is quite impossible and indefensible. The cumulative effect is such that the provisions will be impossible to be carried out by the Germans.' The widespread unease within the British camp was not helped by the comprehensive German critique of the terms delivered on 29 May and Robert Cecil spoke for many when, at the meeting in the Majestic on 30 May to found the Institute of International Affairs (later the Royal Institute of International Affairs – Chatham House), he stated 'There is no single person in this room who is not disappointed with the terms we have drafted.'[30]

Britain's attempt to revise the Treaty

Lloyd George's own concerns that the Germans might not sign the Treaty were reinforced by the disquiet expressed by Barnes, Cecil, Smuts and Henry Wilson, while Bonar Law wrote to him on 31 May: 'I have read the German reply … The document is a very able one and in many particulars is very difficult to answer.' He decided to consult his cabinet, and called his colleagues to Paris for a series of joint meetings with the British delegation from Friday 30 May until Sunday 1 June. The key meetings were held on 1 June. In the morning Smuts mounted a powerful attack on the draft Treaty. It was, he said, 'an impossible document [and] that to sign it would be a real disaster, not only to the British Empire but to the whole world.'

All present (when asked individually by Lloyd George) were agreed that some concessions must be made, but none went as far as Smuts, who advocated what amounted to a complete revision of the Treaty. Churchill suggested 'splitting the difference' between the draft Treaty and the German counter-proposals. Hughes, was, characteristically, less conciliatory: 'he considered that the Germans had not a leg to stand on ... He was in favour of conceding something, but there was no evidence except statements emanating from the German nation – a nation of liars – that they would not sign.' There was widespread concern about the military occupation of Germany, some support for the idea of a fixed sum for reparations, provided there was also an inter-Allied agreement about distribution, and general agreement that some alterations had to be made to the boundaries of eastern Europe.[31]

Lloyd George dominated the afternoon session. He complimented his colleagues on their magnanimity: *The members of the Delegation represented a great victorious Power with a most formidable enemy at their mercy after long and cruel fighting. The whole discussion had taken the form of an earnest and sometimes a passionate plea for justice for the fallen enemy.* He pressed for a just peace: *They must have no hesitation in admitting that they were wrong, if they were wrong, and in modifying the terms accordingly. But they must also see that the terms imposed were expedient as well as just.* He thought the Germans had inflicted losses on the Allies of some £30,000,000,000. He did not expect Germany could pay it all, but he was adamant that: *Somebody had to pay. If Germany could not pay, it meant that the British taxpayer had to pay. Those who ought to pay were those who caused the loss, and we should not water down our claim just when we were being assured that Germany could pay.*[32]

Lloyd George was authorized to return to his main allies and to demand a series of modifications to the draft Treaty.

These included: plebiscites in Upper Silesia and other areas disputed between the Germans and Poles; the early admission of Germany to the League; concessions on reparations; and the scrapping of the Rhineland occupation. He could, if necessary, withdraw the navy from blockading Germany, and refuse to allow British troops to participate in a renewal of hostilities to force German compliance. Smuts was not impressed, dismissing these changes as 'concessions which I consider paltry'.[33]

Lloyd George was not very successful in his attempt to redraft the Treaty. He did persuade Wilson (with some difficulty) that the principle of self-determination demanded a plebiscite in Upper Silesia. The Four agreed to an anodyne form of words offering Germany the prospect of joining the League after a period of probation, and he obtained some minor concession on the costs, but not the length, of the military occupation of Germany. When it came to reparations, on which he was decidedly lukewarm in his approach, he resisted Wilson's irritated attempt to name a fixed sum, and, with Clemenceau's aid, modified the treaty only to the extent that it authorised the Germans to make their own proposal within four months of the signature of the Treaty. It is interesting that Bonar Law's advice was 'to fix a sum, even £5,000,000,000 – though that would probably cause an outcry here'. Lloyd George had hardly delivered the changes his colleagues had approved or which, apparently, he had deemed necessary to obtain Germany's signature to the Treaty.[34]

In the short term it was of little importance. The French, with their microphones, telephone and wire taps, were well aware of the mood of bitter resignation in the German camp, and, although the German government fell, its successor signed the treaty on 28 June. In the longer-term, however, the criticisms of Smuts, Keynes and Headlam-Morley, amongst many others, would encourage British policy-makers to regard Lloyd George's limited success in his June 1919 attempt to revise the treaty as only a preliminary skirmish in the battle to appease Germany. They certainly did not regard the ceremony in the Hall of Mirrors as the final act in the drama, despite receiving free (if bad) champagne, and an extra course at dinner that evening. Nicolson retired 'To bed, sick of life.'[35]

ooooo

This chapter has offered an account of the main stages of the peacemaking process from the opening of the conference in January until the signature of the Treaty of Versailles in June. The next three chapters will consider, in greater detail, some of the key components of those negotiations, most notably the punitive elements of the Treaty, the difficulties of applying Wilson's revolutionary principle of national self-determination within Europe, and the broader imperial settlement.

4
Making Germany Pay

The 1919 election had revealed – unsurprisingly – deep resentment against Germany and a clear intention that, both metaphorically and literally, it should pay dearly for the war. The desire for revenge and punishment was, however, always part of a complex mixture of other emotions and policies and it was not always clear who should be targeted. Some people simply blamed 'the Germans' – 'Germany Can Pay: Germany Must Pay. Germany forced the war on the world' – others made a distinction between them and the responsibilities of their leaders. As Lloyd George put it on 5 January 1918, *We are not fighting a war of aggression against the German people ... The destruction or disruption of Germany or the German people has never been a war aim with us from the first day of this war to this day.*[1]

The nuances were neatly summarised on the night of the Armistice. Sir Henry Wilson recorded a dinner conversation: 'Lloyd George wants to shoot the Kaiser. F.E. [Smith – then Attorney General] agrees. Winston [Churchill – then Minister of Munitions] does not'. Yet, at the same dinner, Churchill and Lloyd George discussed rushing 'a dozen great ships crammed with provisions' to Hamburg to relieve German suffering.[2]

Lloyd George wavered between the popular demand to punish Germany and fear of promoting Bolshevism. He told his cabinet colleagues *It was not vengeance but justice ... whether we ought not to consider lashing her [Germany] as she had lashed France* but warned the peacemakers, *The greatest danger that I see in the present situation is that Germany may throw in her lot with Bolshevism ... If we are wise, we shall offer to Germany a peace, which, while just, will still be preferable for all sensible men to Bolshevism.* Finding policies that would accomplish both objectives was a challenge worthy of the Welsh Wizard.[3]

There were five main ways to punish Germany: occupation and loss of territory, both of which are discussed in the next chapter; cutting its armed forces; the trial of prominent Germans for political as well as operational war crimes; and forcing it to contribute to the Allies' war costs.

Disarmament

Grey was clear: 'The moral is obvious: it is that great armaments lead inevitably to war .... The enormous growth of armaments in Europe, the sense of insecurity and fear caused by them – it was these that made war inevitable.'[4] One of Britain's declared war aims was the destruction of Prussian militarism but, perhaps strangely, Britain had not prioritised the reduction of Germany's army even if the removal of Germany as a naval rival was an almost unspoken policy assumption. On 30 March 1919 Lloyd George boasted to his friend Lord Riddell, the press magnate, *The truth is that we have got our way. We have got most of the things we set out to get ... The German Navy has been handed over; the*

German mercantile shipping has been handed over and the German colonies have been given up.[5] He had not mentioned the German army. British wartime governments had given no serious thought to a major or permanent reduction of Germany's military power. It seems to have been Foch's crippling armistice terms that created the opportunity.

Lloyd George's thinking on Germany's military future had three main foundations. His radical philosophy naturally disposed him to all-round reductions in armaments and military expenditure. *We must disarm Germany. It is good for her as well as for us. Peace guns can do no good to anyone and they are better off out of the way.* This thinking permeated the Allied reply of 16 June 1919 to the German observations on the draft Treaty terms and became the preamble to the disarmament section of the Treaty itself – 'In order to render possible the initiation of a general limitation of the armaments of all nations, Germany undertakes strictly to observe the military, naval and air clauses which follow.' Article 8 of the Covenant of the League of Nations looked forward to 'the reduction of national armaments to the lowest point consistent with national safety …'. There was, at least on paper, a commitment that, although German disarmament would be unilateral in the first instance, it would lead to a wider international reduction in armaments.[6]

The second and third elements needed more skilful presentation – all-round disarmament sounded attractive – who could object? – but defending the idea of a balance of power against Wilson's seductive concept of collective security was trickier. Britain wanted no naval rival to itself, but liked the idea of Germany as a military force restraining France. No British government could say that openly – as Churchill graphically reminded the Prime Minister, 'It would be an enormous shock to the British public, who have 600,000 graves in France, if the statesmen were to tell them that we backed the wrong horse'[7] – but Germany could be presented as a barrier against both Russia and Bolshevism, even if a parallel motive was to act as a check on French ambition. There were thus two key reasons not to weaken Germany too much: to avoid promoting revolution and depriving the Germans of effective means of internal control and to retain Germany as a factor in the continental balance, especially since it was the French who now preoccupied British military and defence thinking.

The French wanted a German conscript army of around 100,000 men. Lloyd George opposed conscription but his advisers, including Haig, suggested a larger army of 200,000 or more. The eventual terms were a trade-off. Lloyd George persuaded Clemenceau to drop conscription and Germany was allowed a long-term volunteer army of 100,000 men, of whom only 4,000 could be officers. The army was limited to seven infantry divisions and three cavalry divisions, and it was allowed no aircraft, tanks, heavy guns, poison gas or chemical weapons. The west bank of the Rhine and the strip of land 50 kilometres to the east of the river were demilitarised. Germany must not improve the existing frontier fortifications on its eastern and southern boundaries, nor its coastal fortifications, and it was banned from having a general staff. Germany's treaty navy was only six pre-dreadnought type battleships, six light cruisers, 12 destroyers and 12 torpedo boats, with no submarines or naval aircraft. It was allowed 15,000 volunteers to meet all the requirements of the service.

These reductions were indeed dramatic. In 1914 Germany had committed 78 infantry divisions and 10 cavalry divisions, or 1.7 million men, to the attack on France and Belgium alone, whilst its pre-war navy had 15 dreadnought battle-ships, five battlecruisers, 22 older battleships, 40 cruisers, 90 destroyers and 29 submarines. In 1914 Germany had some 4,000,000 men under arms, the Treaty now reduced its total armed forces to 115,000. There were real concerns as to whether such a small army could guarantee Germany's external and internal security and the execution of the dis-armament clauses proved to be another area in which British and French views collided in the coming years. But, given the importance attached to the army's role in the creation and development of the Prussian state, and to the navy as a symbol of newly unified Germany, the really serious blows were to German pride.[8]

War crimes

The idea of trying German leaders for political war crimes was a striking departure from the established practice of indicting military personnel for operational breaches of the laws of war. Although a number of the Allied leaders had grave doubts about whether such trials were legal or desir-able, there was a great strength of public opinion that crimes had been committed against humanity and that, with millions dead and injured, someone should be called to account.

Lloyd George was a committed and eloquent supporter of this idea but he was cautious in public. He told the voters in Newcastle only that *the Kaiser must be prosecuted*. Within the Imperial War Cabinet he was much more forceful – *I think this man should be tried for high treason against human-ity* – but the advocates of a trial – Lloyd George, Smith and Curzon – were opposed by Churchill, Austen Chamberlain, Jan Smuts of South Africa and William Hughes of Australia. Hughes, who took a very strong stand on reparations, was dubious about accusing the Kaiser: 'You cannot indict a man for making war. War has been the prerogative of the right of all nations from the beginning, and if you say, well, as a result of this war, millions have died, you can say that much of Alexander and Moses and of almost anybody.' Not to be outdone in hyperbole, Lloyd George responded: *I am not sure that they also ought not to be brought to justice.* The cabinet eventually, on 28 November, accepted Smith's argument that, unless the Kaiser was indicted, it would be impossible to prosecute the lesser offenders. The prosecution of the Kaiser became one of Britain's objectives at the conference.[9]

The Council of Ten established the Commission on the Responsibility of the Authors of the War on 25 January 1919. The members readily agreed that responsibility for the war 'rests first on Germany and Austria, secondly on Turkey and Bulgaria' and that the Central Powers had fought the war 'by barbarous or illegitimate means'. They did not agree to try the Kaiser. Their chairman, Robert Lansing, was adamant that they had no right to establish an international tribunal to try a head of state for a crime Lansing did not believe existed. His objections, and his suggestion that such a court would constitute an 'international Lynch law', were supported by the Japanese but rejected by his European colleagues as 'finespun theories'. They passed the problem to the Council of Four.

The objections to arraigning the Kaiser ranged from the philosophical to the practical. Wilson feared that the legend of a martyred Kaiser could be a more potent menace than the man himself. Sidney Sonnino from Italy did not want the German people to escape their share of blame by heaping all responsibility on their emperor. The Japanese, believing their emperor to be divine, would not welcome the trial of another.

Churchill was concerned that the evidence in the trial might implicate some of the Entente, particularly the Russians, in responsibility for the outbreak of the war, thus tainting the Allied cause. All agreed the Kaiser was a criminal in a moral sense, but Wilson still insisted that no legal precedent existed for trying someone for causing a war. Lloyd George remained firm: *I would like to see the man responsible for the greatest crime in history punished for it.* He was not too concerned about the means – the conference could simply order internment or establish a tribunal – but the Kaiser must be punished: *Send him to the Falkland Islands or Devil's Island. Do whatever you wish – it doesn't matter much to me.*

Eventually, perhaps because he thought that a compromise here might assist his quest to get special status for the Monroe Doctrine in the redrafted Covenant of the League, Wilson agreed to demand the surrender of the Kaiser from the Dutch, after which he would be tried by an international tribunal of five judges, one from each of the principal Allies. Taken together with Article 231 (the 'War Guilt clause'), the demands for the surrender of the Kaiser (Article 227) and other prominent leaders (Article 228) formed the basis of what the Germans termed the 'shame paragraphs' of the Treaty which they judged to be contrary to German honour. They failed in June 1919 to get the Allies to change or drop them. The German government resigned, but its successor had to sign a treaty still containing those demands. This was the beginning and not the end of a story which would eventually become a tragic farce. For whatever motives, Lloyd George was persistent in pursuing his belief that: *There is no right that you can establish, national or international, unless you establish the fact that the man who breaks the law will meet inevitable punishment* and, amidst all the electoral posturing and populist rhetoric, the Paris Conference's decision to endorse the idea of crimes against humanity did make a contribution to the establishment of a world community. [10]

Reparations

One of the most contentious and longest running problems in Paris and afterwards was what Germany could legitimately be required to pay to the Allies for their losses and damage during the war. It involved a tangled series of linked questions: how to calculate the extent of the damage; how much could Germany afford to pay; how (and when) that capacity to pay should be judged; how, and over what period of time, would payments be made; and what share of those payments would be due to each of the Allies?

Taken separately each of those matters was complex enough in its own right, taken together it never quite seemed possible to reach a final agreement – rather like an unruly parcel, issues kept escaping just when they appeared to be wrapped up. The economics of transferring money internationally on such a huge scale posed difficult theoretical and practical problems, but the political implications and complications of any decision, or set of decisions, created even greater obstacles to any settlement. Bundled together in this question were issues of morality, pressing budgetary requirements and conflicting national interests and priorities. As the American banker, Thomas Lamont, himself a participant in the negotiations, declared: 'The subject of reparations caused more trouble, contention, hard feeling and delay at the Paris Peace Conference than any other point of the Treaty.'[11]

The damage was real enough – the war had devastated an area of France as large as the whole of the Netherlands, not to mention Belgium, Serbia, Italy, Romania and Britain's lost merchant shipping – and someone would have to pay to restore it. Should that be Allied taxpayers or the Germans? It was not a hard question for politicians to decide! But any payments the Germans made to repair Allied damage would be money they did not have to build weapons for a war of revenge – so, for the French at least, this was also part of security policy, thus adding another variable to a complex problem.

Lloyd George played a prominent and controversial part in this aspect of the Conference and its aftermath. His own version portrayed him as a moderating influence, seeking to allow time for passions to cool and more rational debate to prevail. He claimed his approach was that of a lawyer in a civil case, whose aim was to gain compensation for his client on the basis, not of his moral or legal entitlement, but of what the offender might realistically be able to pay – a possible settlement rather than an impossible bill. An alternative analysis might stress his responsibility for inflaming public expectations and the significant gaps between his rhetoric and his actions. What is certain is that one of his key objectives in Paris was securing the best possible share of any German compensation.

For what exactly should Germany compensate the Allies? This was a question which caused great debate and dissension in their ranks and disrupted the normal pattern of good Anglo-American relations at the Conference. Expressed in their starkest forms there were two alternatives: Germany should pay the Allies only for the damage done to their civilian populations and their property – reparations; or it should pay their total war costs – an indemnity. Reparations would cover the repair of all damage to civilians and civilian property, for example towns, villages, farms, factories and merchant ships. An indemnity would cover the same civilian losses but also include all the Allied expenditure on men, guns, ships and aircraft, supplies and transport, everything, in fact, that it had cost to fight the war.

Some commentators suggested the distinction was unreal, in that, on whatever basis Germany's debt was calculated, it would probably far exceed its ability to pay. This was itself another area of fraught debate, but the question was not just academic, because the issue of what could, and could not, be charged to Germany might actually determine the amount of compensation each Ally might hope to receive. The interconnected implications of any decision about any aspect of this question were what made it so complex.

Did the pre-armistice agreement embodied in Lansing's note of 5 November 1918 mean that the Allies ruled out any claim to their full war costs? In one sense it was a surprising question because Wilson had been quite specific in his 'Four Principles' of 11 February 1918 that 'There shall be… no contributions, no punitive indemnities' and this seemed to echo Lloyd George's speech of 5 January 1918 which had stressed: *This is no demand for war indemnity, such as that imposed on France by Germany in 1871. It is not an attempt to shift the cost of warlike operations from one belligerent to another, which may or may not be defensible.*

They had both distanced themselves from the usual formula of 'the loser pays' and it seemed that the maximum demands of the United States and the United Kingdom would be limited to the restoration of civilian damage. However (somehow with Lloyd George there is often an 'however'), he had added: *It is no more and no less than an insistence that, before there can be any hope for a stable peace, this great breach of the public law of Europe must be repudiated and, so far as possible, repaired. Reparation means recognition.*

Unless international right is recognised by insistence on payment for injury done in defiance of its canons it can never be a reality. Might 'payment for injury' include a punitive element in addition to simple restoration? [12]

This doubt persisted through 1918 and into 1919 but the key exchanges occurred in October and November 1918, when the Germans requested Wilson to arrange an armistice on the understanding that the eventual peace treaty would be based on his Fourteen Points speech. Clemenceau was sardonic, 'Have you ever been asked by President Wilson whether you accept the Fourteen Points? I have never been asked.' *I have not been asked either* replied Lloyd George but both knew that they had little room for manouevre. Yet, as Lloyd George reminded his cabinet on 25 October, unless they voiced their objections to Wilson's agenda ... *the Germans would have a perfect right to assume that the Fourteen Points were the worst conditions that could be imposed upon them.* [13]

Lloyd George had two particular issues. One was about the Freedom of the Seas, where there was a century-old dispute between the British and American interpretations of what constituted legitimate interference with neutral shipping in wartime. The British believed they had the right to stop and search neutral ships on the high seas for war materials *en route* to their enemies, the Americans always argued that neutrals should be allowed to go about their business without interference. For a brief moment this became the subject of some quite sharp exchanges and veiled threats, but Lloyd George compromised to the extent that he agreed the matter might be discussed at the Conference (in fact it never was).

More significant was the question of interpreting what Wilson had said about potential demands on Germany for compensation. He was clear that the German invasion of Belgium had been illegal and that hence Belgium was entitled to its war costs in addition to any restoration payments, but when speaking of the other invaded Allied territories, he had stipulated only that they be 'evacuated' and 'restored'.

Edward House, sent by Wilson to deal with any Allied concerns arising from his 'program for the peace of the world', agreed a definition of 'restoration': 'By it they understand that compensation will be made by Germany for all damage done to the civilian population of the Allies and their property by the aggression of Germany by land, by sea, and from the air'. The phrasing owed much to Lloyd George, who drafted and redrafted it until he was satisfied, finally substituting 'aggression' for 'invasion' to safeguard British claims for compensation. The definition was incorporated into Lansing's note.

It was thus very clear – Lloyd George and Wilson had both ruled out war costs in their speeches and the pre-armistice agreement with Germany limited their demands to compensation for civilian damage. But everything was not as it seemed because, when the Peace Conference opened, every delegation, except that of the United States, advanced a claim for war costs. Why did Lloyd George propose a commission on 'reparation *and indemnity*' (with the implied claim for war costs) first in London in December and then in Paris in January, meeting firm American resistance on both occasions?

One explanation is that, despite his personal moderation on the issue, he felt the need to enthuse a much expanded electorate, two-thirds of whom had never voted before. David Lindsay, the Earl of Crawford and the First Commissioner of Works, wrote in his diary for 28 December 1918: 'The electoral process has been significant. Lloyd George's original campaign fell rather flat. He pulled himself together on realising he was being left high and dry on the shore. He revised his programme, or rather enlarged it by adding items about indemnities, aliens, punishment of the Kaiser, and pledges to end conscription. Then he got on to the wave again, and with an advancing tide has been borne to victory'. Churchill took a similar line: 'In the hot squalid rush of the event he endeavoured to give satisfaction to mob-feeling and press chorus by using language which was in harmony with the prevailing sentiment, but which contained in every passage some guarding phrase, some qualification, which afterwards would leave statesmanship unchained.'[14]

This is an interesting verdict, because Lloyd George certainly did introduce notes of caution into his speeches, though one might question the extent to which he emphasised them at the expense of the more inflammatory stuff his audience wanted to hear. It was Eric Geddes rather than Lloyd George who wanted to squeeze the German lemon until its pips squeaked, but how loudly, for example, did he say in Newcastle that Germany's capacity to pay was limited, in comparison to the volume of his promise that the Germans *must pay to the uttermost farthing, and we shall search their pockets for it*? There is no doubt that the message that the British and French public took from their politicians was that, as French finance minister Louis-Lucien Klotz allegedly declared, 'L'Allemagne paiera' – Germany will pay. They expected their leaders to ensure this happened.[15]

Like a good lawyer, Lloyd George had formal evidence that he had tried to limit expectations, and this would certainly be the line that he took in his own defence, both for his 1918 speeches and his later policies. He would, for example, claim that, in Paris, his own moderate instincts were severely hampered by the large sums demanded by a powerful body of imperial and domestic opinion. This was personified by William Hughes of Australia and, in particular, the ex-governor of the Bank of England, Lord Cunliffe and a Law Lord, Lord Sumner, who were dubbed the 'Heavenly Twins' because they were always in each other's company and the figures they suggested were astronomical.

Plausibility was always one of Lloyd George's great assets. He managed to convince contemporaries and later historians that he was fettered by the Twins, but there is now the very strong suspicion that he had a much clearer and firmer personal agenda on the size of the bill for Germany and that this remained consistent throughout 1918 and 1919 and beyond. Was it, for example, an embarrassment or an opportunity, when Hughes complained bitterly in November 1918 that a reparations policy would mean an undamaged Australia would receive no compensation, despite losing more men and spending more money than Belgium? Or when the subsequent committee, that he insisted Hughes chair, recommended that Germany could afford to pay £24,000 million in annual installments of £1,200 million including 5 per cent interest?

The committee offered no evidence as to how it had reached this enormous sum. Writing in Paris in January, Hankey informed Lloyd George, 'The figure mentioned to me privately is £25,000,000,000 but I gather from the same source that it is a figure not calculated on any particularly scientific basis but one drawn rather by that peculiar instinct on which, I am told, high financial authorities in the City often work.' Philip Kerr, his private secretary, suggested possible divine inspiration but the general premise, expressed by a member of the Hughes committee, was that, since the cost of the war would ruin either Germany or the Allies, 'On the whole I think we had better ruin them.'[16]

How far was this removed from Lloyd George's own thinking? Did he feel bound by the Lansing note, in whose drafting and negotiation he had played a crucial part? His election speeches in Newcastle and Bristol certainly stressed making Germany pay and Kerr's notes for his apparently moderate Fontainebleau Memorandum had insisted on the need for 'as large an indemnity out of Germany as possible'. When, in June 1919, he was authorised by his cabinet colleagues to seek a revision of the draft German treaty, Robert Cecil noted that he was 'curiously reluctant to make any changes' to reparations, telling Clemenceau and Wilson that *He would not cut out a single one from the categories.* So was he the prisoner of the Twins, stuck with Cunliffe's *wild and fantastic chimera* because he dare not face the electorate with a lower figure without their approval? Or was the boot on the other foot?

This interpretation, which suggests continuity in Lloyd George's policy, argues that, for him, the Lansing note was a deception, a promise given only for the moment, and that he used the Twins as a front, so that he could appear moderate, sheltering behind their 'bad cop' performance whilst, all the while, they were articulating his real wishes. It was he who had appointed them and it was he who retained their services throughout the German settlement and after.

It was not they who were holding him back, it was he who looked to them to provide him with excuses not to moderate his demands. They would not compromise because Lloyd George did not want them to, but they got little thanks at the time – 'You are ordered here and ordered there. Do this and do that. But no-one ever says "Good dog!"' Cunliffe complained. And afterwards they would become the butt of everyone's jokes about their financial incapacity, the poverty of their intellect and the lunacy of their demands, the convenient excuse for a policy that nobody wanted to acknowledge. Lloyd George always seemed to have the knack of having it as many ways as possible![17]

Article 231 and war guilt

Lloyd George and Clemenceau insisted that war costs were a legitimate claim against Germany, but Wilson and his advisers were implacably opposed and a real crisis loomed. It was averted by a classic 'it seemed like a good idea at the time' device which was truly rich in unintended future consequences. Two Americans, John Foster Dulles, Lansing's nephew, and Norman Davis, suggested that they should differentiate between Germany's moral obligation to pay for war costs and the practicality of what it could actually afford. This was the origin of Article 231, the 'War Guilt' clause: 'The Allied and Associated Governments affirm and Germany accepts the responsibility of Germany and her allies for causing all the damage to which the Allied and Associated Governments and their nationals have been subjected as a consequence of the war imposed upon them by the aggression of Germany and her allies.'

Article 232 qualified this liability by recognising 'that the resources of Germany are not adequate … to make complete reparation for all such loss and damage. The Allied and Associated Governments, however, require, and Germany undertakes that she will make compensation for all damage done to the civilian population … and to their property.'

The Allies thought they had found a form of words that would shelter Clemenceau and Lloyd George from public opinion and accommodate Wilson's refusal to allow war costs. They had established that Germany ought to pay an indemnity but that they would limit their actual demands to reparations. They had no intention of passing an historical judgement on Germany and they were certainly not blaming Germany alone – its allies were already mentioned in this clause and similar clauses, highlighting the responsibility of the appropriate state and, in turn, its allies, appeared in all four other original Parisian treaties. But the Germans very successfully exploited what they chose to interpret as a verdict of exclusive guilt, incidentally setting in motion a massive boost to both the historical profession and the printing industry across Europe as states researched, edited (very carefully), and published collections of documents 'proving' their innocence for what had happened in 1914.

Calculations

The fundamental problem the peacemakers faced was that no-one knew the answers to a series of questions, even before adding in the additional complexities of working out their political and economic implications. No-one really knew how much the war had cost, how much damage had been done or what Germany could afford to pay. Any figures they had – the £24,000 million that the British Treasury suggested as the Allied cost of the war, or the £3,000 million to £5,000 million than an American general estimated as the damage done to France and Belgium on the Western Front, or the £24,000 million the Hughes committee said Germany could pay (in stark contrast to the maximum British Treasury estimate of £3,000 million) – were all guesses. No-one wanted to commit political suicide by underestimating their country's claims and few were anxious to tell their electorates that they did not believe Germany could meet those claims. Given that no one really knew how much Germany might be able to pay, not so much now in 1919, but later when its industries and trade had recovered, why settle for a lower guess when there were higher guesses on offer?

Many believed that the only sensible solution was to concede that Germany would not be able to pay everything it owed and to settle for a 'fixed sum' – a total figure, which, although less than Germany's theoretical liability, would be accepted by the Allies as discharging all Germany's debts. If they could agree on a fixed sum and on how the receipts would be divided between them, the peacemakers would cut through a whole series of other problems about how much damage had been done, or what categories of damage should be included. Could this be achieved in Paris?

> Be assured that, whatever this figure, many people in England as well as in France, will immediately exclaim 'This is too small'.
> LLOYD GEORGE

It did not seem very likely because each of the delegations had a very different idea of what a realistic figure meant – the Americans proposed £3,000 million to £5,000 million but were prepared to go as high as £6,000 million in the interests of unity. This did not meet the French claim of £8,000 million, and came nowhere near Cunliffe's original demand of £24,000 million or even his reduced offer of £9,500 million. Given these wide divisions and the weight of public expectations, perhaps it might be better to postpone things – something not lost on Lloyd George: *I see real advantages in not stating now any figure to represent the total sum owed to us by the Germans. Be assured that, whatever this figure, many people in England as well as in France, will immediately exclaim 'This is too small'.* In mid-April Lloyd George, who had received a sharply worded telegram from 233 MPs reminding him of the need to present the British Empire's full claim to Germany, returned to the Commons with a bravura performance that routed his critics – but it was a reminder that his hands were not entirely free.[18]

The desire (or need) to put things off also affected the negotiations about the division of payments. Lloyd George's original suggestion was 50 per cent for France, 30 per cent for Britain and 20 per cent for the rest and this contrasted quite sharply with Louis Loucheur's opening gambit of a 72:18 Franco-British division but, although the Paris figures soon settled somewhere in the range of 55:25 or 56:28, no final agreement was reached until June 1920 when a deal was struck at 52:22 between Britain and France. This was thus yet another unknown but important consideration during the 1919 negotiations.

Since no-one would commit to actual figures, the list of what should be included in the damages demanded under Article 232 became more significant, leading to one of the most controversial of many disputed decisions in Paris. Lloyd George used Smuts to persuade Wilson that claims for pensions and allowances paid to Allied servicemen and their dependants constituted a legitimate claim under the heading of civilian damage because soldiers were simply civilians in uniform. This was an important matter for Britain and its empire because, if German compensation was calculated purely on what was needed to repair material damage, their claims would be severely limited – mainly to merchant shipping losses and whatever damage Britain had sustained in Zeppelin and air raids or in coastal towns during raids by the German High Seas Fleet. Most of the money would go to France and Belgium.

Smuts argued mainly on the basis that conscripts (and

volunteers who had joined for the duration of the war) had no choice but to become soldiers. The President's advisers found his apparently ludicrous claim sufficiently plausible not to dismiss it out of hand, but none accepted it. Acknowledging its weakness, Wilson declared: 'Logic? I don't give a damn for logic, if you will excuse my French. I am going to include pensions.' He did so under the assumption that he was not increasing the amount Germany would have to pay, but that he was helping to create a fairer basis for the distribution of either a fixed sum or some other limited German payment.

Postponing a final decision about Germany's debt proved an attractive option, not just for Lloyd George but also Clemenceau, and, effectively by the end of March, it was clear that there would be no final figure named in the Treaty. Instead a Reparation Commission of five members from Britain, France, Italy and the United States, plus, as appropriate, Belgium (for German claims), Japan (for maritime matters) or Yugoslavia (for Austro-Hungarian claims) would determine Germany's debt by 1 May 1921 by adding up the sums due under the approved categories. It would then decide how and when Germany was to pay, and at what rates of interest. The other way to limit Germany's liability was to put a time limit on payments – for both actuarial and moral reasons 30 years was the usual period mentioned – but this too was ruled out because the Commission had the power, in certain circumstances, to postpone payments and extend the time limit. On important matters like the cancellation of any of the debt, or on lengthy postponements of payment – and, at Wilson's insistence, any German bond issue to cover its debts – the Commission had to be unanimous, thus giving each state a veto. Germany's war was ending, as it had begun, with the signature of a 'blank cheque'.

Lloyd George now suggested that the Commission could, within 48 hours of the signature of peace, calculate a considerable proportion of the German bill and the German government could then issue bonds to cover that amount. It was a typical Lloyd George manoeuvre – if it succeeded it would mean the Allies would get their money faster, but there would be a safety net against any criticism that he had settled for too little, because this was not the final bill. Since the only viable market for the bonds was the United States, this would also have the effect of ensuring that America would continue to take an active interest in the problem. Wilson's exasperation is understandable: 'He was mystified by this discussion. Months had been spent in trying to reach a figure, then it had been decided to drop the attempt. Now it was proposed to ask the Commission to name it right away.' The idea was dropped.

Nobody – not even the Germans – disputed that compensation was due to the Allies. The question was how much? When Lloyd George went back to his colleagues in the Council of Four in June, in an attempt to renegotiate parts of the draft Treaty, one of the things his cabinet had pressed him to do was to have the treaty name a definite figure. Wilson, taking him at his word, suggested £6,000 million, but Lloyd George, in reply, neatly encapsulated the dilemmas: *The conclusion he had come to was that if figures were given now they would frighten rather than reassure the Germans. Any figure that would not frighten them would be below the figure with which he and M. Clemenceau could face their peoples in the present state of public opinion. ... The statement of a figure at the present time would also raise inconvenient questions between the Allies.*[19]

The Conference thus shelved the problem, naming no final

sum in the Treaty, although it did leave an opening for the Germans to make their own offer. Lloyd George would play a prominent role in future negotiations. The question was one which caused deep and bitter divisions between the Allies and the Germans and between the Allies themselves, because, as Sally Marks has reminded us, the stakes were high: 'At heart, reparations were about two fundamental and closely related questions: who won the war and who would pay for it, or at least the cost of undoing the damage ... If the Allies, and especially France, had to assume reconstruction costs on top of domestic and foreign war debts, whereas Germany was left with only domestic debts, they would be the losers, and German economic dominance would be tantamount to victory. Reparations would both deny Germany that victory and spread the pain of undoing the damage done.'[20]

She could have added that the division of any receipts amongst the Allies might also impact on their relative prosperity and power, further exacerbating the complex nature of this issue.

The Allies did have a strong case for appropriate compensation, but they undermined it with some dubious claims and their self-inflicted problems of over-expectant electorates which anticipated massive German contributions. Making Germany pay would, in this case as in others, be easier said than done.

5
Redrawing the Map of Europe

As British troops arrived in August 1914, the French joked that 'If the English get into Calais [an English possession until 1558] they will never leave it at the end of the war. They were much too upset when they lost it before', but Britain in 1919 had no new direct territorial claims in Europe. With Germany's defeat, its traditional concern that no great power should dominate the Low Countries was no longer threatened and the main aim of British decision-makers was to produce a settlement which would be accepted by as many people as possible, be self-enforcing, allow Britain to trade freely, and, eventually, relieve Britain of responsibility for European security, permitting it to return to its perceived proper imperial role.[1]

Different British elite groups had conflicting views on how to attain such happy outcomes. Younger members of the Foreign Office put their faith in nationalism as a stabilising force in Europe, welcomed the demise of the multi-national empires and were enthusiastic for Wilson's League. Senior men tended to favour older, more tried methods of international diplomacy, and to yearn for old decencies, even if these had not prevented Europe plunging into the most destructive war in the history of mankind with proportionately dramatic results.

In March 1917 the Romanov dynasty lost control of Russia. In November 1918, the Habsburgs in Austria-Hungary and the Hohenzollerns in Germany, lost their thrones (though, unlike Nicholas II and his family, not their lives). The Ottoman Empire would survive, nominally, for another two years. This sudden collapse of four great empires that for centuries had dominated eastern and central Europe and the Balkans presented the Paris Peace Conference with an unprecedented eventuality. Great swathes of Europe were left without any recognised authority beyond that of small, often isolated, groups, claiming to be the legitimate government of new, rarely uncontested, states.

National self-determination

While this apparently offered the perfect opportunity to apply President Wilson's doctrine of national self-determination, it revealed also the complexities and ambiguities of that principle. *En route* to Europe, Wilson gloomily predicted that the forthcoming settlement would be a 'tragedy of disappointment'. He feared that his inspirational speeches in 1918 had raised expectations that could not be fulfilled. Nowhere was this more apparent than in the bitter disputes over territory that soon arose in Paris, whether between old established rivals like France and Germany, or the revived or newly emerging states of eastern Europe.

The principle became synonymous with Wilson, but it was actually Lloyd George who was more explicit about national self-determination in January 1918. Wilson's Fourteen Points address to Congress, on 8 January, implied the concept,

Europe 1914

Petrograd (St Petersburg)

Riga

Moscow

Vilna

Königsberg

zig

RUSSIAN EMPIRE

Warsaw   Brest-Litovsk

Kiev

Budapest

ARY

Odessa

ROMANIA

Belgrade   Bucharest

Black Sea

SERBIA   **BULGARIA**

GRO   Sofia

a

BANIA

Constantinople

GREECE   **OTTOMAN EMPIRE**

Athens

without actually using the words. Three days earlier, speaking to the British Trades Union Congress, Lloyd George stated that: ... *we feel that government with the consent of the governed must be the basis of any territorial settlement in this war.* He emphasised that this applied also to the Middle East and Germany's colonies: *The general principle of national self-determination is therefore applicable in their cases as in those of occupied European territories.* In typical Lloyd Georgian fashion, however, he did not tie himself to precise outcomes.[2]

This was unsurprising. National self-determination was, in the dramatic phrase of Wilson's Secretary of State, Robert Lansing, a concept 'simply loaded with dynamite'. Both sides in the Great War included multinational states and empires, yet each had dabbled with the double-edged weapon of encouraging national rebellions in the enemy camp, whilst fervently hoping that their own discontented nationalities would not notice.[3]

It was Wilson, in his 'Four Principles' speech of 11 February 1918, who transformed a tactical gambit into 'an imperative principle of action'. Aspiring nationalities inevitably read his text selectively, choosing not to notice the potentially inconvenient caveats that he introduced into his undertaking that: 'all well-defined national aspirations shall be accorded the utmost satisfaction that can be accorded without introducing new or perpetrating old elements of discord and antagonism that would be likely in time to break the peace of Europe, and consequently of the world.'[4]

The endorsement of the principle by Wilson's ideological rival, Lenin, was most unwelcome but the collapse of Russia, Austria-Hungary, the Ottoman Empire and Germany left it as, apparently, the only viable moral basis on which to reconstruct Europe.

National self-determination created problems. The most fundamental was its meaning. To Wilson and West European liberals like Lloyd George and Clemenceau, the concept was essentially civic and political. They stressed individual choice. Although language might be a possible badge of nationality, for them citizenship, rather than ethnicity, was the main consideration – in Lloyd George's words *government with the consent of the governed*. For many in Eastern Europe, however, nationality was not a matter of personal choice, it was determined by race, religion and language and this ethnic identity was paramount. Whereas people of varied ethnic backgrounds could become American citizens, to Poles you were either a Pole, or you were not. This conceptual clash between civic and ethnic nationalism haunted the conference and remains a contemporary dilemma.

Lloyd George and Wilson both emphasised that the days of the Treaty of Vienna were gone – there would be no transfers of territory and people simply to give a state a more defensible frontier or to readjust its relative strength and resources. Issues of security nonetheless continued to dominate the thinking of most European leaders. Clemenceau was quite explicit: 'There is an old system of alliances called the Balance of Power – this system of alliances, which I do not renounce, will be my guiding thought at the Peace Conference.' He could have added that France also required adequate territorial defensive barriers against Germany. Such considerations would clearly complicate the application of the principle of self-determination, even if satisfactory answers could be found to the difficult question of what factors constituted nationality. Given the kaleidoscopic mixture of national groupings in eastern and central Europe, no frontiers could ensure that everyone finished up in the state of their choice.

If one added requirements for economic and defensive viability, respect for traditional administrative boundaries and an adequate communications network, then the only predictable result would be that no one frontier could ever satisfy all the desirable criteria.[5]

A spectre haunted Lloyd George throughout the negotiations. In 1871, after the Franco-Prussian War, Germany had annexed Alsace and part of Lorraine from France, creating a running sore in European international politics for nearly half a century. In the Place de la Concorde in Paris there are a number of identical statues representing the major towns of France. After 1871 the French kept the memory of the lost provinces alive by draping the statue of Strasbourg in black. Lloyd George recalled *the strongest impression made upon me by my first visit to Paris was the statue of Strasbourg veiled in mourning. Do not let us make it possible for Germany to erect a similar statue.* Whilst the most direct possibilities of an Alsace-Lorraine in reverse arose in the negotiations over the future of the Rhineland and the Saar, it was a graphic image to which he kept returning whenever he perceived a danger of creating an avoidable national grievance, particularly during the debates on the proposed Polish-German frontiers.[6]

Lloyd George's intentions about the future of Germany's colonies or the Middle East were, deliberately, ambiguous, but in European terms he was the peacemaker who paid most attention to ensuring that the settlement followed Wilson's principle as closely as was practical – sometimes even against

> The strongest impression made upon me by my first visit to Paris was the statue of Strasbourg veiled in mourning. Do not let us make it possible for Germany to erect a similar statue.
> LLOYD GEORGE

the President's own inclinations. *I am*, he wrote in the Fontainebleau Memorandum, *strongly averse to transferring more Germans from German rule to the rule of some other nation than can possibly be helped. I cannot conceive of any greater cause of future war than that the German people ... should be surrounded by a number of small States ... each of them containing large numbers of Germans clamouring for reunion with their native land*. This was a constant theme for Lloyd George throughout the Conference.[7]

Alsace-Lorraine

For France one issue was beyond dispute: Alsace-Lorraine must be restored. Lloyd George and Wilson endorsed this aspiration without making the return of the lost provinces an absolute demand, choosing their words carefully in January 1918. Lloyd George spoke of the need for *a reconsideration of the great wrong of 1871 ... This sore has poisoned the peace of Europe for half a century and, until it is cured, healthy conditions will not have been restored*. Wilson's seventh Point stated that 'the wrong done to France by Prussia in 1871 in the matter of Alsace-Lorraine ... should be righted.' The original draft said 'must'.[8]

When the Germans sought an armistice in October 1918 Lloyd George suggested that Germany should evacuate the provinces without their replacement by Allied troops and, surprisingly, Clemenceau agreed, but the Allied generalissimo, Ferdinand Foch, insisted upon an immediate Allied garrison. Anglo-American suspicions that France might seek more than the restoration of the 1870 frontier were confirmed by Clemenceau's claim for the more ambitious 1814 frontiers. Lloyd George resisted firmly and, on 30 April 1919, the Four agreed to restore the 1870 border whilst emphasising that, unlike all other territorial transfers which dated from the ratification of the Treaty (10 January 1920), the two provinces reverted to France on 11 November 1918. No credence was given to German requests for a plebiscite.

The Rhineland

France could not have a physical barrier of the magnitude of the Atlantic or even the Channel but did argue for further readjustments of Germany's frontiers. The ensuing debates over Germany's western borders were among the bitterest and longest running of the Peace Conference. The most optimistic French commentators hoped that they could simply annex the Rhineland, making the Rhine an obstacle to future German invasion and simultaneously depriving Germany of territory, population and other resources whilst increasing those of France. They pointed out that the peacemakers in 1814 had allowed France to retain the Rhineland, gained during the Revolutionary Wars. Only after Napoleon's return from Elba and final defeat, had they awarded the territory to Prussia in 1815, an action rich with unintended 19th-century consequences. More pragmatic observers suggested that, although the territories could not now be transferred back to France, they should be separated from Germany and made into one or more independent Rhineland republics, thus pushing Germany back beyond the Rhine and, if not adding to French resources, at least denying them to Germany.

Extreme optimists hoped that the Rhinelanders would perceive themselves sufficiently different from Protestant North Germany to endorse plans for secession, whether for reasons of their Roman Catholicism, their supposedly Celtic racial origins, or simply to avoid responsibility for Germany's reparation liabilities. More thoughtful observers, like the French revolutionary historian François Alphonse Aulard, were aware of an acute dilemma: 'Either we annex the left bank of the Rhine and violate principle, or we do not annex it and France remains in perpetual danger of invasion.'[9]

When, on 1 December 1918, Clemenceau promised support for British ambitions in Palestine, this was not a quixotic gesture occasioned, as Lloyd George claimed, by the warmth of the London crowds' reception. He expected Lloyd George, in return, to endorse Foch's proposals to detach the Rhineland from Germany, making it a neutral state, and for Britain to join an alliance of all the states on the west (left) bank of the Rhine against future German aggression. He was to be disappointed both then, and throughout the conference.

Quite apart from Lloyd George's genuine and strong desire to avoid causes of a possible new war, he also shared a deep British suspicion of France and French ambitions in Europe and beyond. Where the French argued that they needed additional territorial protection against an overwhelmingly powerful and still militaristic neighbour, the British perceived annexationist ambition and a continuing desire for continental supremacy. In December 1918 Lord Curzon, the future British foreign secretary, declared that he was 'seriously afraid that the great power from whom we have most to fear in the future is France'. In June 1920 Lloyd George himself pointed out that: *I have been in the House of Commons for thirty years, and during that time the French have often been within an ace of declaring war against us.* The veteran French ambassador to London, Paul Cambon, exasperated by what he saw as a total British misreading of the relative threats to European peace from France and Germany, fumed: 'The misfortune is that the English are not yet aware that Napoleon is dead.'[10]

Mutual Anglo-French suspicion became a familiar theme of the inter-war period. As Clemenceau returned from the ceremony at Oxford at which he had been awarded an honorary degree, he remarked to Lloyd George 'I have to tell you that from the very day of the Armistice I found you an enemy of France.' *Well,* replied the Welshman, *was it not always our traditional policy?*[11]

Thus, when Foch or Clemenceau's trusted adviser, André Tardieu, proposed various schemes to detach the Rhineland from Germany, they found Lloyd George, supported by the Americans, in total opposition. As Clemenceau himself put it, 'When confronted with the Rhineland question Mr Wilson shook his head in unpromising fashion, and Mr Lloyd George assumed a determined air of antagonism.' An impasse threatened. The French demanded security against a Germany that, whatever the outcomes of the Peace Conference, would have a larger and younger population and greater resources. Tardieu was adamant: 'France would never be content unless it was secured against a repetition of 1914 and ... this security could only be given by drawing the frontier along the Rhine.'[12]

The British and Americans would not hear of it. Wilson's close confidant, Colonel Edward House, summarised the problem well: 'The French have but one idea and that is military protection. They do not seem to know that to establish a Rhenish Republic against the will of the people would be contrary to the principle of self-determination.' The fate of the Rhineland became a key element in a series of separate but interconnecting problems to which the Conference was struggling to reach solutions. Together they formed a log-jam that threatened to reduce it to impotence and failure unless someone could conjure a proposal that could reconcile the apparently irreconcilable.[13]

Guarantees and a Channel Tunnel

It was a situation designed for the Welsh Wizard. He could not concede the principle of self-determination, but he could offer the French security – or at least a sufficiently persuasive illusion of security – to buy their acquiescence and allow the Conference to proceed. On 4 March he told his cabinet colleagues that: *if the United States and ourselves would guarantee France against invasion, France would be satisfied.* On 14 March, with Wilson's backing, Lloyd George offered an Anglo-American 'immediate military guarantee against any unprovoked aggression on the part of Germany against France'. This was later refined into two, separate, guarantees to France, one from the United States and the other from the United Kingdom. He also promised that Britain would build a railway tunnel under the Channel, which would greatly speed the arrival of British troops in France, should the need arise. In return France must abandon its demands for a Rhineland buffer state or a prolonged Allied military occupation of the left bank of the Rhine.[14]

If Lloyd George had hoped that these offers would satisfy Clemenceau he was soon disillusioned, but he had posed the French premier with a dilemma. Clemenceau judged that France's future security depended on a combination of continuing cooperation with the Anglo-Americans and the more tangible territorial and military guarantees demanded by Foch, Poincaré and the French right, but he was unsure about what would constitute an acceptable balance of these two desirables. He demanded further safeguards for France – all Germany's territory on the left bank of the Rhine and within a 50-kilometre strip parallel to the river on the right bank should become a demilitarised zone in which the Germans could keep no military establishments at all, and Allied military forces should occupy the entire left bank and three right bank bridgeheads for 30 years.

Lloyd George readily conceded the demilitarised zone, but did not want a lengthy military occupation of Germany. He opposed this partly because of the drain on British resources, but mainly because of the resentment he believed it would cause in Germany. In his absence, dealing with parliamentary critics in London, Clemenceau persuaded Wilson to trade American agreement to a 15-year occupation, with one third of the occupied territory being evacuated every five years, for French acceptance of the other Rhineland conditions. Faced with a *fait accompli,* and still very reluctantly, Lloyd George acquiesced. Clemenceau was delighted 'I have the fifteen years. I now consider that the peace is made.'[15]

His delight was based on two premises. He believed that Germany would not execute the Treaty and that this would offer any future French government that could hold its nerve, the right to reimpose or continue the occupation beyond the 15 years – and he had secured continued Anglo-American support in the shape of the guarantee. Whilst only time would reveal whether Germany had either the ability or the intention to execute the Treaty, there were earlier indications that the Anglo-American guarantees were not as secure as Clemenceau believed. House took a cynical view: 'I have my doubts as to the Senate accepting such a treaty but that is to be seen. Meanwhile, it satisfies Clemenceau and we can get on with the real business of the conference.' Lloyd George's sincerity in the promise of a Channel tunnel and in offering the guarantee is also questionable – both had an element of 'Now you see it, now you don't' about them.[16]

Although there had been serious discussion about building a Channel tunnel before 1914, and the wartime links with

France had given the project new impetus, Lloyd George was well aware that British opinion, both at governmental and popular level, was deeply divided over the question of whether to join Britain to the Continent – and especially to France – in such a concrete fashion. It can have come as little surprise when Lord Hardinge, the Permanent Under Secretary of the Foreign Office, effectively scotched the project by declaring, in March 1920, 'our relations with France never have been, are not, and probably never will be, sufficiently stable and friendly to justify the construction of a Channel tunnel'. As his former chief Arthur Balfour put it, there was a deep reluctance 'to put an end to our position as an island Power' and a preference for the thought that 'as long as the ocean remains our friend do not let us deliberately destroy its power to help us'. In 1922 George Curzon told the French that economic difficulties prevented Britain from building the tunnel. Privately he admitted 'It is a dishonest answer. The real reason is strategical.' But in 1919 it was a useful rabbit to pull out of Lloyd George's hat.[17]

The guarantee was equally illusory. As Lloyd George pointed out to Louis Botha this was no general commitment to intervene in every European quarrel: *We ourselves shall be the sole judges of what constitutes unprovoked aggression and I cannot conceive that we could be legally bound to come to France's aid except as the result of unpremeditated aggression as clear cut as that of 1914.* The next day, 27 June, on the eve of the signature of both the Treaty of Versailles and the Anglo-French Treaty of Guarantee, Lloyd George slipped, without Clemenceau noticing it, one word – *only* – into the latter treaty. The British treaty would become operative 'only when' the American treaty was ratified. This ensured that the British obligation was totally dependent on the Americans

honouring their commitment first. When, as House anticipated, the Senate rejected the treaty, Lloyd George's sleight of
hand meant that Britain was left with a legal, if perhaps not a
moral, excuse for reneging. Not surprisingly, Clemenceau and
the French felt cheated and lost trust in Britain.[18]

The Saar

The French had a further claim against Germany for territory that had been lost to Prussia in 1815, this time in the Saar
district. After a rather feeble attempt in late March to base
a case on historical grounds, Tardieu soon reverted to the
much more persuasive economic and moral argument that
France should have the right to work the Saar coalmines in
compensation for the deliberate destruction of French mines
by the retreating German army in 1918. The difficult question faced by the peacemakers was how to reconcile this
reasonable French claim for compensation with national self-
determination – a problem further exacerbated because they
were divided as to whether it would be possible for France to
exploit the coal if Germany still governed the territory. Clemenceau was adamant that France must own the mines and the
territory, but Wilson was convinced that France could use
the mines without owning them or removing German sovereignty. Lloyd George, whilst dismissing any French historical
claim, was more sympathetic to Clemenceau's position. In
contrast to his staunch defence of self-determination in the
Rhineland, he suggested that France be given the Saar. The
mines would remain German but France could have their use
for ten years, and after that Germany must place no barrier
to exporting their coal to France.

Faced with a tricky issue the peacemakers' tactic of choice
was to appoint an expert committee. Charles Haskins from

the United States, James Headlam-Morley from Britain and Tardieu for France proposed that Germany should cede sovereignty of the Saar to the League of Nations and the ownership of the coalmines to France. A League government would enable France to exploit the mineral resources. After 15 years the Saarlanders could choose, in a plebiscite, whether they wanted their district to return to Germany, become part of France, or maintain the League's sovereignty. If Germany regained the Saar it would be obliged to repurchase the coalmines from France. Lloyd George thought this a good compromise, but Wilson became extremely stubborn on the issue, at one point summoning the uss *George Washington* to Brest and threatening to return to the United States. Eventually he relented and the Council of Four accepted the experts' proposals on 9 April.

Belgium

These French successes posed a problem for Britain in its relationship with Belgium. As Balfour put it to Lloyd George: 'it would be most unjust, and in the long run, most inexpedient, that France should get Alsace-Lorraine and the Saar coal – and Belgium *nothing*'. The difficulty was that Belgium's direct claims against Germany in the districts of Moresnet, Malmédy and Eupen were tiny. What Belgium really wanted was a readjustment of its admittedly illogical 1839 frontier with the Netherlands and permission for the Dutch to recompense themselves at Germany's expense for the territory ceded to Belgium. But this was 1919 not 1815, Versailles not Vienna, and such bartering of peoples and provinces was no longer acceptable. Lloyd George was not sympathetic and may have missed an opportunity to further Belgium's case for a controlling interest in the affairs of Luxemburg by making

British support for French claims in the Saar dependent on French acceptance of the Belgian position. Instead Luxemburg voted to maintain its status as a Grand Duchy and the continuation of the current ruling family, whilst opting for economic union with France.[19]

Denmark

There was one other minor territorial adjustment in northwestern Europe when the peacemakers enforced the plebiscite in northern Schleswig which Bismarck had promised in 1867 after annexing Schleswig-Holstein, but then never held. Indeed, rather to Danish embarrassment, France sought a bigger plebiscite area than Denmark had suggested, though the subsequent results vindicated the Danish position. A new frontier between Germany and Denmark was suggested in April 1920 and accepted two years later.

Italy

The future shape and size of Italy was much more contentious. Britain, Russia and France had purchased Italy's support in the April 1915 Treaty of London with extravagant promises of Trieste, the Trentino, the Tyrol, Istria, Dalmatia, part of Albania, some of the Dodecanese islands and a share of the Ottoman Empire if it was partitioned. Italy's entry into the war was both deeply divisive internally and disappointing in terms of military results. Bismarck's judgement that 'she has such a huge appetite and very poor teeth' was much quoted. But, as Balfour admitted 'a treaty is a treaty' and Britain and France felt obligated to fulfil their bargain, even if its spirit clearly came from an age devoid of Wilsonian principles. Yet strangely the President made a very early concession in accepting the strategic argument for the Brenner frontier between Italy and Austria, even though this meant that 250,000 German-speakers in the South Tyrol would be transferred to Italy in apparent contradiction of his ninth Point, which spoke of 'a readjustment of the frontiers of Italy along clearly recognisable lines of nationality'. Wilson later admitted he had not studied the problem in sufficient depth, but he was much less accommodating when it came to Italy's claims against Yugoslavia.

Here the fate of the port of Fiume (Rijeka), which was not part of the London bargain, became a sticking point of huge proportions. Italy would not relinquish its claim to a town, in which, expressed in simple terms, the population was mainly Italian, though that in the surrounding coun-tryside was mainly Croatian. Yugoslavia needed Fiume as a port, Italy had alternatives and Wilson dug in his heels over this issue in a way in which he did not over others. Clem-enceau supported Lloyd George's view expressed in a letter to Orlando on 11 June: ... *the Treaty of 1915* [the Treaty of London] *was a bargain rather than a settlement based upon justice, and as a bargain, the Government of Great Britain is prepared to honour its bargain, even though it considers that in the interests of Italy no less than in the interests of Europe modifications in the Treaty ought to be made* ...[20]

None of their suggested compromises was acceptable, and Orlando, reduced to tears, marched out of the Conference on 21 April but was forced to return humiliated, without any resolution of the issue, on 6 May. The dispute dragged on long after the Four had departed, but even after his stroke, Wilson remained adamant: Italy should not have Fiume. Meanwhile, as international negotiations remained stalled, Gabriele d'Annunzio, an Italian poet and war hero, seized the city in September 1919, remaining in control until he was expelled by the Italians in December 1920. Fiume was, for a brief period an independent city, linked to Italy, rather on the model of Danzig, but in January 1924 Benito Mussolini annexed it.

Poland

Esme Howard, who visited Posen in early March, reported: 'Certainly after 150 years of oppression the Poles show wonderful moderation. All German monuments are respected only the statue of Bismarck was one morning found with an old hat on his "pickelhaube" and a fourth class ticket to Berlin in his hand!'[21] Despite this initial optimism, however, the bitterness of the Rhineland and Saar debates were, at the very least, matched by those on the new frontiers of Eastern Europe, especially that between Poland and Germany.

It was remarkable that the question of a Polish-German border even arose. It did so only because of the remarkable sequential collapse of Russia, Austria-Hungary and Germany, the three great empires that had shared out and swallowed Poland over 100 years before, ending its existence as an independent state. Poles found themselves in opposing armies in 1914, whilst the possibility of encouraging a Polish insurrection in the enemy camp offered obvious advantages – and dangers – to both sides. The most Polish nationalists could realistically expect was that the victors might create an autonomous Polish area in territory taken from the losers. Only the collapse of the three empires, and the ensuing power vacuum, created the possibility of an independent Polish state.

Britain's policy towards Poland was guided by its interpretation of the significance of events and perceptions of British national self-interest, though those interpretations and perceptions were not necessarily shared by all the main policy makers. Most agreed, however, that Britain had few direct interests at stake, but that it was important for the general peace of Europe that the settlement contained as few seeds of new wars as possible. Lloyd George, who was torn between his sympathy for Poland's suffering and his exasperation at what he considered to be its greedy demands, argued that *we must not create a Poland alienated from the time of its birth by an unforgettable quarrel with its most civilized neighbour.*[22]

Was an independent Poland desirable from a British viewpoint? A Foreign Office report in 1916 suggested that a barrier between Russia and Germany could be to Britain's advantage. Arthur Balfour, however, argued that concerns about their mutual frontier helped to restrain Germany in the west and Russia in the east and that its removal could lead, in particular, to greater pressure on the British Empire from a less constrained Russia. Hence he favoured an autonomous Poland, within the Russian empire. After 1917 and the triumph of the Bolsheviks the question changed and, by January 1918, Britain and America accepted that there would be an independent Poland. Both Lloyd George and Wilson made this point in their speeches that month but with important qualifications. Lloyd George declared that *We believe, however, that an independent Poland, comprising all those genuinely Polish elements who desire to form part of it, is an urgent necessity for the stability of Western Europe.* Wilson's 13th Point was even more loaded with potential pitfalls: 'An independent Polish state should be erected, which should include the territories inhabited by indisputably Polish populations, which should be assured a free and secure access to the sea, and whose political and economic independence should be guaranteed by international covenant.'

The definition, identity and location of 'genuinely Polish elements' or 'indisputably Polish populations' offered massive scope for disagreement, but one glaring difficulty was that there was a big gap between the central area that most would concede was 'Polish', and the sea. Wilson's promises were contradictory – on the one hand, secure access to the Baltic, and on the other national self-determination. Danzig – the obvious port – was – equally obviously – German, and Poles were in a minority in the lands that would be needed to make a 'corridor' to Danzig.[23]

His demand for international guarantees for Poland was problematic. Knowing that Eastern Europe would be unsettled and full of disappointed people whatever decisions the Conference took, who would commit themselves to defending the settlement? Lloyd George's final point was therefore very interesting. A persistent theme in British inter-war policy was that events in Eastern and Western Europe were not connected – an idea most famously expressed by Neville Chamberlain on 27 September 1938: 'How horrible, fantastic, incredible it is that we should be digging trenches and trying on gas-masks here because of a quarrel in a far-away country between people of whom we know nothing.' Although the French were convinced that any future German assault on the Paris settlement would begin in the east, it was rare for British policymakers to acknowledge the importance of Eastern Europe to West European security. Austen Chamberlain had already declared Britain's lack of interest in Poland's frontiers at Locarno – the Polish Corridor, he said, was 'not worth the bones of a British grenadier'.[24]

Poland already existed when the Conference began and the infant state found itself in territorial disputes with all its neighbours. As with many other aspiring new states, the responsibility of the peacemakers was less to decide whether or not it should exist, rather it was to adjudicate disputed frontiers and to determine the conditions for its recognition as a member of the international community.

There were plenty of disputed frontiers and conflicting claims. The American expert, Isaiah Bowman, graphically recalled the rival presentations of Roman Dmowski and Eduard Beneš on 29 January: 'When Dmowski related the claims of Poland, he began at eleven o'clock in the morning and in the fourteenth century, and could only reach 1919 and the pressing problems of the moment only as late as four o'clock in the afternoon. Beněs followed immediately afterwards with the counter claims of Czechoslovakia, and, if I remember correctly, he began a century earlier and finished an hour later.'[25]

The peacemakers knew that Poland's claims would not be modest. Wilson told his colleagues that 'I saw M. Dmowski and M. Paderewski in Washington and I asked them to define Poland for me ... and they presented me with a map in which they claimed a large part of the earth.' Dmowski's opening bid was for Poland as it had existed at the time of the first partition in 1772, supplemented by Upper Silesia, which had not been Polish since the 14th century, and the surrender of land and the port of Danzig so it could have access to the Baltic. The Conference's expert commission's report of 19 March, based, it was claimed, mainly on ethnographical considerations, but additionally on religious, economic, strategic and historical grounds, was very favourable to Poland. It proposed that Poland should gain most of Upper Silesia, Danzig, both railway lines from Danzig into central Poland and a corridor linking the interior to the sea, thus granting most of Poland's claims, though it did recommend that Allenstein, on the edge of the proposed corridor, be allowed a plebiscite.[26]

Clemenceau and Wilson agreed with the findings but Lloyd George did not and, briefed by a number of his advisers, he set about disputing and amending the recommendations in a dogged and determined manner over the next three months. Bowman witnessed Lloyd George's transformation from bored spectator to crusader as he shocked his colleagues: *Gentlemen, if we give Danzig to the Poles the Germans will not sign the treaty, and if they do not sign our work here is a failure. I assure you that Germany will not sign such a treaty.* He claimed the report would reassign over two million Germans living in Marienwerder, Danzig and elsewhere to Poland. With his usual keen eye for an effective argument, he exaggerated the numbers but made his point – he *agreed that it was hardly possible to draw any line that would not have Germans on both sides of it but ... to hand over millions of people to a distasteful allegiance merely because of a railway line was ... a mistake.*[27]

When the experts stuck to their guns, so did Lloyd George, and by 1 April, using all his skills, he persuaded Wilson to suggest a plebiscite in Marienwerder and convinced him that Headlam-Morley's idea of making Danzig a Free City under the League was really the President's own. Wilson proposed that an expert committee should consider 'his' idea. Haskins, Tardieu and Headlam-Morley – who had already proposed a similar solution for the Saar – duly endorsed the plan to make Danzig autonomous but linked economically to Poland. On 9 April the Four accepted the Saar and Danzig proposals. Lloyd George's persistence had prevailed – and Marienwerder, like Allenstein, would later vote to remain part of Germany.

It was certainly something on which Lloyd George felt very strongly. He wrote to Andrew Bonar Law on 31 March 1919: *I have never cared for the handing over of two or three million*

Germans to Polish rule … The Germans would never accept permanently this transference. There would be trouble within the next twenty years. We should either have to wage war to enforce the treaty or accept its abrogation in this respect – neither of these alternatives offer a very acceptable prospect to contemplate.[28]

Headlam-Morley was also very concerned about the fate of Upper Silesia, awarded to Poland in the draft Treaty. He persuaded Lloyd George to take up the issue. It was Lloyd George's only major success in his June attempts to revise the draft Treaty, but it was not easily achieved. Wilson and Clemenceau both resented him undermining painfully constructed agreements. Wilson was exasperated by Lloyd George's refusal to stick to his bargains. Clemenceau's anxiety was based on a more concrete concern – he wanted as strong and large a Poland as possible to the east of Germany to act as a substitute threat now that Russia was no longer there. He did not want Lloyd George nibbling away at Poland or returning assets to Germany.

> I have never cared for the handing over of two or three million Germans to Polish rule...The Germans would never accept permanently this transference.
>
> LLOYD GEORGE

Once again Lloyd George was more Wilsonian than Wilson, arguing that the need to consider the self-determination of the people of the area required a plebiscite: *I am doing nothing other than abiding by your Fourteen Points.*[29] Wilson, rather grudgingly and with increasing doubts as to Lloyd George's motives and sincerity, was persuaded that he had to be true to his principle and Clemenceau and the Poles, with great reluctance, had to acquiesce. The plebiscite would be held in the next two years, and, in the interim, Upper Silesia would be under international supervision, so that the Poles could have some chance to put their case to people who had been under German rule for so long.

It is an interesting point whether the later Lloyd George would have thanked himself for changing the Treaty. It certainly did nothing to improve Anglo-French relations. Faced with post-war difficulties in Ireland and the Empire, Britain's resources became overstretched and, to his embarrassment, it could no longer provide troops to police the plebiscite area. This left the task to the French, who had not wanted a plebiscite in the first place and whom the British now accused of favouring the Poles. When the plebiscite was held in 1921 the outcome provoked a further fierce Anglo-French dispute about its interpretation, and very unusually for a matter of Treaty enforcement, they called upon the League of Nations in 1922 to make an adjudication which gave most of the land to Germany but most of the mines and industry to Poland.

Central and Eastern Europe

Lloyd George was consistent in his approach to Poland, and indeed to the situation in eastern and central Europe generally. He wanted to be as generous to the new states as possible, but to avoid weakening them, as he would argue, by burdening them with too many unwilling minorities: *The task of the Parisian Treaty-makers was not to decide what in fairness should be given to the liberated nationalities, but what in common honesty should be freed from their clutches when they had overstepped the bounds of self-determination.*[30] In particular he feared the consequences of leaving too many Germans outside Germany but, despite his best efforts, some 13 million former German citizens, or people of German language, found themselves in Poland, Czechoslovakia, France,

Denmark and elsewhere. Many were unhappy with their new lot. The Conference did try to provide such reluctant citizens with an internationally supervised minority protection scheme under the League but this neither satisfied the minorities nor their host states, which found their sovereignty undermined at the very moment that they became independent. The new states particularly resented the slur that they required minority treaties when the Great Powers exempted themselves and Germany from similar obligations on the grounds of their supposedly superior moral standing.

The Sudetenland, a German-speaking area from the former Austro-Hungarian empire, claimed by Germany and Czechoslovakia, was an example of territory over whose fate the peacemakers agonised – should the industrial and defence needs of the new state prevail over the linguistic argument that suggested that its three million people should belong to Germany? Perhaps equally important, and particularly when it came to the eight million German-speaking remnant of the empire itself, should losers be rewarded, and were those who had had great difficulty in defeating Germany prepared to see it acquire even more people and resources? On the other hand, might union with Austria dilute what was generally viewed as the negative influence of Prussia in the new Germany?

British views on the two issues tended to move in opposite directions. There was a general consensus in the Foreign Office that, in the case of Austria, national self-determination should rule – as Namier pointed out 'We cannot exterminate the Austrian Germans; we cannot make them cease to feel Germans.' The French were adamant – Austria must not be allowed to join Germany – and Britain conceded the point, though Hardinge spoke for many: 'If German Austria wishes to join Germany no clause in the Treaty of Peace will prevent its ultimate consummation.' On the Sudeten question the strategic arguments prevailed, Czechoslovakia must not lose its defensible frontier. Thus the Czechs gained the Sudetenland and Austria was forced to become independent against its expressed wish. Hitler would reverse both decisions, using Konrad Henlein, the leader of the Sudeten German Party, to foment nationalist discontent amongst the Germans in the Sudetenland. The resulting crisis destroyed Czechoslovakia in 1938 and undermined international confidence in group rights for minorities. After 1945 the emphasis would be on human, or individual rights, partly on the grounds of the threat posed by groups to their host state and the fear that 'every protected minority will ultimately find its Henlein'.[31]

Russia

The Conference faced all sorts of difficult dilemmas about new frontiers, sometimes made even more complicated when the direct or perceived interests of one of the major Allies were at stake or when two friendly powers sought the same lands. Its decisions left disappointment and resentment along borders throughout eastern and central Europe and the Balkans, but the situation in Russia proved beyond its capabilities to resolve. Henry Wilson once declared 'The root of evil is that *the Paris writ does not run*'. Nowhere was this truer than in Russia and its borderlands, though Lloyd George had to beat off Winston Churchill's determined attempt to wage war on the Bolsheviks in support of various White Russian groups whose attempts to defeat the revolutionaries were undermined by their lack of coordination and inability to understand the need for change.[32]

Lloyd George had little love for the Bolsheviks but had no

intention of plunging Britain into an unwinnable war. The British, French, American and Japanese troops that had intervened in Russia in the hope of maintaining an eastern front against Germany were mostly withdrawn in 1919 and 1920. Russia's fate, and its new frontiers, would be determined by civil and foreign wars, rather than the decisions of the peacemakers as the fate of the Curzon line, the border between Poland and Russia proposed by the conference, starkly illustrated. After a war of dramatic movement in 1920, where the Poles first reached Kiev, then were pushed back to the gates of Warsaw, before successfully counter-attacking, the Russo-Polish frontier was drawn much farther to the east than the Paris recommendation, though the Curzon Line did become, with some amendments, the frontier between the USSR and Poland after 1945.

The results

In 1914 Europe there were some 60 million people living in states in which they were not the dominant nationality. After 1919 this figure was reduced to about 30 million, though the problem was not halved. The states of 1914 did not claim to be based on national self-determination but the new map of Europe was supposed to embody that principle. Every person left on the wrong side of a redrawn frontier felt themselves a living proof of the settlement's failure. In eastern and central Europe the settlement reduced the proportion of minority nationalities from 50 per cent to 25 per cent. Given the impossibly mixed nature of those populations and the constraints under which the peacemakers operated, most notably their reluctance to force people to move to fit maps, they probably did as much as they practically could. This was little consolation to those, often the previous majority, left as minorities in

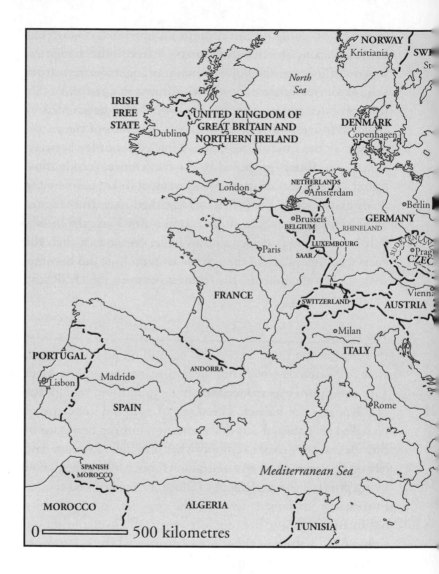

Europe 1923

FINLAND

Petrograd (St Petersburg)

Tallinn
ESTONIA

Riga
LATVIA

ea

LITHUANIA

zig

Vilnius

Königsberg
EAST
PRUSSIA

Warsaw

Brest-Litovsk

POLAND

Kiev

MOSCOW

UNION OF SOVIET
SOCIALIST REPUBLICS

VAKIA

Budapest

GARY

Odessa

ROMANIA

Belgrade

Bucharest

Black Sea

OSLAVIA

BULGARIA

Sofia

ıa

BANIA

Istanbul

GREECE

TURKEY

Athens

IRAQ

SYRIA

CYPRUS

states that did not want them and where they did not wish to become the underdog.

Lloyd George's record of defending the principle was good. His motivation was partly pragmatic, to reduce as far as possible the future causes of tension, but it was an ideal to which, as a Welshman, he did feel a strong commitment. In the Rhineland, Danzig, the Polish Corridor and Upper Silesia he fought hard, and with striking success, to prevent more Germans than necessary being transferred to another state. Elsewhere British negotiators did their best to keep new minorities to a minimum, but it was often a vain struggle. Sadly, Lansing's December 1918 predictions about national self-determination have proved, if anything, to be too optimistic in the remainder of the 20th century: 'It will raise hopes that can never be realised. It will, I fear, cost thousands of lives. What a calamity the phrase was ever uttered! What misery it will cause.'[33]

6

The Imperial Settlement

Lloyd George was, on the face of it, an unlikely British imperialist, given his experiences as an opponent of the Boer War, but his objections to that war were based on its cost and its justification rather than any fundamental opposition to Britain's empire. His imaginative and sensitive inclusion of the increasingly independently minded Dominions in an Imperial War Cabinet after he became Prime Minister in 1916 was an important indication of the way he wished to see the Empire develop. He was also clear when, on 10 May 1917, he told a secret session of the House of Commons that Germany's captured colonies would not be returned and that the Ottomans must forfeit Palestine and Mesopotamia. He and his colleagues were kept aware of imperial issues through a variety of contacts, one of whom, Leo Amery, of the War Cabinet secretariat, congratulated himself at the end of 1917 on 'all the work on Peace terms which gradually drove into their heads the importance of East Africa, Palestine, and Mesopotamia and the Imperial outlook generally'.[1]

On 6 October 1918 Hankey recorded that: 'Ll G took a very *intransigeant* attitude and wanted us to go back on the

Sykes-Picot agreement, so as to get Palestine for us and to bring Mosul into the British zone, and even to keep the French out of Syria ... He also thought it would attract less attention to our enormous gains in the war if we swallowed our share of Turkey now, and the German colonies later.'[2] Not surprisingly then, at the Peace Conference Lloyd George was an enthusiastic and committed defender of the wider interests of Britain and its Dominions. He boasted to Riddell: *I have returned with a pocket full of sovereigns, in the shape of the German Colonies, Mesopotamia etc.*[3]

One of his problems, however, was that the defence of those interests seemed to require greater and greater commitments and the acquisition of even more territory. Arthur Balfour commented on 9 December 1918 that 'Every time I come to a discussion – at intervals of, say, five years – I find there is a new sphere which we have got to guard, which is supposed to protect the gateways of India. Those gateways are getting farther and farther from India.'[4] There was the added complication that, in addition to whatever ambitions Britain might have, particularly in the Middle East, its Dominions had their own, sometimes conflicting agendas, for which each expected British support.

There was also the unspeakable thought that another power might acquire territory somewhere – anywhere – even if Britain had little current interest in it. Writing to Balfour on 28 December 1918, Edwin Montagu satirised this problem splendidly: 'And then there is the rounded Lord Curzon, who for historical reasons of which he alone is master, geographical considerations which he has peculiarly studied, finds, reluctantly, much against his will, with very grave doubts, that it would be dangerous if any country in the world was left to itself, if any country in the world was left to the control of any other country but ourselves, and we must go there, as I have heard him say, "for diplomatic, economic, strategic and telegraphic reasons." So we go on. It is fatal to let the French here. It is appalling to think even of ourselves as mandatories there. The idea of an American fleet in the Mediterranean is unspeakably horrid.'[5]

Thus the question of what to do with the former German possessions in Africa and Asia, amounting to over 1,000,000 square miles and nearly 14,000,000 people, and the territories of the Ottoman Empire in the Balkans, Asia Minor and the Middle East, was both daunting and complex.

As with many other aspects of the Conference, the standards that Wilson in particular had set for the peacemakers appeared to further complicate the situation. On the one hand several of the British Dominions were very anxious, for security reasons, to obtain outright sovereignty of neighbouring former German colonies but, on the other, Wilson had insisted that there would be no colonial carve-up. He did not object to Germany losing its colonies, most of which had been conquered by Allied forces by 1916 – with the notable exception of German East Africa, where isolated German forces were still fighting after the armistice was concluded in Europe – but demanded that there must be some recognition of formal responsibilities before territory changed hands. The conference decided on 24 January that Germany's colonies were forfeit, but it did not determine their new masters until much later.

Wilson envisaged a system of international trusteeship, applying the principle of self-determination, and monitored by the League in 'a free, open-minded and absolutely impartial adjustment of all colonial claims'. This was not necessarily what Australia, New Zealand and South Africa had in mind and they had the support of some key players in London, including Lloyd George's private secretary, Philip Kerr with his strong connections to Lord Milner, Lionel Curtis and the *Round Table* group, who wanted to see the Empire strengthened as a much more practical and cohesive alternative to Wilson's League. Once again Lloyd George had to try to find solutions that would satisfy Wilson's idealism and the practical demands of his Dominion supporters.

The mandate system

With the sterling support of Smuts, another lawyer with a flexible mind and an inventive imagination, Lloyd George came up with some deft manoeuvres to overcome these difficulties. One approach was to suggest that there was no problem for Britain to adhere to Wilson's principles, because the British Empire already embodied them. Demands for self-determination of colonial peoples could be met by consulting tribal rulers. They were able to adapt Smuts' original conception of mandates, under which the League would assign responsibility for governing territories freed from Russian, Austro-Hungarian and Turkish rule to international trustees, to meet Wilson's requirement that Germany's African and Asian colonies could only be assigned once their new rulers agreed to some form of international supervision.

This proposal that Germany's colonies should become League mandates, with their new rulers undertaking international commitments, did not meet universal approval and Billy Hughes of Australia was quite adamant in his objections. He was characteristically blunt when Wilson put him on the spot by asking whether Australia would refuse the appeal 'of the whole civilised world' to accept the former German colonies under the obligations of a League mandate, replying 'That's about the size of it, President Wilson'. William Massey, the New Zealand premier grunted assent. An exasperated Maurice Hankey declared: 'Hughes and Massey … are our principal difficulty, but President Wilson … is even more obstinate.'[6]

Again Lloyd George and his colleagues on the League of Nations commission found an answer. Cecil, supported by Smuts, suggested that there should be three classes of mandate, each requiring annual reports from the mandatory to the League: 'A', where only minimal assistance would be needed for a people close to self-government; 'B', where the mandatory power would administer the territory, subject to League rules banning militarisation and the trade in slaves, arms and liquor; and 'C', which fell little short of annexation, subject only to the same conditions as the 'B' mandates.

Smuts really wanted the Pacific islands and South-West Africa excluded from any mandate scheme but he cooperated with Cecil to find a compromise. Others were less collegial and it took some hard words from Lloyd George on 29 January to quell Hughes, who fought 'like a weasel – which he somewhat resembles – for annexation in the Pacific'. Finally, losing his temper, he told Hughes that he had no intention of quarrelling with the United States over the Solomon Islands. Grudgingly, after reassurances about the rights of a mandatory to control immigration and trade, Hughes accepted that the terms of a 'C' mandate differed only 'from full sovereign control as a nine hundred and ninety nine years' lease differs from a fee simple'.[7]

It looked as though Lloyd George had found an answer acceptable to all, but then, on 30 January, Wilson took offence at a critical newspaper article written by Hughes, and, although he said he found the British plan helpful, he refused, in a fit of pique, to assign the German colonies to specific states. He needled Hughes into an indignant outburst by suggesting that Australia might not necessarily be the mandatory for New Guinea and it required calm moderation by Louis Botha, the South African premier, to restore equanimity on the tacit understanding that the Dominions would get what they wanted – but not yet. The terms of the mandates were defined in Article 22 of the League Covenant.

The assignment of mandates

It was only on 6 May, significantly just before the Italians rejoined the conference, that Wilson relented and agreed to assign mandates. On 7 May, just prior to the Germans receiving the draft Treaty at the Trianon palace, the Four accepted Lloyd George's proposals for the distribution of mandates. Despite the spats between Wilson and Hughes, they went, in almost every case, to the power that occupied the territory and thus the Dominions obtained control of adjacent former German colonies – 'C' mandates for Australia in New Guinea, the Bismarck Archipelago and the German islands south of the Equator, and for South Africa in South-West Africa, with a 'B' mandate for New Zealand in Samoa. Apart from South-West Africa all the Central and sub-Saharan African mandates were in the 'B' category. Britain gained German East Africa (Tanganyika), and reached an agreement in December 1920 sharing Togoland and the Cameroons with France, which gained most of both.

The fate of Germany's concessions in Jiaozhou, Qingdao and Shandong in China proved an embarrassment for both Lloyd George and Wilson because the Chinese claim for their return seemed irrefutable. Instead the Japanese demanded the territories. They based their case on their occupation of the areas in 1914, the acceptance by China of their 'Twenty-One Demands' in May 1915, and the 1917 agreement with Britain to supply naval assistance in exchange for British support for their claims in China and for the German islands north of the Equator. With reluctance Lloyd George accepted that a deal was a deal, clinging to the hope that this might limit Japan's ambitions to north of the Equator and prevent the militarisation of its new territories. When the French also supported Japan, Wilson was isolated in his objections. He felt his position was hopelessly compromised by the Italian walk-out in late April, which coincided with these discussions, and hence that he could not afford a similar boycott by the Japanese. Lloyd George failed to persuade Japan to accept a 'C' mandate for these

Japan's list of Twenty-One Demands were presented to China on 18 January 1915. In essence they demanded that China should no longer lease territory to other foreign powers and accept Japanese control over Manchuria and Shandong. Reluctantly the Chinese agreed in May 1915.

areas, so they were, unusually, awarded in outright posses-sion, though Japan did promise, at an unspecified future date, to return Jiaozhou to China. Now China refused to sign the Treaty, but, uncomfortable though this was, Japan proved once again that power could count for more than morality.

In a former age Germany would have lost its colonies simply because it had lost the war but such a justification was no longer felt to be valid in the new Wilsonian era. Instead the Allies advanced the dubious argument that the Germans, whose colonial record did have blemishes but overall was little different to that of other powers, were incompetent rulers and, on this basis, should be judged unfit to possess colonies. As with reparations, twinges of unease that this case was not sustainable afflicted the British from an early stage, though whether many Germans were really as disgruntled about their

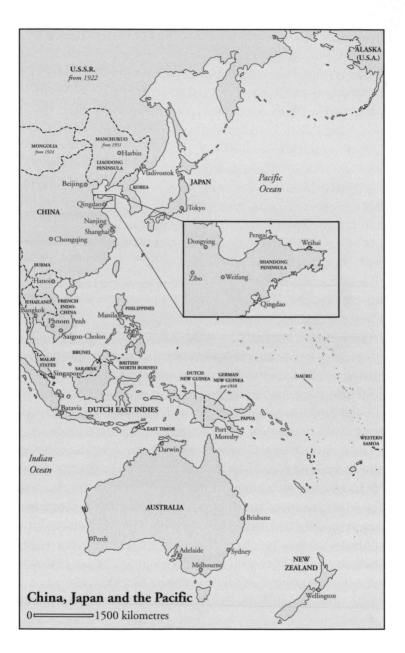

U.S.S.R.
from 1922

MANCHUKUO
from 1931

MONGOLIA
from 1924

○Harbin

LIAODONG
PENINSULA

Vladivostok

Beijing○

KOREA

JAPAN

*Pacific
Ocean*

Qingdao○

CHINA

○Tokyo

Nanjing

Shanghai○

○Chongqing

BURMA

Hanoi○

THAILAND

FRENCH
INDO-
CHINA

Bangkok○

Phnom Penh

Manila○

PHILIPPINES

Saigon-Cholon

BRUNEI

MALAY
STATES

SARAWAK

BRITISH
NORTH BORNEO

○Singapore

DUTCH
NEW GUINEA

GERMAN
NEW GUINEA
pre-1918

NAURU

Batavia○ **DUTCH EAST INDIES**

EAST TIMOR

PAPUA

Port○
Moresby

WESTERN
SAMOA

*Indian
Ocean*

○Darwin

AUSTRALIA

○Brisbane

○Perth

Adelaide○

○Sydney

Melbourne○

**NEW
ZEALAND**

China, Japan and the Pacific

Wellington○

0⬛⬛⬛⬛1500 kilometres

Dongying○

Pengai○

Weihai

**SHANDONG
PENINSULA**

Zibo○

○Weifang

Qingdao○

ALASKA
(U.S.A.)

loss of empire as some revisionist leaders would later claim is doubtful. Equally doubtful is whether Hitler ever treated the colonial issue with the same seriousness as British leaders in the 1930s judged (or hoped) when they sought to appease him with promises of an imperial redistribution.[8]

The Middle East

In Africa and Asia Britain's direct demands were limited and much of Lloyd George's effort went towards achieving satisfactory outcomes for the Dominions. Such was not the case in the Middle East, where the demise of the Ottoman Empire opened potential new spheres of influence for Britain. Its traditional concerns in the area – the security of the Suez Canal and of the routes to India, together with the restriction of Russian access to the Mediterranean and influence in the region – were supplemented by the opportunity to obtain control of supplies of the new strategic resource, oil, and the intangible but powerful psychological lure of controlling the Holy Land.

Just as in Eastern Europe, the settlement in this region at the end of the war would have enormous and far-reaching consequences. It created the broad outline of the Middle East as we know it today, with a number of new states emerging from the defunct Ottoman area. Iraq (then Mesopotamia), Jordan (then Transjordan), Saudi Arabia (then the Hejaz), Israel (then Palestine), Syria and Lebanon were all products of the peace or subsequent adjustments in the 1920s. Unlike Eastern Europe however, very little of this region emerged in the short term as independent, much of it falling into the ambit of either France or Britain.

Britain's policies in this area were complicated, multifaceted and, at times, downright duplicitous. One verdict was

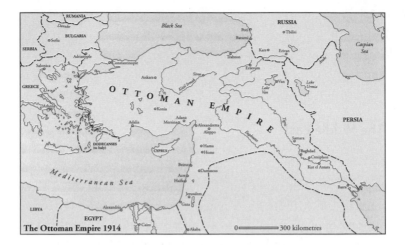

The Ottoman Empire 1914

that they consisted of selling 'the same horse, or at least parts of the same horse, twice' but this, if anything, underestimates the conflicting natures of deals struck with the French, the Russians, the Italians, various Arab leaders and the Jews at different times during the war: deals which were often then adapted, distorted or disregarded as the fortunes of battle and the pressing concerns of the moment changed.

As the war drew to an end, Lloyd George hinted at ambitious plans for British expansion. On 3 October 1918 he told the War Cabinet that *he had been refreshing his memory about the Sykes-Picot Agreement, and had come to the conclusion that it was quite inapplicable to present circumstances, and was altogether a most undesirable agreement from the British point of view.* It was over two years old and *it entirely overlooked the fact that our position in Turkey had been won by very large British forces, whereas our Allies had contributed but little to the result.* Balfour and Bonar Law tried to remind him that the different Allies fought in different theatres, not all of which offered immediate rewards, but all were engaging

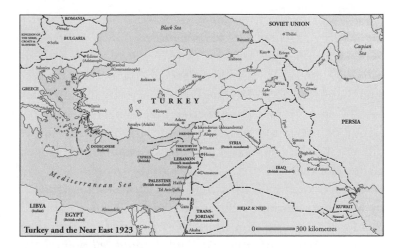

Turkey and the Near East 1923

in a common struggle. Hence it would be fair to treat the settlement, like the war effort, as a whole, but Lloyd George was clearly intent on making Britain the major beneficiary of the former Ottoman Empire in the Middle East.[9]

Palestine

Arnold Toynbee, one of the British PID experts, was enthralled to catch the Prime Minister unawares during the conference: 'Lloyd George, to my delight, had forgotten my presence and began to think aloud.

> Mesopotamia ... yes ... oil ... irrigation ... we must have Mesopotamia; Palestine ... yes ... the Holy Land ... Zionism ... we must have Palestine; Syria ... h'm ... what is there in Syria? Let the French have that.
>
> LLOYD GEORGE

Mesopotamia ... yes ... oil ... irrigation ... we must have Mesopotamia; Palestine ... yes ... the Holy Land ... Zionism ... we must have Palestine; Syria ... h'm ... what is there in Syria? Let the French have that.' Lloyd George certainly had no problem when, in December 1918, Clemenceau *asked me what it was I specially wanted from the French. I instantly replied that I wanted Mosul attached to Irak, and Palestine from Dan to Beersheba under British control. Without hesitation he agreed.* It was not necessarily the decisive concession that Clemenceau intended. His generosity did not deter Lloyd George from seeking further amendments in Britain's favour of previously agreed wartime arrangements and it did not produce his expected British support for French claims elsewhere.[10]

Lloyd George had a fascination with Palestine, sparked by his Nonconformist religious background. He reminisced that *I was taught far more about the history of the Jews than about the history of my own land. I could tell you all the kings of Israel. But I doubt whether I could have named half a dozen of the kings of England, and not more of the kings of Wales.*[11] Unfortunately, despite this knowledge, he could not find Dan on a map – as an Italian diplomat observed: 'A common sight at the Peace Conference in Paris was one or other of the world's statesmen, standing before a map and muttering to himself: "Where is that damn'd … ?" while he sought with extended forefinger for some town or river that he had never heard of before'.[12] When Dan was eventually located it was considered to be too far south, so Britain argued for a new frontier. This was typical of the vague and ambiguous territorial definitions agreed with various parties during the war, and of the incomplete and fragmentary knowledge of the peacemakers. It was also typical of the fate of agreements that had become outdated or inconvenient.

There was no doubt that the Sykes-Picot agreement was the most important – and inconvenient – of these. Sykes himself recognised that its provisions now stood in the way of Britain's ambitions in the area and he sought, unsuccessfully, to get the French to swap their interests in the Arab region, apart from the Lebanon, for new ones in Kurdistan and Armenia. This was but one of many unsuccessful, often deeply divisive, attempts by Britain to renegotiate its agreement with France.

In fact very little of the final Middle Eastern settlement was completed in Paris whilst the main leaders were there and it was not until April 1920, by which time conditions were very different, that these questions were decided. Palestine and Syria were inextricably linked, because the Arab definition of Syria included Palestine, and the conflicting nature of the Allied wartime commitments and territorial understandings were further complicated by the potential of the clash between the indigenous populations of Palestine and incoming Jewish settlers. Emir Feisal and Chaim Weizmann, two of the leaders who considered that Britain had pledged Palestine to them, and whose ambitions were clearly contradictory, nonetheless enjoyed cordial personal relations when they met in 1918 and again at the Peace Conference, but it seemed unlikely that this would be the normal pattern of Arab-Jewish relationships in Palestine. Curzon gloomily, and accurately, predicted that whoever received the mandate for Palestine would have to keep the two groups from killing each other.

Feisal, who had transformed his accommodation in Paris into an approximation of an Arabian sheik's tent, presented the Arab case for Syria to the Council of Ten on 6 February. Some alleged that Feisal's address consisted of quotations from the Qu'ran while Colonel Lawrence's 'translation' represented his, rather than the Arab, vision of the post-war world. Either way the French were having none of it, and Lloyd George's various attempts to offer them less than the Sykes-Picot bargain merely provoked Clemenceau, usually indifferent to

France's imperial ambitions, to declare: 'Lloyd George is a cheat. He has managed to turn me into a "Syrian".'

On 27 February it was Weizmann's turn. His argument that 'in Palestine there was room for an increase of at least 4,000,000 to 5,000,000 people, without encroaching on the legitimate interests of the people already there' formed part of a larger, ambiguous debate. Quizzed by Lansing as to whether a Jewish national home meant an autonomous Jewish government, Weizmann said no, but then amplified this by saying: 'Later on, when the Jews formed the large majority, they would be ripe to establish such a government as would answer to the state of the development of the country and to their ideals.'[13] Lloyd George, who was not present, would have admired the dexterity and obscurity of the response. The Council of Ten and the Council of Four left the Palestinian question for others to resolve.

Syria

The Four also reached no decision on Syria. On 20 March the French insisted that they must have the mandate, and Lloyd George, allegedly on behalf of the Arabs, resisted. Wilson proposed a fact-finding mission to Syria, which Clemenceau, thinking he was being adroit, accepted, provided the British areas of interest were also included. His advisers – painfully aware of the lack of support for France amongst the Syrians – were devastated. Paul Cambon exploded 'They must be drunk the way they are surrendering'.[14] Lloyd George persuaded Wilson not to include Mesopotamia. In the event the Europeans refused to send representatives on the commission led by two Americans, Henry King, a college president, and Charles Crane, a businessman – who would have an important part to play later in the development of the region's oil resources.

King and Crane's findings, which were not made official to the Conference but which were well-known, confirmed that the Syrians would prefer America or Britain if they had to have any mandatory at all, and indeed that anyone would be preferable to the French. They also revealed, unsurprisingly, that the Arabs in Palestine were 'emphatically against the entire Zionist program' and recommended limiting Jewish immigration and dropping the idea of a Jewish national homeland there. Their recommendations were ignored and Curzon's hopes that the American commission would rescue Britain from its Palestinian commitments were dashed.

The British refused to evacuate their troops from Syria to allow the French to replace them, and they also cancelled the Long-Berenger agreement which had divided the region's oil between them. Anglo-French relations sank to a low point and Clemenceau actually threatened Lloyd George with a duel, which, given their relative experience of such matters, Lloyd George was wise to ignore.

Post-Versailles developments

By the time the German treaty was signed little had been resolved, but Lloyd George now became concerned that the damage to Anglo-French relations was too great and that the need to maintain cooperation across the wide range of their interests outweighed any commitment to the Arabs. It was also increasingly clear that the United States was unlikely to become a mandatory power in the former Ottoman Empire – the British and French would have to sort this out between themselves. In September Lloyd George agreed to evacuate Syria and Cilicia in favour of the French, whose occupation forces moved in by November. In October Feisal was told to reach the best deal he could with France and he and

Clemenceau agreed secretly that France would exercise only nominal control in Syria. Even this was not acceptable to the rising tide of Arab nationalism, which, in the shape of the General Syrian Congress, declared itself willing to fight both Britain and France. In March 1920 Feisal accepted, reluctantly, the throne of an independent Greater Syria, including Lebanon and Palestine, offered to him by the Congress in Damascus. His brother, Abdullah, became king of an independent Iraq, while in Palestine, an Arab delegation demanded to be part of Syria.

Although Lloyd George enjoyed indications of French discomfiture in Syria, these developments, particularly in the context of increasing problems in Turkey and the potential threat of an anti-European *jihad,* were too menacing and revealed the underlying community of Anglo-French interests in the region, no matter how much they might squabble over particulars. This paramountcy of the Anglo-French relationship was emphasised when, in London in February 1920, they agreed the frontiers between Palestine and Syria, and Syria and Turkey, without reference to the local wishes. At San Remo in April they concluded a new agreement on the division of oil and assigned the mandates for Syria and Lebanon to France, and for Mesopotamia and Palestine to Britain, though the boundaries between them were not finalised until December and it was only in July 1922 that these deals were sanctioned by the League. Meanwhile the withdrawal of British support, and the military incompetence of Feisal's forces proved decisive. French troops routed the Arabs in July 1920 and Feisal fled.

The collapse of Ottoman power

In addition to the problems of how to dispose of the wider possessions of the defunct Ottoman Empire the peacemakers had to decide what should happen at the centre of that empire. In theory this had nothing to do with the imperial settlement – beyond requiring the internationalisation and neutralisation of the Straits. Lloyd George, in January 1918 had declared: *we do not challenge the maintenance of the Turkish Empire in the homelands of the Turkish race with its capital at Constantinople* and, despite not being at war with the Ottoman Empire at all, Wilson, in his Fourteen Points stated 'The Turkish portion of the present Ottoman Empire should be assured a secure sovereignty'. Both reserved the right of Turkey's wider empire to some form of autonomy, but both had suggested that the core of its Turkish territory would be untouched. The practice would be rather different and Hankey recorded on 6 October 1918 that Lloyd George was 'very contemptuous of President Wilson and anxious to arrange the division of Turkey between France, Italy and G.B. before speaking to America'.[15]

This was partly because the Turkish collapse at the end of the war was sudden and complete. The defeat of Bulgaria in September 1918 opened to gates to the Turkish heartlands and the government in Constantinople sought an armistice. So total was its demoralisation that the British admiral sent with a list of 24 armistice conditions, of which he was told only the first four were essential, found ready acceptance of his complete terms without negotiation. Nicolson recorded the extent of this triumph, which seemed final and irreversible: 'The Ottoman Empire lay at our feet dismembered and impotent, its capital and Caliph at the mercy of our guns.'[16]

The Treaty of Sèvres in August 1920 suggested that the Allies were still in complete control, but this was not the case. The Sultan signed, but did not dare to ratify the treaty, which clearly did not reflect the realities of the situation. Delay, the ebbing away of the formidable British military presence in the Middle East after 1918, the nationalist revolt in Turkey led by Mustafa Kemal, the defeat of the Greek invaders and a near-renewal of hostilities with Britain meant that, in 1922, a revitalised Turkey, from a position of strength, was the only one of the former Central Powers to negotiate a peace settlement with the Allies.

The signature of the Treaty of Lausanne in July 1923 ended a process of peacemaking that had lasted longer than the Great War itself and that had seen the political demise of all the Big Four before its conclusion. Their last survivor fell victim in October 1922 to the danger of a new war with Turkey that, coming on top of growing rank-and-file Tory opposition to Lloyd George's policies towards the Soviet Union and Ireland, destroyed the coalition government and consigned the still young Prime Minister to a political wilderness in which he never held office again.

Making peace with Turkey

Lloyd George, at the start of the process, said that the peace with Turkey would take a week. Even had the peacemakers devoted their full attention to the matter, this was unrealistically optimistic, but the Ottomans came well down the Allied list of priorities. There were some brief discussions about the future of Syria and Palestine and one meeting, in June, with representatives of the Turkish government, but neither the Ten nor the Four devoted much time to Asia Minor (Anatolia) and the future of Turkey. It could wait, there were more urgent matters to settle with Germany and the successor states in eastern and central Europe.

The Allies did take one crucial decision which had far-reaching and disastrous consequences. Both the Italians and the Greeks had aspirations to take parts of Anatolia and the Greek premier, Eleftherios Venizelos, formulated the considerable Greek ambitions to the Ten on 3 and 4 February 1919. In addition to wanting territory from Albania and Bulgaria, he demanded, from Turkey, eastern Thrace, islands in the eastern Mediterranean, Smyrna (Izmir), which had a substantial Greek population, and Aidan and Bursa, which did not.

In the inevitable expert committee set up to examine these claims, Greece had the great advantage of British sponsorship, whilst the French could be relied upon to oppose anything the Italians wanted. In exasperation the Italians began a unilateral occupation of Adalia (Antalya), which did not endear them to their colleagues, and, in conjunction with their boycott of the conference over Fiume, delivered the verdict to Greece. On 6 May, still in the absence of the Italians, Wilson (against the advice of his experts), Clemenceau and Lloyd George authorised temporary Greek landings in Izmir, ostensibly to prevent massacres of the Greek population but really to punish the Italians, to reduce their influence in Asia Minor and, certainly in Lloyd George's case, to further Greek ambitions.

Lloyd George, Frances and Hankey (amongst others) were charmed by Venizelos – *the greatest statesman Greece had thrown up since the days of Pericles* – but there was a strategic opportunity at stake as well. Britain needed a substitute for the Ottomans as a partner in the eastern Mediterranean and thus Lloyd George was willing to support Venizelos and his vision for a greater Greece. Many of his advisers were not convinced: Balfour opposed the partition of Turkey; Churchill and Montagu feared the impact on Muslims throughout the Empire, but especially in India; and the military experts were against the plan. Even Curzon, who disliked the Ottomans intensely and believed that they should lose Constantinople, warned that the practical disappearance of Turkey could give 'a most dangerous and unnecessary stimulus to Moslem passions throughout the Eastern world and that sullen resentment may easily burst into savage frenzy'.[17]

Mustafa Kemal and the nationalist revolt

Henry Wilson's verdict proved accurate: 'The whole thing is mad and bad.'[18] The Greek landings on 15 May provoked more, not less, unrest in Izmir, but crucially converted many Turks to the cause of Mustafa Kemal and the Nationalists. Ironically it was the Allies who had urged the Sultan to send someone into the interior to quell the growing numbers of dissident Ottoman forces in Anatolia. On 19 May he sent Kemal, the hero of the Gallipoli campaign, to restore order. Instead Kemal organised the resistance more effectively, though this was ignored for too long by the British, who dismissed him as a bandit.

Kemal benefitted from Allied neglect and rumours of their plans for the further dismemberment of Turkey – the Greek and Italian landings in Asia Minor, the possibility of independent states in Armenia and Kurdistan, even the detachment of the Straits area and Constantinople, all provoked a nationalist backlash born of desperation. Kemal's position was never secure but his base in Anatolia was remote and elections in January 1920 returned a Nationalist majority, thus adding democratic legitimacy to his growing military strength. The National movement demanded a sovereign, independent and secular Turkish state and, from the spring of 1919 onwards, Kemal manouevred to become its undisputed leader, which he effectively accomplished in January 1921 when his new parliament in Ankara (Angora), the Grand National Assembly, declared him president, with complete responsibility for the affairs of the state.

The Treaty of Sèvres

While Kemal was consolidating his position and changing realities on the ground, Britain and France were making decisions in late 1919 and early 1920 about what they believed should be the future shape of the region. They left Turkey nominal sovereignty over Anatolia, but the real power was to lie with the French and Italians, each of whom was granted a sphere of influence. The Greeks were to gain most of Thrace and to govern Izmir for five years, before a plebiscite decided its destiny. They toyed with expelling the Turks from Europe and creating a new independent state on the Straits, but abandoned this in favour of controlling the waterway by an international commission.

These decisions formed the basis of the Treaty of Sèvres drafted at the London Conference from February to March 1920 and then finalized at the San Remo Conference on 24 April. There were many bitter pills for the Turks to swallow – the loss of their Arabian territories, the limitation of their armed forces, requirements for minority protection, the continuation of foreign financial control and a commitment to an, as yet territorially undefined, independent state of Armenia and hints of an independent Kurdistan. The Sultan had little choice but to sign, since he was both the client and the virtual prisoner of the Allies, who had emphasised their dominance by occupying Constantinople on 16 March 1920. He duly did so 10 August 1920, but there were already serious doubts as to whether this really was the final act of peacemaking at the end of the First World War.

Both in Anatolia and the Middle East there seemed to be broad discrepancies between what the Allied negotiators believed they had decided and incorporated in international treaties and what was happening in the real world. The violent developments in both regions in the following years confirmed that there were still many issues to settle.

Lloyd George in January 1935, when he announced the formation of his Council of Action for Peace and Reconstruction.

III

The Legacy

7

Coping with the Aftermath

The signature of the Treaty of Versailles, disappointing and anti-climactic though it was for some members of the British delegation, did mark the end of the most intensive period of peacemaking after the First World War. On 29 June Wilson and Lloyd George headed for home, leaving Clemenceau as the only member of the Four still in Paris. It was certainly not the end of the process. Many questions in eastern and central Europe and further afield in the Middle East, Africa and Asia were unresolved and, even when the treaties covering the other belligerents were signed, the fraught question of their execution remained. Headlam-Morley's prediction was that now '[n]o doubt things will become more orderly, but they will be much duller.' He was wrong on both counts. The confusion that had been the hallmark of the Peace Conference from its outset continued and the following months and years of Lloyd George's premiership were certainly not dull.[1]

The world of 1914 had been transformed. Austria-Hungary had vanished, the Ottoman Empire was about to be partitioned, and Russia's future remained uncertain, though the Bolsheviks seemed gradually to be taking control. Defeated

Germany was menaced by internal revolution from both left and right. New or revived states replaced the collapsed empires in eastern and central Europe. The United States, after vital interventions in the war and the peace negotiations, seemed about to withdraw into isolation. Japan was confirmed as a major regional power with an increasing world role and lingering resentments from the Conference. Italy, in a world of fewer powers, perhaps seemed stronger than it was. Just as Lloyd George lost power it joined a growing group of states whose conduct of foreign affairs was influenced, perhaps dominated, by considerations of ideology, thus adding a whole new dimension to international relations. At the centre of Britain's post-war world remained France, both an ally and a rival, a paradox reflected in the complexity of Anglo-French relations across a wide range of issues.

He had also to return to personal and political domestic concerns, which were less exciting than international summit diplomacy. He had promised *to make Britain a fit country for heroes to live in.*[2] He now had to deliver. He faced labour problems, particularly in the coal and railway industries. The cabinet received regular reports on revolutionary activity in Britain, and the Irish question required urgent attention. These questions were important, but did not match the intensity and fascination of the conference in which he had thrived.

His political future was uncertain, depending as he did on Conservative support for the Coalition and with the Liberal Party split between Asquith's followers and his own. Should the reformist members of the traditional rivals for power in Britain now combine forces in a new Centre party to oppose the rise of Labour – the politics of Fusion? The idea collapsed in 1920, destroyed, much to Tory relief, by his own Liberal supporters. Once again he had underestimated the deep roots of British political parties.

Lloyd George returned in triumph to London on 29 June to a royal welcome from the King and the Prince of Wales, who defied precedent to greet him at the station. Frances recorded their regret at leaving Paris: 'D. [Lloyd George] hates returning home' – not least apparently because of his wife's frugality. As she rather cattily put it, 'I have never seen anyone with such a capacity for making a place uncomfortable as Mrs. Lloyd George.' She got a souvenir for consolation – someone in the crowd threw a laurel wreath into the royal carriage, which the King said was for Lloyd George. 'D has given it to me, and though it will fade, I will keep it all my life.' It still survives in the Lloyd George Memorial Museum at Llanystumdwy.[3]

Winding down the Conference in Paris

Lloyd George left Balfour in Paris as Britain's representative on the Supreme Council, now the main decision-making forum. After the summer Eyre Crowe, from the Foreign Office, replaced Balfour. Lloyd George could not find another political heavyweight willing to undertake the task, but appointing an official rather than a political leader also signalled that he was determined to end the Paris proceedings which gave the French the advantage of always playing at home.

The Treaty of Versailles was signed on 28 June 1919, but only entered into legal existence with its ratification on 10 January 1920. This required ratification by Germany and three of the major Allies. Germany ratified on 10 July, Britain by 31 July, and Balfour expected to complete the process by mid-August. Why then, did it take until January? Longer parliamentary processes in France and Italy caused some delay and, although it was not legally necessary, Britain waited for each of the Dominions to approve the treaty. Even so, by 6 October, Britain, its Dominions, the French and Italians had all ratified the Treaty and hence the Allies were in a position to bring it into effect.

They did not do so. There were a number of outstanding problems: the refusal of the Germans to evacuate the Baltic provinces; to surrender alleged war criminals like Bethmann-Hollweg, Hindenburg, Tirpitz and the Crown Prince Wilhelm; or to pay compensation for the scuttled ships at Scapa Flow. The Allies were unsure how to resolve these without the sanctions available under the armistice – Foch suggested further occupations of Germany – but most Allied leaders expected the Germans would eventually agree to their demands.

There was panic in London when Clemenceau's draft note of 6 December 1919 threatened 'to place Germany in face of a rupture of armistice with all consequences which would follow there from' unless Berlin agreed to the conditions for final ratification. Lloyd George sent Philip Kerr to Paris to negotiate an amended draft. The Germans backed down, a resumption of hostilities was averted, terms were agreed, the treaty entered into force on 10 January 1920 and the Paris Peace Conference ended on 21 January 1920, one year and three days after it had opened. From now on governments would decide 'large questions of policy' and the Allied Conference of Ambassadors, meeting in Paris, would handle 'questions of detail'. Typically neither type of question was defined.

Of more immediate and pressing importance was the refusal of the United States Senate to ratify the Treaty. In an attempt to overcome the fierce opposition to what were seen as the entangling commitments of the League and dangerous concessions to the Japanese in the Pacific, Wilson had undertaken a whistle-stop campaign in September 1919. The strain proved too much, and he suffered a stroke, paralysing both himself and the presidency. House and Edward Grey, sent specially to Washington to help the process, both hoped for the compromises required to gain the necessary two-thirds Senate majority but Wilson refused to budge and, on 19 November, the Treaty was rejected. The Senate again, and finally, rejected the Treaty on 19 March 1920. The United States eventually made separate peaces with Germany, Austria and Hungary in August 1921. It is almost impossible to overestimate the consequences of this American refusal to accept responsibility for a settlement in which its president had played a crucial role, but to cite just the most obvious examples, the prospects for the League and a new order of international relations, the future of the Middle East and the outcome of the reparations imbroglio would all be deeply affected.

Confusion in the ranks

On 20 January 1920, Clemenceau, rejected as the new French president by French parliamentarians anxious not to replace Poincaré with a second successive strong leader, became the second of the Big Four to leave office. With Wilson very ill and the government of America carried on by communication through his wife, Lloyd George became their last effective political survivor. The focus shifted to London, where the now peripatetic Supreme Council met to draft the peace treaty with Turkey and to deal with issues about the execution of the German treaty. The aftermath of a failed right-wing coup in Germany on 13 March, nominally led by Wolfgang Kapp, a civil servant, caused great confusion in the Allied ranks. A Bolshevik threat in the Ruhr, part real part imaginary, led both the legitimate and insurrectionary German governments to request permission for extra troops to be allowed into the demilitarised zone to restore order.

Kapp's request was ignored, but the legitimate government received contradictory answers from two Allied meetings, each believing it had the overall authority. In Paris the Ambassadors' Conference refused, in London the Supreme Council approved, neither prevailed. Curzon, who had replaced Balfour as Foreign Secretary in October 1919, championed the authority of the Supreme Council, but in Paris the new French premier, Alexandre Millerand, argued vigorously (though unsuccessfully) that the ambassadors had the power and duty to act for the Allies. Curzon commented acidly, 'M. Millerand not only regards the Peace Conference as sitting in Paris, but as I have before remarked, he regards himself as the Peace Conference.' There was thus chaos at the highest level about the overall control of peace enforcement. The Germans did send in extra troops and, in retaliation, the French, taking independent action in the face of British opposition, occupied five German towns on 5/6 April 1920.[4]

GEORGE NATHANIEL CURZON (1859–1925)
A Conservative who served as Viceroy of India and Foreign Secretary, but never, as he had hoped, Prime Minister. The First Marquess Curzon of Keddleston was, according to a piece of Oxford doggerel 'A most superior person'.

Uneasy Anglo-French relations

This provoked the first serious post-war crisis between the two powers now, in America's absence, the main enforcers of the treaty. The Anglo-French relationship had become the pivotal point of international diplomacy, with an involvement in almost every major aspect of world affairs. In December 1921 Curzon pointed out that: 'As a result of the war there remain only two really great powers in Europe – France and our-selves …. For a considerable period, therefore, a combination of Great Britain and France would be so strong that no other likely combination could successfully resist it. It follows that a definite and publicly announced agreement between the two countries to stand by one another in case either were attacked would offer a guarantee of peace of the strongest kind.'

Yet, despite this, he was not convinced that Britain would benefit sufficiently to justify an alliance, and, at the very least, he expected a good price for any agreement: 'I earnestly hope it will not be proposed to give the guarantee for nothing.'[5] The history of the many Anglo-French discussions on this matter indicates clearly that neither intended to sell itself cheaply, with the result that no final bargain was concluded.

There were deep divisions about the idea of a French alli-ance. Those in favour, including Austen Chamberlain, Lord Derby and Henry Wilson, argued that this would make France more secure and hence more amenable to the more lenient policies towards Germany often suggested by Britain. The more cynical also pointed out that since, for reasons of its own security, Britain could not afford to see France crushed in any future war, an alliance would mean that Britain would get credit and leverage for something it would have to do anyway. Opponents, including Arthur Henderson (the Labour leader), Smuts – and, as a late convert – Churchill, argued that a France secure in the knowledge of British support would become more, not less, intransigent in dealing with Germany. One of their most persistent members, Hankey, pointed out that the French were no more amenable after Lloyd George's 1919 offer of a guarantee than before. 'It is doubtful', he wrote, 'if France could be bought, and even if she were bought it is doubtful if she would stay bought.'[6]

Yet, simultaneously, ministers were invited by Balfour to consider the 'hardly conceivable' prospect of the French air force dropping 84 tons of bombs daily on London. He warned that: 'A war with France would be a world calamity which seems almost unthinkable: but where national security is concerned even the unthinkable must be faced.' That the Committee of Imperial Defence could dutifully consider air defence and naval contingency plans for an eventuality is an indication of the deeply rooted suspicion of France held by many of the British elite, amongst them Lloyd George himself.[7]

This suspicion resurfaced every time a question arose about taking forcible action to ensure German fulfilment of the Treaty. For France the default method was to suggest an occupation of the Ruhr basin, heart of the German mining and metallurgy industries. This rekindled British concerns about France's intentions to undermine the unity of Germany and about its dreams of Napoleonic European domination. Curzon told the Imperial Conference in 1921: 'There has never disappeared from her imagination the lure of the Ruhr Valley ... with Lorraine, the Saar and the Ruhr Valley in her occupation she becomes the mistress of Europe.' These fears of French ambition – which the French categorised as concerns for their own security – were a cancer at the heart of the relationship.

The unilateral French action in April 1920 was but the first of many instances of major disagreements, each posing the same fundamental problem – should Britain oppose or cooperate with France? Lloyd George feared that: *We may be landed one day in war with Germany through French action. Or we may have to repudiate our Allies.* There was no real choice. As Curzon pointed out on 5 October 1923: 'If France and ourselves permanently fall out, I see no prospect of the recovery of Europe or of the pacification of the world.' The relationship had to function, whatever its frustrations, personal dislikes and thorny problems. Whilst some yearned for the days of splendid imperial isolation, the reality was that Britain needed to work with France, if only to restrain it. In Curzon's words: 'We go about arm in arm with her, but with one of our hands on her collar.' Lloyd George and Millerand met at San Remo in April. They papered over the cracks, Mill-erand promised no further French independent action, but the tensions remained, even if, as Curzon remarked: 'These are things which I cannot possibly say in public.'[8]

> 'If France and ourselves permanently fall out, I see no prospect of the recovery of Europe or of the pacification of the world.'
> LORD CURZON

Diplomacy by conference

Lloyd George distrusted traditional diplomatic methods – *diplomatists were invented simply to waste time*, he said. San Remo began the era of 'casino diplomacy', as inter-Allied and, exceptionally, international gatherings involving the Germans, were held in desirable seaside resorts, capitals and watering places. The next three years saw successive conferences in Hythe, Boulogne, Brussels, Spa, London, Paris, London, Cannes, Genoa, London and Paris. Lloyd George approved: *I have been a constant advocate of negotiation by conference in preference to negotiation by Notes.* 'Conference diplomacy' suited his style and enabled his quick-witted skills of communication and persuasion to be used to great effect, at least in the context of the meetings themselves.[9]

However, as Curzon told the new British government in

November 1922, Lloyd George's 'superior cleverness' may have been a short-term asset but was frequently a long-term liability in that his conference successes could create later resentments, particularly if he had been economical with the truth in his dealings. Unkind critics suggested that the Washington Naval Conference in 1921, which Lloyd George did not attend, was the only successful example. A further potential problem was that conferences frequently broke up with expressions of goodwill but without discovering lasting solutions to the persistent problems of Treaty execution. Conference diplomacy might be an effective way to round off longer-term negotiations, or to force an issue to a head, but it also needed to be incorporated into a continuous process of review and implementation. Frequently these high profile gatherings were not effectively linked to the more mundane business of day-to-day diplomatic exchanges.

Lloyd George and Curzon

This was one of the major bones of contention between Lloyd George and his Foreign Secretary, George Curzon. In theory the marriage of their respective talents for intimate negotiation and immediate results and attention to prosaic detail and the long-term view, should have been ideal. It was not. An exchange in 1919 encapsulates very neatly their characteristic approaches. Lloyd George was regaling colleagues about a Turkish retreat towards Mecca when Curzon corrected him: 'Ankara'. *Lord Curzon is good enough to admonish me on a triviality*, responded the Prime Minister, with a lighthearted disregard for geographical accuracy.[10]

The problem was partly personal, Curzon, the exaggeratedly aristocratic product of an ancient lineage, stood for everything that Lloyd George's radical soul rejected: *The only man I ever bullied was Curzon and that was because he was so pompous.* Curzon, who was better at delivering slights than receiving them, believed Lloyd George treated him 'as a valet, almost a drudge' and deeply resented this. It was too late for Lloyd George to write, on 16 October 1922, that *whatever befalls politically I am anxious that there should be no personal misunderstandings amongst men who have worked together for the nation in great days.*[11]

> **The only man I ever bullied was Curzon and that was because he was so pompous.**
> LLOYD GEORGE

It was also institutional. Curzon saw the Prime Minister, the new Cabinet Office, and his array of personal advisers, as threats to the Foreign Office's function to be the government's main source of advice on foreign policy. In certain fields, particularly with regard to the Near East and Russia, they disagreed deeply over policy and Curzon was alarmed, both by Lloyd George's penchant for personal and secretive diplomacy, and by the incursions of other ministers into what he regarded as his exclusive sphere of influence.

These frustrations, coupled with the Prime Minister's real or imagined insults, frequently drove Curzon to the brink of resignation. Lloyd George was dismissive: *Curzon was always sending me letters of resignation. He would send them by a messenger afflicted with a club foot. A second and more nimble messenger would thereafter be despatched with a second letter.* Once the threat was withdrawn Lloyd George instinctively knew that, in this situation as in so many others, he was the master.

Finally, in October 1922, Curzon deserted the coalition, thus ensuring his continuing role as Foreign Secretary in the new Conservative government led by Bonar Law, and potentially keeping the door to the premiership open for the future. Although Balfour sought to reassure him that 'it's the rarest thing when the Prime Minister and the Foreign Minister don't clash', the stormy nature of the Curzon-Lloyd George relationship was notorious at the time and endured in the institutional memory. When Anthony Eden fell out with Neville Chamberlain in 1938, the Marquess of Zetland (Curzon's biographer), attempted to persuade him remain in the government, citing it as a precedent. Eden said it was a parallel of which he did not care to be reminded and resigned.[12]

Executing the Treaty

Lloyd George and Curzon were certainly faced by sufficient issues of substance to make these personal and institutional disputes unwanted distractions. It was rapidly becoming obvious that, tricky though it had been, drafting the Treaty with Germany was the easy part. Now it had to be interpreted and enforced and, if the British inclination, from June 1919 onwards, was generally (but not exclusively) to look for ways to soften its impact, they were aware that the French wished to enforce it and perhaps revise it by making it tougher.

Lloyd George, except when driven to exasperation by German intransigence or diplomatic ineptitude, tended to be sympathetic to claims that aspects of the Treaty could not be executed. Curzon did not necessarily disagree, but despite his belief that, since every aspect of Treaty enforcement had international political implications, and hence their handling should be overseen by the Foreign Office, he came, with great reluctance, to accept that certain issues would be handled mainly by the Prime Minister. These included reparations and disarmament, two of the key areas of contention with Germany and France. In addition the Cabinet Office administered Britain's relations with the League. All of this was deeply resented within the Foreign Office, which felt itself to be in eclipse.

Lloyd George faced several enduring problems of Treaty execution. We have already noted the difficulties over the holding of the Upper Silesian plebiscite and then the subsequent Anglo-French clashes over the interpretation of its results. The Germans either could not, or would not, meet the terms and deadlines set by the Treaty for disarmament, or, even more seriously, for the payment of reparations. The non-delivery of people accused of war crimes created a further, though shorter term, dispute. All these problems interfaced with others in a complex and changing pattern of international relationships in an era when there was still great uncertainty about the shape of Europe and the world after the war.

Disarmament

In the aftermath of a war which had ended in great confusion it was never going to be possible to account for every rifle, machine gun or bullet, although battleships were quite difficult to hide. Furthermore the Allies were relying on German governments to disclose and then deliver their arsenals and reduce their forces when they had no great wish or incentive to do so. It was a vicious circle. If the German government complied it risked popular and political discontent and hence became weaker. The weaker it was, the less able it was to enforce its will, particularly on industrial giants like Krupp, seeking to maintain as much of their machinery and expertise by whatever means they could – concealment, falsification of records, licensing arrangements with foreign countries or the illegal export of material. Britain and France clashed frequently over their interpretations of German inability or unwillingness to execute the treaty.

In January 1921 the Air Ministry declared 'The aerial disarmament of Germany may be regarded as virtually accomplished and whatever material may still be concealed cannot be regarded as constituting a menace to the Allies.' Naval disarmament had already received a tremendous start when the Germans created the still-unbroken record for the most tonnage lost in a single day with the scuttling of much of their High Seas Fleet in Scapa Flow on 21 June 1919. The Allies argued about how Germany should compensate them for those sinkings, and about the disposal of German ships and submarines, with the Americans and British anxious to sink or break them up and the French and Italians wanting to incorporate some units into their fleets to compensate for the wartime interruption of their building programmes. By mid-1921, with compromise solutions agreed, naval disarmament was also virtually complete.

Reducing the German army to its Treaty size was much trickier. In theory 10 April 1920 was the deadline for reaching its limit of 100,000 men. This was not achieved and many in Britain also believed that it was undesirable, judging 100,000 men insufficient to maintain even internal order in a country of Germany's size, with its widespread political discontent, millions of trained men, paramilitary groups and readily available arms. Since its neighbours were not required to disarm, Germany had also to consider its external security. Others, less sympathetic to the Germans, like the French, perceived a premeditated intention to evade the Treaty.

In 1920 and 1921 Lloyd George negotiated a number of new deadlines for Germany to reduce its army to the Treaty level. A number of major paramilitary organisations – potential shadow sources of recruitment and training – also had to be disbanded. The British feared that disarming these groups, which were mainly conservative or right-wing, might open the door to communism.

Lloyd George had to steer between the more optimistic British War Office view of January 1921 that 'Germany has ceased to be a military danger to the Allies for a considerable period of time' and the French judgement that the 'German Government has put itself in opposition both to the spirit and the letter of the Treaty'. Tougher Allied stances in February and May 1921 encouraged the German government to clamp down on the remaining paramilitaries and to complete at least the appearance of Treaty compliance.

There was deliberate and continuing Treaty evasion, but, by September 1921, Lord d'Abernon, Britain's first post-war ambassador to Berlin considered that 'Germany is incapable of entering upon a campaign against the *Entente*, or even against an isolated France with the smallest chance of success'. Any final assessment as to whether Germany was fully disarmed entailed a complex set of judgements about its actual and potential industrial, military and psychological capacity. It could never be an exact science. No-one denied that Germany could rearm, probably quite rapidly, but this could not be done in secret, and it would be for the Allies then to react. By the time Lloyd George left office in October 1922 Germany posed no military threat to its neighbours. He was not responsible for the later decisions of his successors.[13]

Reparations

Lloyd George's long and ambiguous involvement with reparations continued after the Peace Conference. He criticised French leaders for not being open about what Germany could pay but showed little inclination to set such an example himself in Britain. Having established a Reparation Commission to postpone any decision on what Germany should pay, he now spent much of 1920 and the early part of 1921 trying to pre-empt the decisions of a body that, in the absence of the planned American chairman, he feared would be too heavily influenced by the French and their close allies the Belgians. In a commission of four, Britain could not expect to prevail – the Italians could see little point in antagonising the certain winners by splitting any vote and thus the French chairman's casting vote was both decisive but unused.

Lloyd George feared the Franco-Belgian combination would produce a ruinous reparations bill, but his own 'moderate' suggestions during conferences at Boulogne, in July 1920, and at Paris, in January 1921 exceeded the £6,600 million set by the Commission in April, and were much higher than the London Schedule of Payments in May 1921. This required Germany to issue three sets of bonds, A, B and C, of which the C bonds made up over £4,000 million. The C bonds were 'phoney money' – camouflage to make the reparations bill look big enough to satisfy the Allied public. Germany's real, as opposed to paper liability, was the £2,500 million of the A and B bonds, roughly what the British Treasury and American expert estimates had suggested it could pay, and less than the £5,000 million that Germany had itself offered that March, admittedly hedged about with unacceptable conditions.

Lloyd George and the French wanted to link reparations to the question of inter-Allied debt, most of which was owed to America, but the Americans would have none of it. The Europeans argued that this was the main contribution of the United States to a joint war effort – the Americans paid in cash, the Europeans in blood. The ideal solution, from a European perspective, was an all-round cancellation of debts. The American view was strictly commercial. In the words of President Calvin Coolidge: 'They hired the money, didn't they?'

Some British ministers argued that Britain should cancel the debts of its European allies, in the hope this would produce a reciprocal American gesture. In theory Britain was a creditor nation. It was owed £1,600 million by various European states, it owed the United States £800 million but, whereas the Americans expected to recover their loans, the British credits were unlikely to materialise. Here was another dilemma – should Britain be generous to France and its other debtors and cancel, thereby buying goodwill, or should it use its hold over its debtors to encourage them to follow its policies? Lloyd George tended to the second option.

In 1922 his government brought the two issues of debt and reparations together. The Germans claimed they could not meet their May 1921 obligations and requested a moratorium on payments. The Americans pressed Britain to repay its debts over 25 years at 4.5 per cent interest. At Genoa in April 1922 Lloyd George suggested to Louis Barthou, the French justice minister, that if America would drop its claims on Europe, then Britain would cancel all European government debts. Britain and France should abandon their pension claims against Germany. His statement that *if this plan were adopted, the position would be that ... the claims against Germany would be confined to reparation* was, even for him, a remarkable piece of cheek – Keynes had been right all along, pensions and allowances were not 'reparations'![14]

The Americans would not play and Balfour, temporarily back as Foreign Secretary for the indisposed Curzon, was set to draft an alternative policy whereby Britain would only seek to recover from reparations and European debt repayments what it was required to pay to America. What at first glance looked eminently reasonable was, in fact, an international disaster. The Balfour Note of 1 August 1922, which Lloyd George claimed as his own, castigated American selfishness, thus removing much of their room for manoeuvre, implied that any shortfall in German payments would require larger demands upon France, and wrecked any slim chance of resolving the chronic reparations crisis without the French occupying the Ruhr. Sir Edward Grigg, who had replaced Kerr as Lloyd George's adviser, was scathing: 'How can we demean ourselves so much as to range ourselves with the pitiful European bankrupts and to declare our credit dependent on theirs'?[15] By the end of the Coalition Britain's reparations policy was in tatters and was certainly not one of Lloyd George's successes.

War criminals

Article 227 of the Treaty, which arraigned 'William II of Hohenzollern, formerly German Emperor, for a supreme offence against international morality and the sanctity of treaties' might have created an interesting precedent in international law had the trial taken place. Perhaps fortunately for all concerned – certainly for the Kaiser who did not want to be dragged through London or Paris, to be spat upon 'so that those bastards can cut off my head' – the Dutch refused to surrender their unwanted guest and he remained in exile until his death in 1941, even after the German occupation of the Netherlands in 1940.

On the face of it Article 228, recognising the right of the Allies to try, before military tribunals, 'persons accused of having committed acts in violation of the laws and customs of war', was less revolutionary, though normally peace treaties extended amnesties for some of these violations. What was especially shocking to the Germans – and, eventually, to some of the Allies – was the sheer scale of the numbers suggested, and the extension of the principle from operational acts to political and command decisions involving some of the most prominent German leaders.

The initial Allied lists totaled over 3,000 names and even Lloyd George baulked at the reduced demand for 853 men and one woman, Elsa Scheiner, who had guarded imprisoned Frenchwomen during the war. It was too much – had the boot been on the other foot with the Germans seeking the surrender of 800 officers *he did not believe they would ever comply with it. No British or French Government could do so.* His advice was that *we should confine our demands to surrender of the most important and notorious offenders and let the rest go.*[16]

British soldiers and diplomats in Germany warned that the question was highly emotive and dangerous in the volatile atmosphere of the time – it was one of the contributing factors to the Kapp *putsch* in March, even though the Allies had, in February, agreed to a German compromise suggesting that the accused should be brought before Germany's highest tribunal, the Supreme Court, in Leipzig. The original figures were slashed to 45 test cases but the outcomes were very unsatisfactory, particularly for the French who saw General Stenger acquitted of ordering the murder of French soldiers, even though no-one denied that they had been murdered, and another officer, said to be suffering from stress, was given a derisory sentence for actually killing them. Lieutenant Karl Neumann was acquitted of sinking a British hospital ship, *Dover Castle*, because he had been ordered to do so, though two others, acquitted of sinking a further British hospital ship, *Llandovery Castle,* were convicted of machine-gunning the survivors because this was judged contrary to international law.[17]

Acquittals and lenient sentences were condemned as a parody of justice by British and French leaders, but Lloyd George's initial enthusiasm for the project rapidly dissipated and his moral crusade to punish the wicked collapsed into farce, or worse. His strong words after the armistice, or during the Conference, were soon forgotten in late 1919 and early 1920. Whether this should be seen as the triumph of pragmatic politics based on concern for a weak German democracy, or simply the dropping of an inconvenient election pledge, is a moot point.

Enforcing the Treaty

For all its 440 articles the Treaty was remarkably vague about penalties and sanctions. It was especially weak in measures to encourage Germany to act with any urgency. Article 430 of the Treaty allowed an extension of the occupation of the Rhineland beyond the original 15 years if Germany did not pay reparations. Article 429 suggested a similar extension if there were doubts about the adequacy of the Anglo-American guarantees. Neither was calculated to be of major immediate concern to a German government in the early 1920s.

Many of the actions taken by the Allies between 1920 and 1923 were of dubious legality, relying upon adaptations of clauses intended for other purposes or upon interpretations of Treaty provisions disowned by their original authors. In March 1921, Article 270, which permitted the Allies to make special customs arrangements for their occupied areas of Germany 'to safeguard the economic interests of the population of those territories', was invoked to justify a customs barrier around the Rhineland designed to penalise the German government for not making an adequate effort to comply with the Treaty. It was used again for a similar purpose during the Franco-Belgian occupation of the Ruhr beginning in January 1923.

That occupation was itself justified by an interpretation of Part VIII (reparations) Paragraph 18, Annex II. The paragraph stated that the Allies had the right to take measures in the event of a voluntary reparations default by Germany which 'may include economic and financial prohibitions and reprisals and in general such other measures'. The French argued that 'such other measures' could include territorial occupation, whereas the British government, and one of the original drafters, the American lawyer John Foster Dulles, argued that the phrase clearly applied only to sanctions of an economic or financial nature.[18]

British legal objections to the 1923 Franco-Belgian occupation of the Ruhr were compromised by Lloyd George's exasperated agreement in March 1921 to an Allied occupation of three German towns. He did so, despite his own eloquent arguments that *from a technical point of view the Allies' case might be weak,* because he perceived no other way of persuading a German government he saw as intransigent.[19] He had already conceded in 1920 that occupying the Ruhr was the only effective sanction: *there was no other method available for enforcing the Treaty*[20] – but was it legitimate? H W Malkin, the Foreign Office's deputy legal adviser, was doubtful: 'It may be that some of the means of pressure adopted are of such a nature that Germany would be entitled, if she thought fit, to treat them as involving a state of war.'[21] Treaty enforcement was not easy, legally or practically, and Lloyd George, in common with others, struggled.

Ireland

Strictly speaking Ireland was an internal, not an international, matter, but it typified the dilemma of self-determination and events in the war had helped bring the issue to a head. Neither Wilson nor Clemenceau would receive an Irish nationalist delegation in Paris. It departed empty-handed, but Lloyd George knew that this problem would not be disposed of so easily. In Ireland the situation deteriorated, particularly once the 1920 Government of Ireland Act (successor to the 1914 Home Rule Act) established a separate parliament for six of the nine counties of historic Ulster in the north. Nationalists ignored the sister institution in the south, instead creating their own parliament, the *Dáil*.

1920 saw an increasingly vicious cycle of violence and counter-violence, with assassinations perpetrated by the Irish Republican Army (IRA), led by Michael Collins, matched by reprisals carried out by British forces. Lloyd George shocked and alienated many of his Liberal supporters, including his old friend C P Scott, by his adoption of violent counter-terrorism. *We have murder by the throat* he boasted in November 1920 *… the terrorists are now complaining of terror* but he was distracted by foreign affairs and only really gave Ireland his full attention in 1921.[22]

Serious discussions only began in late October when an Irish delegation came to London. In familiar fashion Lloyd George charmed, threatened, bullied and bluffed his way to an agreement, partitioning Ireland into a Free State in the south, whilst Northern Ireland remained part of the United Kingdom. At the crucial point on 5 December 1921 he mesmerised the Irish delegates into forgetting the existence of the telephone. He brandished two letters, one of which recorded an agreement, the other the breakdown of the talks, and demanded an answer by 10 p.m. that night as to which he should send by special train to Holyhead and destroyer to Belfast. He told Collins that the proposed Boundary Commission to settle the question of the six counties would end partition and the Ulster leader, James Craig, that it would perpetuate it. But he achieved a settlement which, whilst it did not solve all the problems, and indeed provoked an immediate civil war in the new Free State and long smouldering resentment amongst the Catholic minority in Northern Ireland, did largely remove the Irish question from British politics for nearly 50 years until the outbreak of the Troubles in 1968.

Genoa

Lloyd George's last great attempt to solve many of the residual problems of the First World War came at the Genoa Conference in April and May 1922. It was the culmination of his efforts to create a working relationship with the Soviet Union, and to solve or alleviate Europe's problems by a revival of prosperity. He had already negotiated an Anglo-Soviet trade agreement and *de facto* recognition of the Soviets in March 1921, much to the displeasure of some of his cabinet, but particularly his Liberal colleague, Churchill. Even more marked was grass-root Conservative opposition in the constituencies. The French too, still seeking repayment of their massive Tsarist debts, were furious. Lloyd George was anxious to move on from the British military interventions of 1918–19, and the uncertainties caused by British policy during the 1920 war between the Soviets and Poland, and to open economic links with Russia to revive British industry.

If Russia could be reintegrated into the European economy and Germany encouraged to exploit the opportunities this would produce, then Germany could pay reparations, France could repay Britain its war debts, perhaps eventually even Russia could be persuaded to honour the debts of the previous Tsarist regime. Britain could repay the United States, prosperity would assist Europe to build a more peaceful future and Germany and the Soviet Union, the two pariahs of the post-war era, could be take their proper places in the League and the affairs of the world. As he told the delegates

Europe ... needs rest, quiet, tranquility ... It needs peace.
LLOYD GEORGE

of *the greatest gathering of European nations which has ever been assembled on this continent ... we meet on equal terms to seek out in common the best methods for restoring the shattered prosperity of this continent ... It is true that the actual fighting has ceased but the snarling goes on ... Europe is deafened with this canine clamour ... It needs rest, quiet, tranquility ... It needs peace.*[23]

Sadly it all went wrong even before the conference opened on 10 April. He needed French cooperation and was prepared to make significant concessions over an Anglo-French alliance to the flexible Breton, Aristide Briand (with whom it was alleged he could communicate in Welsh). An ill-fated golf lesson at the Cannes conference in January 1922, which seemed to show that Briand was also Lloyd George's pupil in diplomacy, led to his resignation. He was replaced by Britain's least favorite Frenchman, Raymond Poincaré, whose negotiating style consisted of making a list of impossible demands and then treating any reduction of that list as a great concession. Poincaré refused to permit any discussion of reparations at Genoa. Like the Tory die-hards in Britain, he was deeply sceptical about negotiations with the Soviets. He sent his deputy prime minister, Louis Barthou, to wreck the conference.

He did not need to. Genoa got off to a disastrous start when Germany and the Soviets departed to Rapallo to agree the first of several Russo-German pacts over the next two decades that, on the face of it, were ideologically inconceivable. The two pariahs cocked a snook at the victors. The conference continued for a further month but achieved none of its dramatic intentions. Genoa was a classic Lloyd Georgian venture. It had vision and, in many ways, admirable goals, but it was ill-conceived, poorly prepared and a striking example of what happened when Lloyd George's faith in conference diplomacy and his ability to create harmony from cacophony went awry.

The Near and Middle East

Lloyd George's policy in the Near East came under increasing pressure in 1920 and 1921, eventually collapsing in 1922, bringing down the Coalition in October. In Turkey Kemal's revolt continued and the international tide seemed to be moving in his direction. In Greece Venizelos fell, after King Alexander died from a pet monkey's bite in October 1920 leading to the return of Constantine, deposed as pro-German in 1917. The French and Italians resented British advantages under Sèvres and there was increasing British criticism of Lloyd George's pro-Greek policies. Kemal also skilfully exploited a relationship with the Soviet Union, which he kept at arm's length, but which brought substantial aid in 1922.

The triumph of Kemal

In early 1921 Lloyd George failed in his attempt to revise Sèvres at a London conference of Greeks, the Nationalists and the Constantinople government. He reverted to supporting the Greeks, who claimed they could enforce the treaty, but his secret encouragement for a renewed attack was discovered, much to British embarrassment, when the French intercepted and deciphered the Greek telegrams. The March Greek offensive collapsed and, with the Italians and French prepared to negotiate with Kemal, the alliance began to crack. Britain's attempts to mediate failed, the Greeks attacked again in the summer but were held at Ankara in August 1921. Although they retreated in good order in September this marked the high point of their attempt to defeat Kemal.

Curzon now tried to negotiate a Greek withdrawal from Asia Minor in return for Thrace remaining Greek. It looked in March 1922, that he had succeeded but the compromise disintegrated. Kemal was encouraged when Poincaré intimated that its terms were not necessarily final. Curzon was flabbergasted: 'Here is Poincaré telling the Turks to tear up the agreement on which his signature is still wet. And these are our allies.' Hardinge was not surprised: 'I regard him as a dirty dog, a man of very mean character.'[24] All this was not helped by strong British suspicions that the French and Italians were supplying Kemal with arms.

Kemal's August offensive drove the Greeks out of Asia Minor, amid atrocity and counter-atrocity, taking Izmir on 9 September. His continued advance threatened the British forces guarding the Straits at Chanak. War seemed possible, but Britain's allies, and most of its empire, made it clear they would not fight. An exasperated Curzon accused Poincaré of betraying the alliance. Poincaré responded vigorously, and Hardinge escorted a badly mauled Curzon from the room: '"Charley", he panted, "I can't bear that horrid little man. I can't bear him". He wept.'[25] They patched it up, the Turks were invited to renegotiate the peace settlement, and hostilities were averted at Chanak by a combination of luck and good sense despite an enthusiastic group in the British cabinet, including Lloyd George, Churchill and Chamberlain, who seemed bent on war. After the Prime Minister's dealings with the Soviets, and the Anglo-Irish treaty, this proved the last straw for rank-and-file Tories. Their revolt destroyed the Coalition. Kemal swept on to Constantinople, renamed it Istanbul, deposed the Sultan in November and then successfully negotiated a revised peace settlement in the two-stage Lausanne conference between November and July 1923.

Muddle in the Middle East

Lloyd George also faced serious and unresolved problems in the Middle East. The early promise of the 1918 victory seemed to be dissipating as the imperial schemes there ran into the sands of expense, unrest and increasing Jewish-Arab communal problems. In January 1921 Lloyd George appointed Churchill Colonial Secretary to sort out the mess.

He set about reducing Britain's costs (by September 1922 he had cut expenditure from £45 million to £11 million) and looking for alternative solutions to maintain Britain's influence in the area. His proposal was to instal the Hashemite brothers, Feisal and Abdullah, as rulers of two Arab areas. Feisal, in compensation for his discomfiture in Syria in 1920, would become king of Iraq (Mesopotamia), preferably at the invitation of its inhabitants. Meanwhile Palestine would be divided by the Jordan river, to its west the Jewish national home could be established and to its east Abdullah would take temporary control of an Arab territory in order to restore order before handing power to a local governor. Churchill also planned to substitute air power for military occupation in an attempt to reduce the costs of controlling the region.

Feisal, with British support, was crowned King of Iraq on

23 August 1921 but proved a difficult client. In May 1923 the British installed Abdullah as the permanent leader of Transjordan, thus partially reneging on the Balfour Declaration's promise to the Jews to make Palestine their national home. The promised land now became the partitioned land. The Hashemites' great rival, Ibn Saud, the Sultan of Nejd, who was also on the British payroll, began attacking Abdullah in 1922. Britain intervened, established frontiers between Iraq, Kuwait and Ibn Saud's territory, but eventually he conquered the Hejaz, took Mecca and created the Kingdom of Saudi Arabia by joining the Hejaz and Nejd. In 1927 Britain recognised the new state.

Lloyd George's fascination with the Middle East, the ambitions of various British politicians, officials and military leaders, the safeguarding of imperial arteries and the desire to secure strategic supplies of oil all contributed to the hope that Britain could gain a long-term mastery of the region. In 1919 T E Lawrence wrote: 'My own ambition is that the Arabs should be our first brown dominion, and not our last brown colony' but there was little evidence to suggest this was a possibility. Many of the key decisions that shaped the modern Middle East, not least those of 1922, many of which sprang from contradictory wartime promises, were taken under Lloyd George's leadership. It is dubious whether it was be a legacy of which he could be proud.[26]

8
Keeping out the Welshman

In *Guilty Men,* a vitriolic attack on the appeasers, 'Cato' records a brief meeting at Crewe station during the 1929 election campaign. As they parted Ramsay MacDonald said to Stanley Baldwin 'Well, whatever happens we shall keep out the Welshman.'[1] The two men, who alternated as prime minister from 1923 to 1937, shared an intense dislike for Lloyd George. When MacDonald stayed at Chequers, the prime minister's country house, he consigned Lloyd George's picture to a drawer. Baldwin, not normally a violent man, defaced his photographs in his albums.

From 1922 until his death in March 1945 Lloyd George would never again hold office, confounding the predictions of not only George V but many others who did not believe that they had seen the last of that 'dynamic force'. In one sense they had not, Lloyd George cast a long shadow over the 1920s and 1930s, characteristically looking for unorthodox solutions to the problems of unemployment and depression, intervening intermittently on foreign affairs and becoming a focal point for some younger, independently minded MPs. There were moments when he might have returned to government

– almost certainly in 1931 had he not been incapacitated following a prostate operation, possibly under Churchill in 1940, or, hypothetically, as the leader of a defeated Britain attempting, like Marshal Pétain in France, to be its shield, even if he could no longer be its sword.

His reconciliation with Asquith, brought about by Baldwin's sudden conversion to protection and imperial preference in 1923, was dogged by distrust, personal animosity and wrangling over the use of the Lloyd George Fund – some of which derived from money raised by the sale of honours. The 1923 election saw the Liberals reduced to third place, a position from which they have yet to recover over 80 years later. Lloyd George became Asquith's deputy, succeeding him as party leader in October 1926 after disagreements over the General Strike, with Lloyd George much more sympathetic to the strikers.[2] Once again he assembled experts and men of experience into a 'brains trust' to try to break away from conventional approaches to the chronic problems of the British economy. The result was an impressive series of publications, some on themes close to his heart, like *The Land and the Nation* and *Towns and the Land* in 1925. *Britain's Industrial Future* (1928) resulted from a two-year enquiry that he financed, drawing, amongst others, on the expertise of Keynes, despite the unkind words of *Economic Consequences of the Peace*. In 1929 the pamphlet, *We Can Conquer Unemployment*, offered imaginative counter-cyclical job-creation suggestions for investments in public works.

Lloyd George's willingness to embrace the unconventional proved a political weakness. Charles Masterman, despite himself, approved: 'I have to confess, when Lloyd George came back to the party, ideas came back to the party.'[3] Others, however, did not and this further fragmented the Liberals, with younger, radical members welcoming Lloyd George's innovative approach, at the cost of the support of many older colleagues like Alfred Mond, who joined the Tories. For a brief moment in 1928 Lloyd George's Centre party idea had a final flicker of life, but soon collapsed. He invested heavily in the 1929 election campaign, which saw the Liberals poll over five million – almost a quarter of the total vote – but the workings of the electoral system meant this produced only 59 MPs.

Two years later MacDonald's Labour government was split by the budget proposals to tackle the financial crisis in August 1931. MacDonald joined Baldwin to form a National Government, with the political aftermath dividing both the Labour and Liberal parties. Now aged 68, Lloyd George was the 'leader' of a tiny family group of four – his children Gwilym and Megan, himself and a relative, Goronwy Owen, all representing Welsh seats. Whilst never abandoning all hope, he was sufficiently realistic about his chances of returning to power to devote much of his energy to writing his memoirs. Many old scores were settled and he was rather cavalier with his promise to tell the whole truth but his prodigious output was striking evidence of his resilience.

There was one last flurry of action in January 1935 when he launched the Council of Action for Peace and Reconstruction which rebranded some of the 1929 programme into a British version of Roosevelt's 'New Deal'. The government flirted with him, but eventually sidelined him into a morass of fruitless meetings. In October the National Government won a comfortable mandate and Lloyd George went back to travelling, farming, writing his newspaper articles, his war and peace memoirs and breeding a new raspberry.

He did retain an interest in foreign affairs, the fate of the settlement he had negotiated and the rise of the dictatorships in Europe. Whereas he was hostile to Mussolini, advocating the use of force through the League to defeat the Italian attack on Abyssinia in 1935, he was intrigued by the rise of Hitler, regarding him as someone willing to try innovative and daring solutions to the problems besetting Germany. He did not approve all his methods – *I need hardly say that I am no advocate of the immuring of political opponents in concentration camps,* these, and religious persecution were *a terrible thing to an old Liberal like myself* – but he was persuaded to visit Hitler in September 1936, after the remilitarisation of the Rhineland in March and Germany's earlier breaching of the disarmament clauses of the Treaty.[4]

The meeting went well: Hitler gave him a signed photograph, dedicated to 'the man who won the war'; he called Hitler *the greatest living German.* He returned deeply impressed, though his eulogy in the *Daily Express,* despite some toning down from the original, was still rather excessive. Hitler, he wrote, *is a born leader of men. A magnetic dynamic personality with a single-minded purpose, a resolute will and a dauntless heart … He is the George Washington of Germany.* Apart from the last statement, this could also be a self-portrait.[5]

Churchill condemned the visit as a monumental misjudgement, believing Hitler had hoodwinked Lloyd George, though there must be a question-mark over who was fooling who in this encounter between two consummate showmen and accomplished liars. Lloyd George and, reflecting later, Frances, both believed he could have reached an arrangement with Hitler that would have averted a new, even more terrible conflict. In 1942 Hitler suggested that Lloyd George in power in 1936 might have secured an Anglo-German understanding – crucially, however, he did not specify upon what terms.

Lloyd George's condemnation of the Munich agreement suggests that he would not have settled for a one-sided bargain but the viability of any deal with Hitler had to be questionable. Increasingly alarmed at German ambitions, Lloyd George, like Churchill, favoured an alliance with the Soviet Union. He criticised Neville Chamberlain's March 1938 guarantee to Poland as worthless without one, but was such an alliance ever on offer, on terms that would be acceptable to Britain? There seemed little purpose in saving Eastern Europe from the Nazis if the price was delivering it to the Soviets.

When war returned in September 1939 Lloyd George was not enthusiastic. He had asked, in Paris in 1919, if the Allies would *die for Danzig*? Always critical of the Poles, his Commons speech after their surrender on 3 October conveyed an impression far beyond the words he used, hinting at the possibility of an immediate peace conference with Germany. He dropped the idea but it is an important reminder that the notion of an absolutely determined and resolute Britain in 1939–40 was, partially at least, a myth. Many, like Lloyd George, considered reason and reality called for a less heroic stance.

> I say solemnly that the Prime Minister should give an example of sacrifice.
> LLOYD GEORGE

In May 1940 he made one of his last great parliamentary speeches (no doubt delivered with some personal satisfaction), urging Chamberlain to go: *I say solemnly that the Prime Minister should give an example of sacrifice, because there is nothing which can contribute more to victory in this war than that he should sacrifice the seals of office.* Some advocated bringing the 76-year-old back into government but he refused Churchill's tentative 1940 offers of becoming Food

Controller or Britain's ambassador in Washington. His ostensible reason was Chamberlain's continuing role in the government – *I won't go in with Neville* – but he and Churchill may have shared the thought that, in the case of disaster, he might be able to do what Churchill could not, negotiate with 'That Man'. His luck held and, unlike Pétain, he emerged with his Great War laurels relatively intact, though he remained rather detached and pessimistic as the war progressed, making only rare appearances in the House.[6]

In January 1941 Maggie died. Perhaps symbolically Lloyd George failed to reach her in time, becoming trapped in snow *en route*. Two years later in October 1943 he married Frances. By now increasingly frail and suffering with cancer he came home to Wales where on 26 March 1945 he died, Megan holding one hand, Frances the other. His grave, by the banks of the Dwyfor at Llanystumdwy, is marked by a Welsh boulder. There is no inscription.

Conclusion

Lloyd George and the Legacy of Versailles

The Treaty of Versailles is still regarded as a failure, and commentators continue to make a direct connection between its shortcomings and the outbreak of a second major European conflict in 1939. Cynical spectators of the Conference observed: 'After "the war to end all war" they seem to have been pretty successful in Paris at making a "Peace to end Peace".'

George Curzon's reflections, written in late 1922 and early 1923 'for the use of my biographer', predicted such an outcome, for which he blamed Britain's principal negotiator: 'So the drama went on throughout that fatal year – Lloyd George was supposed to be holding up

> 'Lloyd George was sowing the seeds of European disaster'
> LORD CURZON

the flag of Britain ... with sustained vigour and brilliance in Paris. In reality Lloyd George was sowing the seeds of European disaster ...'[1]

Foch was also pessimistic, declaring, 'This is not a peace, it is an armistice for twenty years.' He was wrong – by 67 days

– but there are a number of reasons why it is too simplistic to make the direct connection between events in 1919 and 1939. Among the most important are first, that the peacemakers were not handed a blank sheet on which to design their world of perpetual peace and, second, if we accept Harold Wilson's famous dictum that 'A week is a long time in politics', then 20 years in international politics is an infinity.

The Great War ended Anglo-German naval and colonial rivalry by eliminating Germany as a competitor but, beyond that, it produced no clear solutions to the European problems that led to its outbreak in 1914. Its four years of industrialised conflict, producing death and injury on a massive scale, created much bitterness and many new complications and dilemmas. The near-simultaneous collapse of the four empires that had ruled eastern and central Europe for centuries did not mean that the peacemakers could redraw the map as they wished. The further the distance from Paris, the less their actual power to enforce their decisions, most of which were really tinkering at the edges of a series of *faits accomplis* as the quickest and best organised of the aspiring new states staked their claims regardless. Some of the peacemakers' problems were of their own making – the imperial ambitions, wartime deals, promises and expectations that returned to haunt them in Paris and afterwards – but many others were not.

As Lloyd George reminded the Commons in April 1919, peacemaking was much more complex than in 1815: *You then had to settle the affairs of Europe. It took eleven months. But the problems of the Congress of Vienna, great as they were, sink into insignificance compared with those which we have had to attempt to settle at the Paris Conference. It is not one continent that is engaged – every continent is affected.*[2]

Paris 1919 certainly confirms the historical truism that it is easier to start a conflict than to resolve one.

Given all these complexities, John Maynard Keynes' picture of four all-powerful men deciding the shape of the settlement is seductive for its reduction of a chaotic welter of problems into a comprehensible simplicity. *The Economic Consequences of the Peace* was written and published within six months of his disillusioned return from Paris in June 1919, becoming an instant best-seller, not just, predictably, in Germany, but also in Britain where it helped to partly reinforce and partly create a sense of the immorality and impracticability of the Treaty.

Keynes castigated the peacemakers, but particularly Wilson, for their failure to produce a rational Europe in which, in Keynes's idealised portrait, the pre-war English capitalist could travel, trade and invest his money as he wished, unencumbered by the need for passport or foreign currency. Keynes had a number of proposals to rectify the mistakes made in Paris: a European free trade area; the fixing of German total indebtedness for reparation and occupation costs at £2,500 million with Germany to be credited with £625 million for the assets it had surrendered (ships, submarine cables and so on) and to repay the remaining £1,875 million in 30 interest-free annual instalments; the all-round cancellation of inter-Allied debts; and the revival of trade with Russia.

There are hints in Lloyd George's post-Versailles policies that he did make efforts, however inadequate, half-hearted or unsuccessful at times, to deliver at least some of these suggestions or the spirit behind them. His record was not successful in a number of areas; how far this was because of their impracticality or his lack of leadership, is debatable. That debate takes us to October 1922. He survived in power longer than any of the men impugned by Keynes. Orlando departed even before the Treaty was signed, Clemenceau in January 1920 and Wilson, formally in March 1921, in reality probably earlier, given his illness. Even if we accept the premise that statesmen control international relations, to what extent can the Four be held responsible for the decisions of their successors over the nearly 17 years between Lloyd George's resignation and the outbreak of war in September 1939?

Lloyd George's attempt to modify the draft Treaty in June 1919 encouraged those in the British elite sympathetic to the idea of revision, whilst Keynes helped to create a wider sense of public dissatisfaction with a treaty that was perceived to be unfair to Germany. This, together with the very strong popular determination to avoid any repetition of the dreadful costs of the war, and a wish as far as possible to distance Britain from the problems of Europe, encouraged inter-war governments to follow the traditional British policy of seeking the peaceful resolution of international disputes. It was only when that policy was taken to extremes in dealing with Hitler, whose demands, despite his perennial denials, seemed to be insatiable, that appeasement became a dirty word.

Leaving aside questions of what were, and were not, wise and sensible decisions about specific issues, there are two key areas in which confusion in British thinking did not help the peacemakers or later governments to make clear policies. Lloyd George declared *I do not claim that the Treaty is perfect in all respects. Where it is not perfect, I look forward to the organisation of the League of Nations to remedy, to repair, and to redress.*[3] The League was also to replace the balance of power with collective security as the basis for international stability. This exposed a number of ambiguities in British thinking. The British electorate liked the idea of collective security, their political leaders were unconvinced, but realised that to remain in power they must appear enthusiastic for an untried method of international relations. So, whilst most British leaders remained believers in the balance of power, they professed faith in the League and fell into the chasm between what they said and what they thought in the Abyssinian crisis of 1935.

The balance of power and national self-determination were also incompatible, though not everyone seemed to grasp this. Even those Foreign Office men who believed in Wilson's two big ideas of the League and national self-determination, found their wires crossed. On the one hand the PID welcomed the break-up of multi-national states like the Austro-Hungarian Empire, on which the old system of the European balance had been based, declaring that this represented 'a great gain, for there is every reason to hope that states based upon the conscious existence of a common nationality will be more durable and afford a firmer support against aggression than the older form of state, which was often a merely accidental congeries of territories without internal cohesion, necessary economic unity, or clearly defined geographical frontiers.'[4] On the other Headlam-Morley argued that 'we wish to use the League of Nations in order to maintain the existence of the smaller multi-national States such as Belgium and Switzerland. Quite apart from questions of the balance of power, we have had enough of nationalism, and we want the tide to begin flowing in the other direction.'[5]

The hope that national self-determination would produce stable, economically viable and geographically well defined states was an illusion, and the peacemakers were aware that in certain instances, such as Czechoslovakia, they had to abandon the principle to create states with adequate resources and defensible frontiers. But this was not possible on a large scale, as it was in 1815. The Wilsonian 'new world order' deprived them of the means to manufacture a balance of resources and power amongst states in Europe as a whole, so they asserted that nationalism could create the basis for stability. Yet they knew that intense national rivalries, especially between those states disappointed by the new frontiers, constituted a major threat to future peace, and hence suggested that 'we have had enough of nationalism' at precisely the moment that they created that new world order, supposedly grounded on the virtues of nationalism.

Britain was therefore left with a bad conscience about the wrongs of Versailles, uncertainty as to how to best marry the realities of eastern and central Europe to a set of principles, and confusion about the basis of post-war international relations. Its leaders, in common with most other democrats, did believe, however, that war no longer represented a legitimate element in international politics. Unfortunately this was not an assumption shared by all the new leaders – especially in Poland, at odds and at war with all six of its neighbours during and after the Conference – let alone by the growing band of dictators who still perceived war as a possible way to achieve their goals. Neville Chamberlain found it very difficult to believe that Hitler really wanted to repeat the horrors of 1914–18, and therefore sought compromise solutions to international problems. He was also slow to grasp that Hitler did not treat a concession as final, merely as the starting point for a new set of demands. These preconceptions explain much of Chamberlain's policy between becoming prime minister in May 1937 and the outbreak of war in September 1939.

To what extent was Lloyd George to blame for this European disaster predicted by Curzon and Foch? In 1916 he told

Riddell *we must beat the Germans, and when they are beaten I would endeavour to make the peace real and lasting. A great nation like Germany must live.*[6] This theme runs through his January 1918 speech, the Fontainebleau Memorandum and many of his policies in Paris, particularly in his attempted revision of the Treaty in June. He strove to commit as few Germans as possible to alien rule, especially Polish rule, and he was anxious to limit any occupation of Germany to as short a time as possible. He never intended the disarmament of Germany to be unilateral, though he accepted that Germany must disarm first. He was anxious to remove the Allied blockade, arranging for a dramatic report of the effects of food shortages on German children to be sent to the Conference by the British occupation forces. After the Treaty was signed he was generally willing to listen to German requests for more time or for some adjustment of its commitments. His early enthusiasm for punishing Germany's leaders for their part in the outbreak and waging of war dissipated after 1919. He did have a blind spot over reparations, originally believing that this was not a question over which the Germans were too agitated. Later he was concerned that, if Britain was left heavily indebted and Germany got off scot-free, financially at least Britain would have lost and Germany won. His insistence that war-guilt was the basis for reparations was unnecessary and unwise. He did not make strenuous efforts in Paris to fix a final sum for German indebtedness, driven by a determination to secure as much as he could for Britain and a corresponding reluctance to agree to any figure that might prove too low. His apparent 'moderation' in the post-Treaty negotiations to enforce reparations proved to be based more on rhetoric than reality.

The major criticism of the Versailles settlement must be

that it did not solve 'the German problem'; how to create, as Hans-Dietrich Genscher, the West German foreign minister at the time of German reunification in 1992, would put it, 'a European Germany, rather than a German Europe'. If the European Union has provided a framework capable of harnessing Germany's potential without allowing it dominate Europe, it has required a second major conflict, total German defeat, and the ensuing Cold War to bring it about. The key question in 1919 is whether any settlement reflecting a German defeat could ever have been acceptable to a nation that had patently defeated all its enemies in the east and beaten off all its enemies in the west for 4½ years. At the time of the Armistice, its armies were still encamped in France and Belgium, with no Allied soldier with his boot on German soil. The sense of denial, encouraged by the new president, Ebert, when he told German troops in November 1918 that 'you return unvanquished from the field of battle' was maintained even after the Treaty was signed, whilst the idea that its victorious armies had been 'stabbed in the back' by Jews, socialists and communists in Germany and then betrayed by the 'November criminals' who had signed the armistice was both popular and disguised the military shortcomings of the generals. In such an atmosphere it was unlikely that any policy pursued by Lloyd George in defence of British interests would have found favour in Germany.[7]

How well did he defend British interests? He had set out to produce a stable, democratic Europe, preferably one that reverted to Professor Pollard's definition of the balance of power ('according to which Europe was to provide the balance and Great Britain to have the power').[8] He wished to reduce potential areas of discontent to a minimum, to encourage disarmament and to promote a more just international society.

In pursuing these ideals he never lost sight of the practicalities from a British perspective, ensuring that Germany was no longer an imperial or naval rival, whilst the requirement that it deliver much of its merchant fleet in restitution for Allied shipping losses also removed it as a rival to Britain's mercantile marine. It was always his intention that Britain should get a fair share of German reparations. Beyond that, Britain's interests in Europe were limited, though there was an increasing concern at the prospect of French hegemony.

In the short term at least, Britain's post-war situation was as secure as might reasonably be expected in conventional military terms. It had defeated Germany, its other potential rivals were either allies or, like Russia, reduced to powerlessness. Its trade routes and imperial arteries were not threatened by any external force. Its empire reached its fullest extent, boosted by the mandates awarded to it in Africa and, most significantly, in the Middle East, where Lloyd George was anxious to establish a firm British presence. Once again, its only real rival appeared to be its ally, France, with whom it crossed swords in the Middle East and over the enforcement of the treaty with Germany.

It is possible, from the perspective of the 21st century, to criticise Lloyd George's imperial ambitions. That would be unfair: his policies have to be set within the context of the attitudes and assumptions of the time. There are two more telling criticisms that might be made: his attitude to France; and his style of negotiation.

Although he did show an awareness of the French need for security, he never made sufficient efforts to create the closer Anglo-French partnership that he and Curzon perceived to be an important component of future international harmony. Both grasped that every major question had an

Anglo-French angle but neither felt that this required them to listen more closely to French concerns; rather they preferred to be exasperated by France's policies in pursuit of its security. Balfour put their frustrations perfectly, stating of French attitudes to Germany that they 'were so dreadfully afraid of being swallowed up by the tiger, but would spend their time poking it'.[9] Perhaps Lloyd George could have made more effort to probe behind the reasons for this behaviour and to persuade himself and many of his colleagues that a stronger British European commitment was required and that, although rivalry with France was a traditional policy, it might no longer be fit for purpose.

The second criticism might be that, although he could produce inspirational and exciting long-term visions, his real forte was in reaching deals in the present, without necessarily considering whether their medium and longer-term outcomes would aid or hinder his aspirations. Whilst it might be argued that such is the way all politicians – and indeed others as well – often behave in the face of practical problems requiring a solution, there must be some doubt as to Lloyd George's methods which prioritised instant fixes and sometimes sacrificed trust for temporary success.

There can be no doubt as to his brilliance in negotiation, the quickness of his wit, or his ability to absorb complex ideas in verbal briefings. He steered the intricacies of the National Insurance Bill through Parliament on the basis of notes hastily passed to him in mid-speech by his civil servants. He had an eye for the unanswerable question that overcame embarrassing self-erected obstacles. How, he asked, despite the agreed definitions of the Lansing note, ruling out an indemnity, could it be right to compensate a French widow for her destroyed chimney but deny help for a Welsh widow whose husband had died defending it? He could use humour, scorn, drama and deception to achieve his ends and he frequently did so, with great success – in the short term.

Somewhere in every archive or account of Lloyd George, the word 'liar' appears or is implied – sometimes more subtly than others – Aristide Briand said that Lloyd George had only one word of honour but it was so valuable that he gave it many times, and the Belgian statesman, Henri Jaspar, rendered his note of 'liar' less starkly in his actual article as 'Lloyd George was never obsessed by the cult of truth or the logical sequence of ideas'.[10] According to Lord Derby, Clemenceau became very bitter. 'He says that he had been tricked by him ... he says he can't believe a word the PM says!'[11] He deceived too many people too many times, and they did not share his innate belief that every day was a new day. They remembered.

Keynes' charge, that 'this half-human visitor to our age from the hagridden magic and enchanted woods of Celtic antiquity' was 'rooted in nothing', is unjust, though not implausible. As House pointed out: 'With all his faults he is by birth, instinct and upbringing, a liberal.'[12] That liberalism shines through the January 1918 speech, the Fontainebleau Memorandum, many of his interventions in the Council of Four and his post-war pronouncements like the Cannes memorandum in January 1922 or his hopes for the Genoa conference. Unfortunately, whereas Wilson's idealism was undermined by a lack of pragmatic flexibility, Lloyd George frequently suffered a surfeit of it.

Lloyd George's own verdict on the peace settlement was unequivocal in his later memoirs, written as the storm clouds gathered once more over Europe. It was not, he insisted, drawn up in the hour of triumph by vindictive victors; it did not represent a struggle between Wilson's idealism and the rapacious demands of his European colleagues, but it was an honest attempt to deal with the aftermath of the greatest war in the history of mankind, an earthquake of such proportions that the aftershocks would continue for many years to come.

If I had to go to Paris again I would conclude a very different treaty.

LLOYD GEORGE

He was aggressively defensive of his role in the negotiations, putting the best interpretation possible on the outcome of each part of the process. Yet his verdict at the time was much less confident. Within a year of leaving office he admitted to Charles Hardinge *if I had to go to Paris again I would conclude a very different treaty.*[13]

In two recent polls Lloyd George came second. He would have been flattered to be considered second only to Owain Glyndwyr, the last independent Prince of Wales, as the greatest ever Welshman, but probably less pleased to trail behind Churchill as the greatest British prime minister of the 20th century.

He remains frustratingly difficult to pin down. There is much to admire about him: his wit, vision, spirit, energy, charm (he would certainly score well for interpersonal skills); his sheer cleverness; his political acumen and ability to get things done. On the other hand there are many negative qualities: his duplicity, both personal and political; his hypocrisy – before making his great recruiting speech in September 1914 he had written to Maggie, *I am not going to sacrifice my nice boy ...[Gwilym must] on no account be bullied into serving abroad;*[14] the unpleasant vengeful streak evidenced by his selective rendition of 'the truth' in his memoirs. He was the master of 'spin' before it was invented. Six months after the fall of his government, reflecting on developments in the Near

East, the Ruhr occupation and the funding of Britain's debt to the United States, Lloyd George defended his record thus: *As long as we were in office we prevented the Turks from going into Constantinople, the French from going into the Ruhr, and the American hand from coming into our till. Now they have all got there.*[15] As so often with Lloyd George this is plausible, partly true but certainly not the whole truth.

Notes

1. The Rising Star

1. P Rowland, *Lloyd George* (Barrie and Jenkins: 1975) p 13; Letter to Margaret Lloyd George, 16 Aug 1902, K Morgan (ed.), *Lloyd George Family Letters 1885–1936* (University of Wales and Oxford University Press, 1973) p 137, hereafter Morgan, *Family Letters*.
2. Letter c.1885, Rowland, *Lloyd George*, p 14; K Morgan, *Lloyd George* (Book Club Edition: 1974) p 26.
3. L A Atherley-Jones, *Looking Back: Reminiscences of a Political Career* (1925) p 87.
4. Ffion Hague suggests Maggie allowed him the benefit of the doubt: F Hague, *The Pain and the Privilege: The Women in Lloyd George's Life* (Harper: 2008) pp 238–9.
5. Letter 2 Dec 1902, Morgan, *Family Letters*, p 138.
6. Letter 21 Aug 1897, Morgan, *Family Letters*, p 112; Frances Lloyd George, *The Years That Are Past* (Hutchinson: 1967) p 49.
7. R Toye, *Lloyd George and Churchill: Rivals for Greatness* (Macmillan: 2007) p 100, hereafter Toye,

Rivals; Richard Lloyd George, *Lloyd George* (Frederick Muller: 1960) p 57.

8. Lloyd George was the most probable father, the alternative was Thomas Tweed, a close associate of Frances and Lloyd George. Jennifer herself recorded 'In any case Frances could not be sure whose child I was': J Campbell, *If Love Were All: The Story of Frances Stevenson and David Lloyd George* (Jonathan Cape: 2006) p 361.

9. Rowland, *Lloyd George*, pp 740–1; Frances Lloyd George, *The Years That Are Past*, p 272.

10. M G Fry, *Lloyd George and Foreign Policy: Volume One The Education of a Statesman: 1890–1916* (McGill-Queen's University Press: 1977) p 58.

11. Toye, *Rivals*, p 45 and p 56.

12. *Punch* 13 Nov 1907 in *Lloyd George by Mr Punch* (Cassell: 1922) p 24.

13. Toye, *Rivals*, p 62.

14. In January the Liberals won 274 seats, the Conservatives 272; in December the figures were 272 to 271. On each occasion the Irish Nationalists won 82 seats and the Labour Party 40 and 42 respectively, thus continuing its rise since its 2 seats in 1900.

15. Lloyd George Papers in the House of Lords Record Office, C/16/9/1, hereafter LGP.

16. 18 Jun 1913, D M Crieger, *Bounder from Wales: Lloyd George's Career before the First World War* (University of Missouri Press: 1976) p 210.

17. D Lloyd George, *War Memoirs* (2 vol. edition, Odhams: 1938) Vol I, p 60.

18. Morgan, *Family Letters*, p 167.

19. Rowland, *Lloyd George*, p 282.

20. Lloyd George. *War Memoirs*, Vol I, p 26.
21. Morgan, *Family Letters*, p 167.
22. Frances Lloyd George, *The Years That Are Past*, pp 73–4.
23. Lloyd George, *War Memoirs*, Vol I, p 32 and pp 57–8.

2. The Man Who Won the War

1. Speech at the Queen's Hall, London, 19 Sep 1914, Rowland, *Lloyd George*, p 287; Toye, *Rivals*, p 129.
2. Toye, *Rivals*, p 134.
3. Viscount Grey, *Twenty Five Years 1892–1916* (2 vols., Hodder and Stoughton: 1925) Vol II, p 243.
4. T Wilson (ed.), *The Political Diaries of C.P Scott 1911–1928* (Cornell UP: 1970) p 148.
5. T Jones, *Lloyd George* (Oxford UP: 1951) p 72.
6. Jones, *Lloyd George*, pp 75–6 and 78.
7. Lloyd George, *War Memoirs*, Vol I, p 596.
8. Toye, *Rivals*, p 185.
9. National Eisteddfod, Aberystwyth, 17 Aug 1916, Jones, *Lloyd George*, p 264.
10. *Lloyd George by Mr Punch*, p 111.
11. Lloyd George, *War Memoirs*, Vol II, pp 1510–17.
12. C Seymour (ed.), *The Intimate Papers of Colonel House* (4 vols., Ernest Benn: 1928) Vol III, p 350.
13. Wilson's speeches in 1918 are reprinted in H W V Temperley, *A History of the Peace Conference of Paris* (6 vols., Oxford: 1920–4) Vol. I, pp 431–48, hereafter Temperley, *History*.
14. This section is based on R Bunselmeyer, *The Cost of the War 1914–1919: British Economic War Aims and the Origins of Reparation* (Archon Books: 1975) pp 121–56.

15. Frances Stevenson, *Lloyd George: A Diary* (ed. A J P Taylor, Hutchinson: 1971) p 169, hereafter Stevenson, *Diary*.

16. H Nicolson, *Peacemaking 1919* (Constable: 1933) pp 9–10.

17. W R Louis, *Great Britain and Germany's Lost Colonies* (Clarendon Press: 1967) p 154.

18. E Monroe, *Britain's Moment in the Middle East 1914–1956* (University Paperbacks: 1963) p 26.

19. Lloyd George, *The Truth about the Peace Treaties* (2 vols, Victor Gollancz: 1938) Vol II, p 1136, hereafter Lloyd George, *The Truth*.

20. Lloyd George, *The Truth*, Vol II, pp 1128–9.

21. Letter to Lloyd George, 26 May 1919, LGP F/39/1/21.

22. M Dockrill and D Goold, *Peace Without Promise: Britain and the Peace Conferences 1919–23* (Batsford: 1981) p 142. On the wartime history of the Middle East see D Fromkin, *A Peace to End All Peace: The Fall of the Ottoman Empire and the Creation of the Modern Middle East* (Phoenix ed.: 2000); M E Yapp, *The Near East Since the First World War: A History to 1995* (Longman: 1996); and the appropriate chapters of Margaret MacMillan, *Peacemakers: The Paris Conference of 1919 and Its Attempt to End War* (John Murray: 2001).

3. Paris

1. Lord Riddell, *Lord Riddell's Intimate Diary of the Peace Conference and After* (Victor Gollancz: 1933) 29 Jun 1919, p 101, hereafter Riddell, *Intimate Diary*; Stevenson, *Diary*, 5 Apr 1919, p 178.

2. R Vansittart, *The Mist Procession* (Hutchinson: 1958) p 218.

3. This section relies very heavily on Sally Marks, 'Behind the Scenes at the Paris Peace Conference of 1919', *Journal of British Studies* Vol. 9, No.2 (1970) pp 154–80, hereafter Marks, 'Behind the Scenes'. All the quotations are cited by her.

4. Marks, 'Behind the Scenes', p 179.

5. Lord Howard of Penrith, *Diary for 1919* D/HW1/5, Cumbria Archive Service, Carlisle, hereafter Howard, *Diary*; MacMillan, *Peacemakers*, p 158. The mourners included Frances, whose brother Paul was killed in May 1915.

6. Nicolson, *Peacemaking 1919*, pp 44 and 26.

7. Quoted by MacMillan, *Peacemakers*, pp 51–2.

8. Riddell was dismissive: 'It looks as if the Foreign Office has prepared an enormous amount of material that is of no use, or at any rate is never used.' Riddell, *Intimate Diary*, p 14.

9. P Cambon, *Correspondance* (3 vols., Grasset: 1946) Vol III, p 311.

10. Nicolson, *Peacemaking 1919*, p 100.

11. MacMillan, *Peacemakers*, p 1.

12. MacMillan, *Peacemakers*, p 35

13. Howard, *Diary*, 18 Jan 1919.

14. Letter 21 Jan 1919, LGP, F/51/1/6.

15. Howard, *Diary*, 24 Jan 1919; Nicolson, *Peacemaking*, p 241.

16. G Egerton, *Great Britain and the Creation of the League of Nations: Strategy, Politics, and International Organisation, 1914–1919* (Scolar: 1979) p 31.

17. S P Tillman, *Anglo-American Relations at the Paris Peace Conference of 1919* (Princeton UP: 1961) p 133.
18. *Lloyd George by Mr Punch*, p 127; Letter 17 Mar 1919 LGP, F/23/4/37.
19. Letter 19 Feb 1919, LGP, F/89/2/25; Riddell, *Intimate Diary*, p 51.
20. Letter 19 Feb 1919, LGP, F/89/2/25.
21. Stevenson, *Diary*, 5 Apr 1919, p 178; Riddell, *Intimate Diary*, p 51; Seymour (ed.), *Intimate Papers of Colonel House*, Vol. IV, p 405; Nicolson, *Peacemaking 1919*, p 339.
22. J M Keynes, *Economic Consequences of the Peace* (Macmillan: 1919).
23. Hankey to Lloyd George, 19 Mar 1919, LGP, F/23/4/39.
24. Riddell, *Intimate Diary*, p 36; 'Some Considerations for the Peace Conference before they finally draft their Terms' *Cmd. 2169 Papers Respecting Negotiations for an Anglo-French Pact* (HMSO: 1924) pp 78–87, hereafter 'Some Considerations for the Peace Conference'.
25. 'Some Considerations for the Peace Conference', p 79.
26. 'Some Considerations for the Peace Conference', pp 79 and 81.
27. 'Some Considerations for the Peace Conference', pp 80–1.
28. 'Some Considerations for the Peace Conference', p 81.
29. United States Department of State, *Papers relating to the foreign relations of the United States, 1919. The Paris Peace Conference* (13 vols., U.S. Government Printing Office: 1919) Vol. V, pp 112–48, hereafter *FRUS*.
30. A Headlam-Morley, R Bryant and A Cienciala (eds.), *Sir James Headlam-Morley: A Memoir of the Paris Peace Conference 1919* (Methuen: 1972) Letter to John Bailey,

10 May 1919, p 103, hereafter Hedlam-Morley, *Memoir*; A Lentin, *Lloyd George and the Lost Peace: From Versailles to Hitler* (Palgrave: 2001) p 69.

31. Bonar Law to Lloyd George, 31 May 1919, LGP, F/30/3/71; K Bourne and D Watt (eds.), *British Documents on Foreign Affairs: Reports and Papers from the Foreign Office Confidential Print: The Paris Peace Conference of 1919* (7 vols., University Publications of America: 1989) Vol. IV, pp 96–106, hereafter *BDFA*.

32. *BDFA*, Vol. IV, pp 106–16.

33. *BDFA*, Vol. IV, p 116.

34. Bonar Law to Lloyd George, 31 May 1919, LGP, F/30/3/71.

35. Headlam-Morley, *Memoir*, p 180; Nicolson, *Peacemaking 1919*, p 371.

4. Making Germany Pay

1. Advertisement placed by the 'National Party' – a group of Conservative MPs – in *The Times* 28 Oct 1918. Lloyd George's speech, 5 Jan 1918, *War Memoirs*, Vol II, p 1511.

2. W S Churchill, *The World Crisis – The Aftermath* (Butterworth: 1929) pp 20–1, hereafter Churchill, *Aftermath*; Wilson diary, 11 Nov 1918, quoted by Toye, *Rivals*, p 193.

3. P Mantoux, *Les Délibérations du Conseil des Quatre* (2 vols., Editions de Centre Nationale de la recherché scientifique: 1955) Vol. I, pp 58–62, hereafter Mantoux, *Délibérations*; CAB 491B, 26 Oct 1918, in CAB 23/14; Fontainebleau Memorandum in *Cmd*. 2169 pp 80–1.

4. C Kitching, *Britain and the Problem of International Disarmament 1919–1934* (Routledge: 1999) p 9.

5. Riddell, *Intimate Diary*, p 42.

6. Lloyd George to Kerr, 10 Feb 1919, LGP, F/89/2/8.

7. Churchill to Lloyd George, 28 Nov 1921, LGP, F/10/1/48.

8. See D Stevenson, 'Britain, France and the Origins of German Disarmament, 1916–1919', *Journal of Strategic Studies* Vol. 29 No. 2 (2006) pp 195–224 and A Sharp, 'Mission Accomplished? Britain and the Disarmament of Germany, 1918–1923', in K Hamilton and E Johnson (eds.), *Arms and Disarmament in Diplomacy* (Valentine Mitchell: 2007) pp 73–90.

9. G J Bass, *Stay The Hand of Vengeance: The Politics of War Crimes Tribunals* (2nd paperback ed., Princeton UP: 2002) pp 64–75.

10. Bass, *Stay The Hand of Vengeance*, pp 75–6 and 61. See also J F Willis, *Prologue to Nuremberg: The Politics and Diplomacy of Punishing War Criminals of the First World War* (Greenwood: 1982) *passim*.

11. MacMillan, *Peacemakers*, p 191.

12. Lloyd George, *War Memoirs*, Vol. II p 1513

13. Seymour (ed.), *Intimate Papers of Colonel House*, Vol. IV, p 167; WC491A in CAB 23/14.

14. J Vincent (ed.), *The Crawford Papers: The Journals of David Lindsay, 1892 to 1940* (Manchester UP: 1984) p 399: Churchill, *Aftermath*, p 49.

15. Speech, Newcastle, 29 Nov 1918.

16. Hankey to Lloyd George, 21 Dec 1918, LGP, F/23/4/19; Lothian Papers (National Library of Scotland, Edinburgh) GD 40; W A S Hewins, quoted by Bunselmeyer, *The Cost of the War*, p 115.

17. Lentin, *Lloyd George and the Lost Peace*, pp 23–46. Riddell, *Intimate Diary*, p 47.

18. Mantoux, *Délibérations*, Vol. I, pp 58–62.

19. *FRUS* Vol. VI, pp 261–2.

20. S Marks, 'Smoke and Mirrors: In Smoke-Filled Rooms and the Galerie des Glaces' in M Boemeke, G Feldman and E Glaser (eds.), *The Treaty of Versailles: A Reassessment after 75 Years* (Cambridge UP: 1998) pp 237–8.

5. Redrawing the Map of Europe

1. E L Spears, *Liaison 1914: A Narrative of the Great Retreat* (Heinemann: 1930) p 84.
2. Lloyd George, *War Memoirs*, Vol. II, pp 1513, 1515.
3. Note, 30 Dec 1918, R Lansing, *The Peace Negotiations: A Personal Narrative* (Houghton Mifflin: 1921) pp 97–8.
4. Temperley, *History*, Vol. I, pp 437, 439.
5. MacMillan, *Peacemakers*, p 31.
6. P Mantoux, *Paris Peace Conference 1919: Proceedings of the Council of Four, March 24 –April 18* (Libraire Droz: 1964) p 28; A Tardieu, *The Truth about the Treaty* (Bobbs-Merrill Co.: 1921) p 171.
7. *Cmd. 2169*, p 79.
8. Lloyd George, *War Memoirs*, Vol. II, p 1513; Seymour (ed.), *Intimate Papers of Colonel House*, Vol. III, pp 337–8.
9. J C King, *Foch versus Clemenceau: France and German Dismemberment 1918–19* (Harvard UP: 1960) p 8.
10. Eastern Committee, 2 Dec 1918 in CAB27/24; Comte de Saint-Aulaire, *Confession d'un Vieux Diplomate* (Flammarion: 1953) p 536.
11. G Clemenceau, *Grandeur and Misery of Victory* (Harrap: 1930) p 113.
12. Clemenceau, *Grandeur and Misery of Victory*, p 220; *Cmd 2169* p 63.
13. Seymour (ed.), *Intimate Papers of Colonel House*, Vol. IV, p 356.

14. CAB541A, 4.3.19, in CAB23/15.

15. R Poincaré, *Au Service de la France* (11 vols., Plon: 1928–74) Vol. XI, p 337.

16. H I Nelson, *Land and Power: British and Allied Policy on Germany's Frontiers 1916–19* (Routledge and Kegan Paul: 1963) p 229.

17. All the quotations are sourced in A Sharp, 'Britain and the Channel Tunnel, 1919–1920', *Australian Journal of Politics and History* Vol. XXV, No.2 (1979) pp 210–15.

18. Letter to Botha, 26 Jun 1919, LGP, F/5/5/14

19. S Marks, *Innocent Abroad: Belgium at the Paris Peace Conference of 1919* (University of North Carolina Press: 1981) p 231.

20. Letter 11 Jun 1919, LGP, F/55/4/35.

21. Howard, *Diary*, 6 Mar 1919.

22. MacMillan, *Peacemakers*, p 228.

23. Lloyd George, *War Memoirs*, Vol. II, p 1514; Temperley, *History*, Vol. I, pp 434–5.

24. National Broadcast, 27 Sep 1938, N Chamberlain, *The Struggle for Peace* (Hutchinson: 1939) p 275.

25. Isaiah Bowman in E House and C Seymour (eds.), *What Really Happened at Paris* (Hodder and Stoughton: 1921) pp 158–9.

26. MacMillan, *Peacemakers*, pp 222–3.

27. Bowman in House and Seymour (eds.), *What Really Happened at Paris*, pp 160–1; *FRUS* Vol. IV, p 415.

28. Letter 31 Mar 1919, LGP, F/30/3/40.

29. 3 Jun 1919, Mantoux, *Délibérations*, Vol. II, p 278.

30. Lloyd George, *The Truth*, Vol. I, p 91.

31. E Goldstein, *Winning the Peace: British Diplomatic Strategy, Peace Planning and the Paris Peace Conference*

1916–1920 (Clarendon Press: 1991) p 129; I L Claude, *National Minorities* (Greenwood: 1969) p 57.

32. MacMillan, *Peacemakers*, p 7.

33. Lansing, *The Peace Negotiations*, pp 97–8.

6. The Imperial Settlement

1. L S Amery, *The Leo Amery Diaries: Volume I, 1896–1919* (J Barnes and D Nicholson eds., Hutchinson: 1980) p 189.

2. S Roskill, *Hankey: Man of Secrets* (3 vols., Collins: 1970–4) Vol. I, p 609.

3. Riddell, *Intimate Diary*, p 24.

4. Balfour 9 Dec 1918, CAB 27/24.

5. Montagu to Balfour, 28 Dec 1918, FO 800/215.

6. Lloyd George, *The Truth*, Vol. I, p 542; M Hankey, *The Supreme Control at the Paris Peace Conference 1919* (Allen and Unwin: 1963) letter 29 Jan 1919, p 60.

7. A Sharp, *The Versailles Settlement: Peacemaking in Paris, 1919* (Macmillan: 1991) p 162.

8. The colonial settlement is well covered in W R Louis, *Great Britain and Germany's Lost Colonies* (Clarendon Press: 1967) and the relevant chapters of MacMillan, *Peacemakers*.

9. War Cabinet 482A, 3 Oct 1918, in CAB 23/14.

10. MacMillan, *Peacemakers*, p 394; Lloyd George, *The Truth*, Vol. II, p 1038.

11. MacMillan, *Peacemakers*, p 426.

12. D Varè, *Laughing Diplomat* (John Murray: 1938) p 155.

13. BDFA, Vol. II, pp 261–4.

14. Cambon, *Correspondence*, Vol. III, p 323.

15. Roskill, *Hankey*, Vol. I, p 609.

16. H Nicolson, *Curzon: The Last Phase, 1919–1925. A Study in Post-War Diplomacy* (Constable: 1934) p 3.

17. Lloyd George, *The Truth*, Vol. II, p 1204; Nicolson, *Curzon: The Last Phase*, p 80.
18. MacMillan, *Peacemakers*, p 443.

7. Coping with the Aftermath

1. Headlam-Morley, *Memoir*, p 180.
2. 24 Nov 1918 speech in Wolverhampton. Rowland, *Lloyd George*, p 467.
3. Frances Lloyd George, *Diary*, p 187.
4. R Butler and J Bury (eds.), *Documents on British Foreign Policy 1919–1939* (First Series, HMSO: 1954 onwards), Vol. IX, Curzon, minute, 6 Apr 1920, N1, p 328, hereafter *DBFP*.
5. Memo. 28 Dec 1921, *DBFP*, Vol. XVI, p 862.
6. Memo. 25 Jun 1921, LGP F/25/1/48.
7. Committee of Imperial Defence [CID] meeting 108A, 29.5.21, in CAB16/47.
8. Rowland, *Lloyd George*, p 523; Imperial Conference meetings 5 Oct 1923, E3 in CAB32/9 and 22.6.21, E4 in CAB32/2.
9. A L Kennedy, *Old Diplomacy and New* (John Murray: 1922) p 365.
10. MacMillan, *Peacemakers*, p 49.
11. A J Sylvester, *The Real Lloyd George* (Cassel: 1947) p 282; Letter 16 Oct 1922, LGP F/13/2/53.
12. Nicolson, *Curzon: The Last Phase*, p 214; B Dugdale *Arthur James Balfour* (2 vols., National Book Association ed.: 1939) Vol. II, p 215; Cabinet meeting, 20 Mar 1938 in CAB23/92.
13. All the quotations in this section can be found in A Sharp, 'Mission Accomplished? Britain and the Disarmament of Germany, 1918–1923' in K Hamilton

and E Johnson (eds.), *Arms and Disarmament in Diplomacy* (Vallentine Mitchell: 2008) pp 73–90.

14. *DBFP*, Vol. XIX, p 625.

15. Grigg Note 6 Jul 1922, LGC F/86/2/8.

16. Bass, *Stay the Hand of Vengeance*, p 81.

17. Willis, *Prologue to Nuremberg*, pp 133–9.

18. Memo, by R W Wigram on the legal position in the event of a German default, 18 Dec 1922 (C17313/99/18), *DBFP* Vol. XX, pp 344–6; Opinion by the Solicitor-General (Thomas Inskip) on the interpretation of Paragraph 18, Annex II, 28 Dec 1922 (C17791/99/18), *DBFP* Vol. XX, p 358

19. ICP 171, 2 Mar 1921, *DBFP*, Vol. XV, pp 246–7, 251.

20. ICP 137, 14 Jul 1920, *DBFP*, Vol. VIII, p 602.

21. Malkin note, 12 Mar 1921, C5545/2704/18 in Fo317/6018.

22. Toye, *Rivals*, p 221.

23. *DBFP*, Vol. XIX, pp 340–3.

24. Hardinge Papers, Cambridge University Library, Vol. 45, letters of 2 May 1922 and 5 May 1922.

25. Nicolson, *Curzon: The Last Phase*, p 274; Lord Hardinge, *Old Diplomacy* (John Murray: 1947) pp 271–4.

26. Fromkin, *A Peace to End All Peace*, p 501.

8. Keeping out the Welshman

1. Cato, *Guilty Men* (Gollanz: 1940) p 19. 'Cato' was a collective of three journalists; Michael Foot, Frank Owen and Peter Howard.

2. M Pugh, *Lloyd George* (Longman: 1988) p 167.

3. Pugh, *Lloyd George*, p 167.

4. Lentin, *Lloyd George and the Lost Peace*, p 103.

5. Morgan, *Lloyd George* p 188
6. Pugh, *Lloyd George*, p 180; Lentin, *Lloyd George and the Lost Peace*, pp 126–8.

Conclusion: Lloyd George and the Legacy of Versailles

1. Archibald Wavell, Fromkin, *A Peace to End All Peace*. Curzon Papers, British Library, Mss. Eur. F112/3192.
2. House of Commons Debates, 5th series, Vol. 114, Cols. 2936–8.
3. Frances Lloyd George, *The Years That Are Past*, p 166.
4. PID Paper 3, *Europe* in FO 371/4353.
5. Headlam-Morley, 18 Mar 1919, 41/1/1 in FO 608/9.
6. Fry, *Lloyd George and Foreign Policy*, p 247.
7. R Watt, *The Kings Depart: The Tragedy of Germany: Versailles and the German Revolution* (Literary Guild ed.: 1968) p 211.
8. A Pollard, 'The Balance of Power', *Journal of the British Institute of International Affairs* Vol. II (1923) p 60.
9. CID meeting, 13 Feb 1925, CAB2/4.
10. Papiers Henri Jaspar, Dossier 209, Archives du Royaume, Brussels.
11. Derby to Curzon, 16 Oct 1919, Curzon papers, MSS EUR F/112/196.
12. J M Keynes, *Essays in Biography* (Macmillan: 1933) pp 36–7; Lentin, *Lloyd George and the Lost Peace*, p 10.
13. Lloyd George, *The Truth*, Vol. I, pp 17–91; Hardinge, *Old Diplomacy*, p 240.
14. Letter to Maggie, 11 Aug 1914, Morgan, *Family Letters*, p 169.
15. Lord D'Abernon, *An Ambassador of Peace: Pages from the Diary of Viscount D'Abernon (Berlin 1920–1926)* (3 vols., Hodder and Stoughton: 1929–30) Vol. II, p 185.

Chronology

YEAR	AGE	THE LIFE AND THE LAND
1863		17 Jan: David George born.
		Construction of London Underground begins.
1864	1	7 Jun: William George (David's father) dies.
		Elizabeth (Betsy) George (David's mother) and family move to Llanystumdwy, North Wales to live with Richard (Uncle) Lloyd; becomes Lloyd George (LG).
1877	14	Jul: LG articled as solicitor.
		Queen Victoria proclaimed Empress of India.
1884	21	LG qualifies as a solicitor and establishes own law practice in Criccieth.
1888	25	24 Jan: LG marries Margaret (Maggie) Owen.
		Dec: LG wins Llanfrothen burial case.
		'Jack the Ripper' murders in London.

YEAR	HISTORY	CULTURE
1863	American Civil War: Confederate defeats at Gettysburg and Vicksburg: Lincoln's 'Gettysburg Address'. Schleswig incorporated into Denmark. French capture Mexico City.	Charles Kingsley, *The Water Babies*. Football Association founded, London.
1864	Schleswig War: Austrian and Prussian troops defeat Danes. Archduke Maximilian of Austria crowned Emperor of Mexico. American Civil War: General Grant made Commander-in-Chief of Union Army; Lincoln re-elected; Sherman's march through Georgia.	Charles Dickens, *Our Mutual Friend*. Tolstoy, *War and Peace* (-1869).
1877	Outbreak of Russo-Turkish War. Satsuma rebellion suppressed in Japan.	Henry James, *The American*. Rodin, sculpture 'The Age of Bronze'.
1884	Germans occupy South-West Africa. Gold discovered in the Transvaal.	Mark Twain, *Huckleberry Finn*. *Oxford English Dictionary* begins publication (-1928).
1888	Kaiser Wilhelm II accedes to the throne. Suez Canal convention.	Rudyard Kipling, *Plain Tales from the Hills*. Van Gogh, painting 'The Yellow Chair'.

YEAR	AGE	THE LIFE AND THE LAND
1889	26	Jan: LG elected alderman on the new Caernarvon County Council. 15 Feb: Son, Richard, born.
1890	27	10 Apr: LG elected as MP for Caernarvon Boroughs. 2 Aug: Daughter, Mair, born. Britain exchanges Heligoland with Germany for Zanzibar and Pemba.
1892	29	3 Apr: Daughter, Olwen, born. Britain and Germany agree on Cameroon.
1894	31	4 Dec: Son, Gwilym, born.
1897	34	LG cleared of fathering Kitty Edwards' child. Queen Victoria's Diamond Jubilee.
1899	36	11 Oct: Outbreak of Second Boer War: British defeats at Stormberg, Magersfontein and Colenso ('Black Week'). LG sits on Parliamentary Select Committee on Old Age Pensions.
1900	37	28 Sep–24 Oct: General Election (Conservative victory) Salisbury remains prime minister. Second Boer War: relief of Mafeking and capture of Johannesburg and Pretoria.

YEAR	HISTORY	CULTURE
1889	Austro-Hungarian Crown Prince Rudolf commits suicide at Mayerling. London Dock Strike.	Jerome K Jerome, *Three Men in a Boat*. Richard Strauss, symphonic poem 'Don Juan'.
1890	Bismarck dismissed by Wilhelm II. First general election in Japan. German Social Democrats adopt Marxist Erfurt Programme.	Oscar Wilde, *The Picture of Dorian Gray*. Mascagni, opera 'Cavelleria Rusticana'. First moving picture shows in New York.
1892	Pan-Slav Conference in Cracow.	Bernard Shaw, *Mrs Warren's Profession*. Israel Zangwill, *Children of the Ghetto*. Tchaikovsky, ballet 'The Nutcracker'.
1894	Sino-Japanese War begins: Japanese defeat Chinese at Port Arthur.	Anthony Hope, *The Prisoner of Zenda*.
1897	Russia occupies Port Arthur. Zionist Congress in Basel, Switzerland.	H G Wells, *The Invisible Man*. Edmond Rostand, *Cyrano de Bergerac*.
1899	First Peace Conference at the Hague. Germany secures Baghdad railway contract.	Rudyard Kipling, *Stalky and Co*. Elgar, 'Enigma Variations'.
1900	Assassination of King Umberto I of Italy. Boxer Rising in China.	Freud, *The Interpretation of Dreams*. Anton Chekhov, *Uncle Vanya*.

YEAR	AGE	THE LIFE AND THE LAND
1901	38	22 Jan: Queen Victoria dies, Edward VII becomes king.
		Negotiations for Anglo-German alliance end without agreement.
1902	39	30 Jan: Anglo-Japanese alliance.
		22 Apr: Daughter, Megan, born.
		11 Jul: Salisbury resigns, Arthur Balfour becomes prime minister.
		Treaty of Vereenigung ends Boer War.
1904	41	8 Apr: Anglo-French *entente*.
1905	42	4 Dec: Balfour resigns as prime minister.
		5 Dec: Henry Campbell-Bannerman becomes prime minister.
		10 Dec: LG becomes President of the Board of Trade
1906	43	12 Jan–7 Feb: General Election (Liberal landslide).
		Edward VII of England and Kaiser Wilhelm II of Germany meet.
		Britain grants self-government to Transvaal and Orange River Colonies.
		Launch of HMS *Dreadnought*.
1907	44	31 Aug: Anglo-Russian *entente*.
		Oct–Nov: LG averts national rail strike.
		29 Nov: Mair dies after an operation.

YEAR	HISTORY	CULTURE
1901	US President McKinley is assassinated: Theodore Roosevelt sworn in as President. First transatlantic radio signal transmitted.	Thomas Mann, *Die Buddenbrooks*. Rudyard Kipling, *Kim*.
1902	Triple Alliance between Austria, Germany and Italy renewed for another six years. USA acquires perpetual control over Panama Canal.	Arthur Conan Doyle, *The Hound of the Baskervilles*. Elgar, 'Pomp and Circumstance March No 1'.
1904	Outbreak of Russo–Japanese War. Roosevelt wins US Presidential election.	J M Barrie, *Peter Pan*. Thomas Hardy, *The Dynasts*.
1905	Port Arthur surrenders to Japanese. 'Bloody Sunday' massacre in Russia.	George Santayana, *The Life of Reason*. E M Forster, *Where Angels Fear to Tread*. Edith Wharton, *House of Mirth*.
1906	In France, Dreyfus rehabilitated. Major earthquake in San Francisco USA kills over 1,000.	John Galsworthy, *A Man of Property*. O Henry, *The Four Million*. Invention of first jukebox.
1907	Rasputin gains influence at the court of Tsar Nicholas II. Peace Conference held in The Hague.	Joseph Conrad, *The Secret Agent*. First Cubist exhibition in Paris.

YEAR	AGE	THE LIFE AND THE LAND
1908	45	5 Apr: Campbell-Bannerman resigns, Herbert Asquith becomes prime minister.
		12 Apr: LG becomes Chancellor of the Exchequer.
		Jul: Old Age Pensions Act.
1909	46	12 Mar: LG wins libel case against the *People* newspaper.
		29 Apr: LG introduces the 'People's Budget'.
		30 Jul: LG delivers Limehouse speech.
		30 Nov: House of Lord rejects Budget.
1910	47	14 Jan–9 Feb: General Election (virtual tie, IPP hold balance); Constitutional Conference on the House of Lords.
		6 May: Edward VII dies, George V becomes king.
		17 Jun–31 Jul: Constitutional Conference.
		2–19 Dec: General Election (virtual tie, IPP hold balance).
1911	48	4 May: LG moves National Insurance Bill.
		10 Aug: Parliament Act.
		21 Jul: LG's Mansion House Speech.
		Jul: LG first meets Frances Stevenson.
1912	49	Marconi Scandal.
1913	50	Land Campaign.

YEAR	HISTORY	CULTURE
1908	Union of South Africa is established. William Howard Taft elected US President.	E M Forster, *A Room with a View.* Kenneth Grahame, *The Wind in the Willows.*
1909	Kiamil Pasha, grand vizier of Turkey, forced to resign by Turkish nationalists. Plastic (Bakelite) is invented.	H G Wells, *Tono-Bungay* Marinetti publishes *First Futurist Manifesto.*
1910	Egyptian Premier Butros Ghali assassinated. South Africa becomes a dominion within the British Empire with Botha as Premier.	E M Forster, *Howard's End.* H G Wells, *The History of Mr. Polly.*
1911	Arrival of German gunboat *Panther* in Agadir triggers international crisis. Peter Stolypyn, Russian Premier, assassinated. Italy declares war on Turkey.	Max Beerbohm, *Zuleika Dobson.* Saki, *The Chronicles of Clovis.*
1912	*Titanic* sinks. First Balkan War. Woodrow Wilson is elected US President.	C G Jung, *The Theory of Psychoanalysis.*
1913	Second Balkan War breaks out. US Federal Reserve System is established.	D H Lawrence, *Sons and Lovers.* Thomas Mann, *Death in Venice.*

YEAR	AGE	THE LIFE AND THE LAND
1914	51	28 Jun: Assassination of Franz Ferdinand at Sarajevo.
		28 Jul: Austria-Hungary declares war on Serbia.
		1 Aug: Germany declares war on Russia.
		3 Aug: Germany declares war on France and attacks Belgium.
		4 Aug: Britain (and its empire) declare war on Germany.
		23 Aug: Battle of Mons.
		5 Sep: Treaty of London; Britain, Russia and France agree not to make peace separately.
		19 Sep: LG delivers Queen's Hall recruiting speech.
		Oct–Nov: First Battle of Ypres.
		5 Nov: Britain and France declare war on Turkey.
1915	52	18 Jan: Japan issues the 'Twenty-One Demands' to China.
		Mar: Battle of Neuve Chapelle.
		25 Apr: Gallipoli campaign begins.
		26 Apr: Treaty of London between Britain, France and Russia and Italy.
		23 May: Italy declares war on Austria-Hungary.
		25 May: Liberal-Conservative Coalition; Asquith remains prime minister, LG becomes Minister of Munitions.
		Sep: Battle of Loos.
		24 Oct: Britain promises Sherif Hussein an independent Arab state.
1916	53	16 May: Sykes-Picot Agreement.
		31 May–1 Jun: Battle of Jutland.
		6 Jul: LG becomes Secretary of State for War.
		July–Nov: Battle of the Somme.
		28 Aug: Italy declares war on Germany.
		5 Dec: Asquith resigns
		6 Dec: LG becomes prime minister.

YEAR	HISTORY	CULTURE
1914	First World War: Russians defeated at Battles of Tannenberg and Masurian Lakes.	James Joyce, *Dubliners.* Film: Charlie Chaplin in *Making a Living.*
1915	Germans sink the British liner *Lusitania,* killing 1,198. Germans execute British nurse Edith Cavell in Brussels for harbouring British prisoners.	John Buchan, *The Thirty-Nine Steps.* Film: *The Birth of a Nation.*
1916	First World War: Western Front: Battle of Verdun. 5 Jun: Arab revolt against the Ottomans begins. US President Woodrow Wilson is re-elected: issues Peace Note to belligerents in European war.	James Joyce, *Portrait of an Artist as a Young Man.* Film: *Intolerance.*

YEAR	AGE	THE LIFE AND THE LAND
1917	54	28 Feb: Death of Uncle Lloyd.
		Jun–Nov: Battle of Passchendaele.
		2 Nov: Balfour Declaration
1918	55	5 Jan: LG's War Aims speech to the TUC.
		Aug: Allied offensives begin on Western Front.
		30 Oct: Armistice with Turkey at Mudros.
		3 Nov: Armistice with Austria-Hungary.
		5 Nov: Lansing Note.
		11 Nov: Armistice with Germany.
		14 Dec: General ('Coupon') election, (Coalition landslide).

YEAR	HISTORY	CULTURE
1917	15 Mar: Tsar Nicholas II abdicates.	P G Wodehouse, *The Man With Two Left Feet.*
	6 Apr: United States Congress declares war on Germany.	T S Eliot, *Prufrock and Other Observations.*
	China declares war on Germany and Russia.	Film: *Easy Street.*
	7 Nov: Bolshevik revolution in Russia.	
	German and Russian delegates sign armistice at Brest-Litovsk.	
	7 Dec: United States declares war on Austria-Hungary.	
1918	First World War.	Gerald Manley Hopkins, *Poems.*
	8 Jan: Wilson's Fourteen Points Speech to Congress.	Luigi Pirandello, *Six Characters in Search of an Author.*
	6 Mar: German-Soviet Russian Treaty of Brest-Litovsk.	
	Mar: German Spring offensive on Western Front.	
	Romania signs Peace of Bucharest with Germany and Austria-Hungary.	
	4 Oct: Germany requests armistice from Wilson.	
	14 Oct: Turkey requests armistice.	
	9 Nov: Abdication of Kaiser Wilhelm II, Proclamation of German Republic.	
	Ex-Tsar Nicholas II and family executed.	

YEAR	AGE	THE LIFE AND THE LAND
1919	56	18 Jan: Paris Peace Conference begins.
		22 Jan: All Russian factions invited to Prinkipo Island, Sea of Marmara, Turkey for a conference.
		8 Feb: LG returns to London (until 5 Mar).
		14 Feb: Draft Covenant of the League approved.
		15 Feb: Wilson returns to the USA (until 13 Mar).
		19 Feb: Assassination attempt on Clemenceau.
		14 Mar: LG and Wilson offer Anglo-American guarantees to France.
		24 Mar: Council of Four meets for first time.
		25 Mar: LG issues Fontainebleau Memorandum.
		21 Apr: Italy walks out of Peace Conference.
		6 May: Italy returns to the Conference.
		7 May: Treaty text presented to Germany.
		21 Jun: Germans scuttle fleet at Scapa Flow.
		23 Jun: Orlando resigns.
		28 Jun: Treaty of Versailles signed in the Hall of Mirrors.
		10 Sep: Treaty of St-Germain-en-Laye signed with Austria.
		12 Sep: D'Annunzio occupies Fiume.
		19 Nov: US Senate refuses to ratify Treaty of Versailles.
		27 Nov: Treaty of Neuilly signed with Bulgaria.

YEAR	HISTORY	CULTURE
1919	Benito Mussolini founds fascist movement in Italy.	Thomas Hardy, *Collected Poems*.
	Irish War of Independence begins.	Film: *The Cabinet of Dr Caligari*.
		Elgar's Cello Concerto in E minor (op.85).

YEAR	AGE	THE LIFE AND THE LAND
1920	57	10 Jan: Treaty of Versailles enters into force.
		16 Jan: First meeting of League of Nations Council, Paris.
		21 Jan: Official end of Paris Peace Conference.
		19 Mar: US Senate rejects Treaty of Versailles for second and final time, American guarantee to France lapses, thus releasing Britain from its guarantee.
		18–26 April: San Remo conference.
		4 Jun: Treaty of Trianon signed with Hungary.
		5–16 Jul: Spa Conference.
		10 Aug: Treaty of Sèvres signed with Turkey.
		25 Oct: King Alexander I of Greece dies.
		10 Dec: Nobel Peace Prizes – Wilson (1919), Léon Bourgeois (1920).
		23 Dec: Government of Ireland Act.
1921	58	16 Mar: Anglo-Soviet Trade Treaty.
		27 Apr: Reparation Commission sets reparations at £6,600 million.
		5 May: London Schedule of Payments for Reparations.

YEAR	HISTORY	CULTURE
1920	Warren G Harding wins US Presidential election.	F Scott Fitzgerald, *This Side of Paradise*.
	Bolsheviks win Russian Civil War.	Rambert School of Ballet formed.
	Adolf Hitler announces his 25-point programme in Munich.	
1921	Irish Free State established.	Aldous Huxley, *Chrome Yellow*.
	Peace treaty signed between Russia and Germany.	D H Lawrence, *Women in Love*.
	State of Emergency proclaimed in Germany in the face of economic crisis.	
	23 Aug: British establish kingdom of Iraq, with Feisal as king.	
	12 Nov–6 Feb 1922: Washington Naval Conference.	

YEAR	AGE	THE LIFE AND THE LAND
1922	59	6–13 Jan: Cannes conference
		6 Feb: Washington naval treaties, Anglo-Japanese treaty lapses.
		10 Apr–19 May: Genoa conference; 29 nations discuss European reconstruction and relations with Soviet Russia.
		16 Apr: Treaty of Rapallo between Germany and Soviet Russia.
		1 Aug: Balfour Note on inter-Allied debts and reparations.
		9–11 Sep: Turks capture Smyrna (Izmir)
		15 Sep: Britain appeals to Dominions and Allies for help for Greeks at Chanak, most refuse.
		11 Oct: Mudania armistice between Allies and Kemal ends Chanak crisis.
		19 Oct: LG resigns as prime minister. Andrew Bonar Law becomes prime minister.
		15 Nov: General Election (Conservative landslide).
		20 Nov–4 Feb 1923: Lausanne conference.
1923	60	4 Feb: Breakdown of Lausanne conference.
		23 Apr–24 Jul: Lausanne conference resumes.
		20 May: Bonar Law resigns.
		22 May: Stanley Baldwin becomes prime minister.
		18 Jun: Anglo-American war debt agreement.
		24 Jul: Treaty of Lausanne between Turkey and Allies.
		23 Aug: Allies evacuate Constantinople (Istanbul).
		Nov: LG rejoins the Liberal Party.
		6 Dec: General Election (no overall majority, Conservatives largest single party).
1924	61	22 Jan: Ramsay MacDonald becomes prime minister of minority Labour government.
		29 Oct: General Election (Conservative victory) Baldwin prime minister.

YEAR	HISTORY	CULTURE
1922	Election in Irish Free State gives majority to Pro-Treaty candidates. IRA takes large areas under its control. Mussolini's 'March on Rome'.	T S Eliot, *The Waste Land.* James Joyce, *Ulysses.* British Broadcasting Company (later Corporation) (BBC) founded: first radio broadcasts.
1923	1 Jan: USSR enters formal existence. 11 Jan: Franco-Belgian occupation of Ruhr. Severe earthquake in Japan destroys all of Yokohama and most of Tokyo. British Mandate in Palestine begins. Adolf Hitler's *coup d'état* (The Beer Hall Putsch) fails.	P G Wodehouse, *The Inimitable Jeeves.* BBC listings magazine *Radio Times* first published.
1924	Death of Lenin. Dawes Plan published. Nazi party enters the Reichstag for the first time.	Noel Coward, *The Vortex.* E M Forster, *A Passage to India.*

YEAR	AGE	THE LIFE AND THE LAND
1925	62	LG commissions *The Land and the Nation* and *Towns and the Land*.
		Pound Sterling returns to the Gold Standard.
		Locarno Treaty signed in London.
1926	63	The General Strike.
		14 Oct: LG succeeds Asquith as leader of the Liberal Party.
1928	65	4 Oct: Birth of Jennifer Stevenson.
1929	66	Mar: LG publishes *We Can Conquer Unemployment*.
		30 May: General Election (no overall majority, Labour largest single party).
		5 Jun: MacDonald prime minister of second minority Labour government.
1931	68	Jul: LG undergoes prostate operation.
		24 Aug: MacDonald becomes prime minister of coalition National Government.
		27 Oct: General Election (National Government landslide).
		3 Nov: LG resigns as leader of the Liberal Party.
1933	70	Sep–Oct: LG publishes first two volumes of *War Memoirs*.
1934	71	Sep–Oct: LG publishes third and fourth volumes of *War Memoirs*.

YEAR	HISTORY	CULTURE
1925	Paul von Hindenburg, former military leader, elected President of Germany.	Virginia Woolf, *Mrs Dalloway*. Film: *Battleship Potemkin*.
1926	Germany admitted to the League of Nations.	Ernest Hemingway, *The Sun Also Rises*.
1928	Herbert Hoover elected US President.	D H Lawrence, *Lady Chatterley's Lover*.
1929	Germany accepts Young Plan at Reparations Conference in the Hague – Allies agree to evacuate the Rhineland. The Wall Street Crash	Erich Remarque, *All Quiet on the Western Front*. Noel Coward, *Bittersweet*.
1931	Nazi leader Adolf Hitler and Alfred Hugenberg of the German National Party agree to co-operate. Bankruptcy of German Danatbank leads to closure of all German banks.	William Faulkner, *Sanctuary*. Films: *Dracula. Little Caesar*.
1933	Adolf Hitler appointed Chancellor of Germany. Germany withdraws from League of Nations.	George Orwell, *Down and Out in Paris and London*. Film: *King Kong*.
1934	Hitler becomes *Führer* of Germany. USSR admitted to League of Nations.	Robert Graves, *I, Claudius*. Films: *David Copperfield*.

YEAR	AGE	THE LIFE AND THE LAND
1935	72	20 Jan: George V dies, Edward VIII becomes king.
		7 Jun: Baldwin replaces MacDonald as prime minister.
		12 Jun: LG establishes Council of Action for Peace and Reconstruction.
		14 Nov: General Election (National Government victory).
1936	73	Sep: LG visits Hitler at Berchtesgaden.
		Sep–Oct: LG publishes fifth and sixth volumes of *War Memoirs*
		11 Dec: Edward VIII abdicates, George VI becomes king.
1937	74	28 May: Baldwin resigns, Neville Chamberlain becomes prime minister.
1938	75	LG publishes the two volumes of *The Truth about the Peace Treaties*.
		Munich Agreement hands Sudetenland to Germany.
1939	76	Mar: British guarantees to Poland, Romania and Greece
		3 Sep: Britain declares war on Germany.

YEAR	HISTORY	CULTURE
1935	Saarland is incorporated into Germany following a plebiscite. League of Nations imposes sanctions against Italy following invasion of Abyssinia.	T S Eliot, *Murder in the Cathedral*. Ivy Compton-Burnett, *A House and its Head*. Film: *The 39 Steps*.
1936	German troops reoccupy Rhineland. F D Roosevelt, Democrat, re-elected president of the USA. Germany and Japan sign Anti-Comintern Pact.	J M Keynes, *General Theory of Employment, Interest and Money*. Film: *Modern Times*. BBC begins world's first television transmission service.
1937	Japan invades China, captures Shanghai. Rape of Nanjing. Italy joins German-Japanese Anti-Comintern Pact.	George Orwell, *The Road to Wigan Pier*. John Steinbeck, *Of Mice and Men*. Film: *A Star is Born*.
1938	German troops enter Austria which is declared part of the German Reich. Kristallnacht in Germany – Jewish houses, synagogues and schools burnt.	Graham Greene, *Brighton Rock*. Films: *Alexander Nevsky. The Adventures of Robin Hood*.
1939	Mar. Germans invade remainder of Czechoslovakia. Japanese-Soviet clashes in Manchuria. Aug. Nazi-Soviet Pact. Soviets invade Finland.	James Joyce, *Finnegan's Wake*. Film: *Gone with the Wind*.

YEAR	AGE	THE LIFE AND THE LAND
1940	77	8 May: LG calls for Chamberlain's resignation after failure of Norwegian campaign.
		10 May: Chamberlain resigns, Winston Churchill becomes prime minister.
		Jun: Dunkirk evacuation of British Expeditionary Force.
		Jul-Oct: Battle of Britain.
1941	78	20 Jan: Maggie dies.
1943	80	Jan. Allies demand unconditional surrender from Germany and Japan at Casablanca Conference.
		23 Oct: LG marries Frances Stevenson.
1945	82	1 Jan: LG becomes Earl Lloyd George of Dwyfor and Viscount Gwynedd.
		26 Mar: LG dies at Ty Newydd.
		7 May: Germany surrenders.

YEAR	HISTORY	CULTURE
1940	Second World War. May: Germany invades Holland, Belgium, Luxembourg and France Italy declares war on France and Britain. British victories against Italians in the Western Desert. Italy invades Greece.	Graham Greene, *The Power and the Glory.* Ernest Hemingway, *For Whom the Bell Tolls.* Films: *The Great Dictator. Pinocchio. Rebecca.*
1941	Second World War. 22 Jun: Germany invades USSR 7 Dec: Japan attacks Pearl Harbor.	Bertold Brecht, *Mother Courage and Her Children.* Films: *Citizen Kane.The Maltese Falcon.*
1943	Second World War. Germans surrender at Stalingrad. Axis forces in North Africa surrender. Invasion of Sicily and Italy.	Rogers and Hammerstein, *Oklahoma!* Film: *For Whom the Bell Tolls.*
1945	Second World War. British troops invade Burma. Yalta Conference.	Evelyn Waugh, *Brideshead Revisited.* Films: *Brief Encounter. The Way to the Stars.*

Bibliographical Note

The two principal characters in this book – Lloyd George and the Settlement itself– could each generate bibliographies of huge proportions, before even considering the possible contributions of the supporting cast. These are the sources that I have found especially helpful in preparing this modest addition to the vast array of literature.

There are many biographies of Lloyd George. Kenneth Morgan's 1974 biography, *Lloyd George,* in A J P Taylor's edited series on British Prime Ministers has been my overall guide in mapping the general outline of his life. Peter Rowland's massive single *Lloyd George* volume is both readable and informative, whilst John Grigg's four books (1973–2002) offer a very full and detailed account of his life and career up to the end of the First World War. Michael Fry analyses his early forays into international relations in *Lloyd George and Foreign Policy: Volume One The Education of a Statesman: 1890–1916* and Richard Toye explores his chequered relationship with Winston Churchill in *Lloyd George and Churchill.* The years of Lloyd George's peacetime premiership are sympathetically analysed by Kenneth Morgan in *Consensus and Disunity* and his career after

1922 by John Campbell in *Lloyd George: The Goat in the Wilderness*.

Lloyd George's relationship with Frances Stevenson is thoroughly covered by John Campbell in *If Love Were All* and A J P Taylor has edited and published Frances Stevenson's *Lloyd George: A Diary* and their letters to each other in *My Darling Pussy*. His wider circle of female friends is the subject of a new book by Ffion Hague, *The Pain and the Privilege: The Women in Lloyd George's Life*. Kenneth Morgan's edition of *Lloyd George: Family Letters 1885–1936* is another useful source of information about his family and friends.

The best historical insights into Lloyd George's performance at the Paris Peace Conference are to be found in Antony Lentin's books on *Guilt at Versailles: Lloyd George and the Pre-History of Appeasement* and *Lloyd George and the Lost Peace: From Versailles to Hitler*, together with Margaret MacMillan's splendid study of the Conference as a whole, *Peacemakers: The Paris Conference of 1919 and Its Attempt to End War*. Both have a tremendous eye for the telling quotation and write in an entertaining as well as an authoritative manner.

The best text of the Treaty of Versailles is the annotated edition *The Treaty of Versailles and After*, published by the United States government. It contains helpful commentaries and information on the execution of the various clauses. The remarkable *History of the Paris Peace Conference*, edited by H W V Temperley in 1920 and largely written by participants, is still an invaluable source of information on all aspects of the treaties, providing maps, statistics and document extracts, as well as an account of the decisions. J M Keynes' *Economic Consequences of the Peace* remains one of the great pieces of 20th-century polemical writing, and his descriptions of

Clemenceau, Wilson and Lloyd George are essential reading. His relationship with Lloyd George underwent several transformations, but when he wrote *Economic Consequences* and *Essays in Biography* he took a very negative view of the Prime Minister's performance and character. Harold Nicolson's *Peacemaking 1919*, James Headlam-Morley's *Memoir of the Paris Conference 1919* and Lord Riddell's *Intimate Diary of the Peace Conference and After* are also excellent contemporary sources for revealing remarks and anecdotes about the principal players.

Lloyd George himself wrote extensively on war and peace, quoting freely from contemporary government papers – something which occasioned Whitehall to evolve new policies for ex-ministers and the use they might make of their official papers. His *War Memoirs, The Truth about Reparations and War Debts,* and *The Truth about the Peace Treaties* are essential reading, but the reader should not take the claim about their being the truth too literally. Michael Fry (see above) has a good section on the 'The Problem: the Man and the Sources' on the way in which these books were written and how he was persuaded to revise some of the comments on his colleagues. Even so many remain both unforgiving and highly quotable.

There have been two major international seminars on the Paris Conference in the last 15 years. One held in 1994 had its proceedings published in 1998 as *The Treaty of Versailles: A Reassessment after 75 Years* edited by Manfred Boemeke, Gerald Feldman and Elisabeth Glaser. Michael Dockrill and John Fisher edited the proceedings of the 1999 conference in 2001 as *The Paris Peace Conference: Peace without Victory?*. Erik Goldstein *The First World War Peace Settlements 1919– 1925* and Alan Sharp *The Versailles Settlement: Peacemaking after the First World War* both offer succinct accounts of the settlement with full bibliographies. David Andelman's *A Shattered Peace: Versailles 1919 and the Price We Pay Today* represents an ambitious attempt to analyse the long-term effects of the settlement, whilst G John Ickenberry's *After Victory: Institutions, Strategic Restraint, and the Rebuilding of Order after Major Wars* seeks to compare the post-First World War experience with those of 1815, 1945 and the post-Cold War arrangements. The international history of the post-war years is brilliantly recorded in Zara Steiner's *The Lights That Failed: European International History 1919–1933*.

Bibliography

Unpublished sources
CAB and FO papers in the National Archive, Kew
Curzon Papers in the British Library
Hardinge Papers in the Cambridge University Library
Howard Papers in the Cumbria Archive Service, Carlisle
Papiers Henri Jaspar in the Archives du Royaume, Brussels
Lloyd George Papers in the House of Lords Record Office
Lothian Papers (Philip Kerr) in the National Library of
    Scotland, Edinburgh

Published official documents
K Bourne and D Watt (eds.), *British Documents on Foreign
    Affairs: Reports and Papers from the Foreign Office
    Confidential Print: The Paris Peace Conference of 1919*
    (7 Vols. University Publications of America: 1989)
Cmd 2169 *Papers Respecting Negotiations for an Anglo-
    French Pact* (HMSO: 1924)
R Butler and J, Bury (eds.), *Documents on British Foreign
    Policy 1919–1939* (First Series, HMSO: 1954 onwards)
A Link (ed.) (with the assistance of M Boemeke), *The
    Deliberations of the Council of Four (March 24–June*

28, 1918): Notes of the Official Interpreter, Paul Mantoux (2 vols Princeton: 1992)

P Mantoux, *Les Délibérations du Conseil des Quatre* (2 Vols Editions de Centre Nationale de la recherché scientifique: 1955)

——, *Paris Peace Conference 1919: Proceedings of the Council of Four, March 24 –April 18* (Libraire Droz: 1964)

The Treaty of Versailles and After: Annotations of the Text of the Treaty (Greenwood reprint, 1968, of original U S Government Printing Office: 1944)

United States Department of State, *Papers relating to the foreign relations of the United States, 1919. The Paris Peace Conference* (13 Vols , U S Government Printing Office, 1919)

Published diaries, letters and memoirs

Lord D'Abernon, *An Ambassador of Peace: Pages from the Diary of Viscount D'Abernon (Berlin 1920–1926)* (3 vols. Hodder and Stoughton: 1929–1930)

L S Amery, *The Leo Amery Diaries: Volume I, 1896–1919* (J Barnes and D Nicholson eds., Hutchinson: 1980)

P Cambon, *Correspondance* (3 Vols. Grasset: 1946)

N Chamberlain, *The Struggle for Peace* (Hutchinson: 1939)

W S Churchill, *The World Crisis – The Aftermath* (Butterworth: 1929)

G Clemenceau, *Grandeur and Misery of Victory* (Harrap: 1930)

Viscount Grey, *Twenty Five Years 1892–1916* (2 vols., Hodder and Stoughton: 1925)

M Hankey, *The Supreme Control at the Paris Peace Conference 1919* (Allen and Unwin: 1963)

Lord Hardinge, *Old Diplomacy* (John Murray: 1947)

A Headlam-Morley, R Bryant, A Cienciala (eds.), *Sir James Headlam-Morley: A Memoir of the Paris Peace Conference 1919* (Methuen: 1972)

E House and C Seymour (eds.), *What Really Happened at Paris* (Hodder and Stoughton: 1921)

A L Kennedy, *Old Diplomacy and New* (John Murray: 1922)

J M Keynes, *Economic Consequences of the Peace* (Macmillan: 1919)

R Lansing, *The Peace Negotiations: A Personal Narrative* (Houghton Mifflin: 1921)

D Lloyd George, *The Truth about Reparations and War Debts* (Heinemann: 1932)

——, *War Memoirs* (2 vol. edition, Odhams: 1938)

——, *The Truth about the Peace Treaties* (2 Vols. Victor Gollancz: 1938)

Frances Lloyd George, *The Years That Are Past* (Hutchinson: 1967)

K Morgan (ed.), *Lloyd George Family Letters 1885–1936* (University of Wales and Oxford University Press: 1973)

H Nicolson, *Peacemaking 1919* (Constable: 1933)

R Poincaré, *Au Service de la France* (11 vols. Plon: 1928–74)

Lord Riddell, *Intimate Diary of the Peace Conference and After, 1918–23* (Victor Gollancz: 1933)

——, *The Riddell Diaries, 1908–23* (edited by J McEwen, Athlone: 1986)

Comte de Saint-Aulaire, *Confession d'un Vieux Diplomate* (Flammarion: 1953)

C Seymour (ed.), *The Intimate Papers of Colonel House* (4 Vols., Ernest Benn: 1928)

E L Spears, *Liaison 1914: A Narrative of the Great Retreat* (Heinemann: 1930)

F Stevenson (ed. A J P Taylor), *Lloyd George: A Diary* (Hutchinson: 1971)

A Tardieu, *The Truth about the Treaty* (Bobbs-Merrill Co.: 1921)

R Vansittart, *The Mist Procession* (Hutchinson: 1958)

D Varè, *Laughing Diplomat* (John Murray: 1938)

J Vincent (ed.), *The Crawford Papers: The Journals of David Lindsay, 1892 to 1940* (Manchester UP: 1984)

T Wilson (ed.), *The Political Diaries of C P Scott 1911–1928* (Cornell UP: 1970)

Biographies

J Campbell, *Lloyd George: The Goat in the Wilderness* (Jonathan Cape: 1977)

——, *If Love Were All: The Story of Frances Stevenson and David Lloyd George* (Jonathan Cape: 2006)

D M Crieger, *Bounder from Wales: Lloyd George's Career before the First World War* (University of Missouri Press: 1976)

B Dugdale, *Arthur James Balfour* (2 Vols National Book Association Ed.: 1939)

M G Fry, *Lloyd George and Foreign Policy: Volume One The Education of a Statesman: 1890–1916* (McGill-Queen's University Press: 1977)

J Grigg *The Young Lloyd George* (Eyre Methuen: 1973)

——, *Lloyd George: The People's Champion, 1902–1911* (Eyre Methuen: 1978)

——, *Lloyd George: From Peace to War, 1912–1916* (Eyre Methuen: 1985)

——, *Lloyd George: War Leader* (Eyre Methuen, 2002)

F Hague, *The Pain and the Privilege: The Women in Lloyd George's Life* (Harper: 2008)

T Jones, *Lloyd George* (Oxford UP: 1951)

J M Keynes, *Essays in Biography* (Macmillan: 1933)

Richard Lloyd George *Lloyd George* (Frederick Muller: 1960)

K Morgan, *Lloyd George* (Book Club Edition: 1974)

H Nicolson, *Curzon: The Last Phase, 1919–1925 A Study in Post-War Diplomacy* (Constable: 1934)

M Pugh, *Lloyd George* (Longman: 1988)

S Roskill, *Hankey: Man of Secrets* (3 vols. Collins: 1970–74)

P Rowland, *Lloyd George* (Barrie and Jenkins: 1975)

A J Sylvester, *The Real Lloyd George* (Cassell: 1947)

R Toye, *Lloyd George and Churchill: Rivals for Greatness* (Macmillan: 2007)

Secondary sources

G J Bass, *Stay The Hand of Vengeance: The Politics of War Crimes Tribunals* (Second, paperback ed. Princeton UP: 2002)

M Boemeke, G Feldman, E Glaser (eds.), *The Treaty of Versailles: A Reassessment after 75 Years* (Cambridge UP: 1998)

R Bunselmeyer, *The Cost of the War 1914–1919: British Economic War Aims and the Origins of Reparation* (Archon Books: 1975)

Cato, *Guilty Men* (Gollanz: 1940)

I L Claude, *National Minorities* (Greenwood: 1969)

M Dockrill and D Goold, *Peace Without Promise: Britain and the Peace Conferences 1919–23* (Batsford: 1981)

G Egerton, *Great Britain and the Creation of the League of Nations: Strategy, Politics, and International Organisation, 1914–1919* (Scolar: 1979)

D Fromkin, *A Peace to End All Peace: The Fall of the Ottoman Empire and the Creation of the Modern Middle East* (Phoenix ed.: 2000)

E Goldstein, *Winning the Peace: British Diplomatic Strategy, Peace Planning and the Paris Peace Conference 1916–1920* (Clarendon Press: 1991)

K Hamilton and E Johnson (eds.), *Arms and Disarmament in Diplomacy* (Valentine Mitchell: 2007)

B Kent *The Spoils of War: The Politics, Economics, and Diplomacy of Reparations 1918–1932* (Clarendon pbk ed.: 1991)

J C King, *Foch versus Clemenceau: France and German Dismemberment 1918–19* (Harvard UP: 1960)

C Kitching, *Britain and the Problem of International Disarmament 1919–1934* (Routledge: 1999)

A Lentin, *Guilt at Versailles: Lloyd George and the Pre-History of Appeasement* (Methuen: 1985)

———, *Lloyd George and the Lost Peace: From Versailles to Hitler* (Palgrave: 2001)

W R Louis, *Great Britain and Germany's Lost Colonies* (Clarendon Press: 1967)

M MacMillan, *Peacemakers: The Paris Conference of 1919 and Its Attempt to End War* (John Murray: 2001)

S Marks, 'Behind the Scenes at the Paris Peace Conference of 1919' *Journal of British Studies* (Vol. 9 No. 2, 1970) pp 154–80

———, *Innocent Abroad: Belgium at the Paris Peace Conference of 1919* (University of North Carolina Press: 1981)

S Marks, 'Smoke and Mirrors: In Smoke-Filled Rooms and the Galerie des Glaces', in M Boemeke, G Feldman, E

Glaser (eds.), *The Treaty of Versailles: A Reassessment after 75 Years* (Cambridge UP: 1998)

E Monroe, *Britain's Moment in the Middle East 1914–1956* (University Paperbacks: 1963)

H I Nelson, *Land and Power: British and Allied Policy on Germany's Frontiers 1916–19* (Routledge and Kegan Paul: 1963)

F Owen, *Tempestuous Journey: Lloyd George, His Life and Times* (Hutchinson: 1954)

A Pollard, 'The Balance of Power', *Journal of the British Institute of International Affairs* Vol II (1923)

Mr Punch, *Lloyd George by Mr Punch* (Cassell: 1922)

H Purcell, *Lloyd George* (Haus: 2006)

A J Sharp, *The Versailles Settlement: Peacemaking at the End of the First World War, 1919–1923* (Second ed. Macmillan: 2008)

——, 'Britain and the Channel Tunnel, 1919–1920', *Australian Journal of Politics and History* Vol. XXV, No. 2 (1979) pp 210–5

——, 'Mission Accomplished? Britain and the Disarmament of Germany, 1918–1923' in K Hamilton and E Johnson (eds) *Arms and Disarmament in Diplomacy* (Valentine Mitchell: 2007) pp 73–90

Z Steiner, *The Lights That Failed: European International History 1919–1933* (Oxford UP: 2005)

D Stevenson, 'Britain, France and the Origins of German Disarmament, 1916–1919' *Journal of Strategic Studies* Vol. 29, No. 2 (2006) pp 195–224

S P Tillman, *Anglo-American Relations at the Paris Peace Conference of 1919* (Princeton UP: 1961)

H W V Temperley, *A History of the Peace Conference of Paris* (6 Vols. Oxford UP: 1920–4)

R M Watt, *The Kings Depart: The Tragedy of Germany: Versailles and the German Revolution* (Literary Guild ed.: 1968)

J F Willis, *Prologue to Nuremberg: The Politics and Diplomacy of Punishing War Criminals of the First World War* (Greenwood: 1982)

M E Yapp, *The Near East Since the First World War: A History to 1995* (Longman: 1996)

Picture Sources

The author and publishers wish to express their thanks to the following sources of illustrative material and/or permission to reproduce it. They will make proper acknowledgements in future editions in the event that any omissions have occurred.

Punch Library: p 54. Topham Picturepoint: pp viii, xii and 166.

Endpapers

The Signing of Peace in the Hall of Mirrors, Versailles, 28th June 1919 by Sir William Orpen (Bridgeman Art Library)
Front row: Dr Johannes Bell (Germany) signing with Herr Hermann Müller leaning over him
Middle row (seated, left to right): General Tasker H Bliss, Col E M House, Mr Henry White, Mr Robert Lansing, President Woodrow Wilson (United States); M Georges Clemenceau (France); Mr David Lloyd George, Mr Andrew Bonar Law, Mr Arthur J Balfour, Viscount Milner, Mr G N Barnes (Great Britain); Prince Saionji (Japan)
Back row (left to right): M Eleftherios Venizelos (Greece);

Dr Afonso Costa (Portugal); Lord Riddell (British Press);
Sir George E Foster (Canada); M Nikola Pašić (Serbia);
M Stephen Pichon (France); Col Sir Maurice Hankey,
Mr Edwin S Montagu (Great Britain); the Maharajah of
Bikaner (India); Signor Vittorio Emanuele Orlando (Italy);
M Paul Hymans (Belgium); General Louis Botha (South
Africa); Mr W M Hughes (Australia)

Jacket Images

(Front): akg Images.
(Back): *Peace Conference at the Quai d'Orsay* by Sir
William Orpen (akg Images).
Left to right (seated): Signor Orlando (Italy); Mr Robert
Lansing, President Woodrow Wilson (United States); M
Georges Clemenceau (France); Mr David Lloyd George, Mr
Andrew Bonar Law, Mr Arthur J Balfour (Great Britain);
Left to right (standing): M Paul Hymans (Belgium); Mr
Eleftherios Venizelos (Greece); The Emir Feisal (The
Hashemite Kingdom); Mr W F Massey (New Zealand);
General Jan Smuts (South Africa); Col E M House (United
States); General Louis Botha (South Africa); Prince Saionji
(Japan); Mr W M Hughes (Australia); Sir Robert Borden
(Canada); Mr G N Barnes (Great Britain); M Ignacy
Paderewski (Poland)

Index

NB All family relationships are to David Lloyd George, unless otherwise stated.

Makers of the Modern World

UK PUBLICATION: November 2008 to December 2010
CLASSIFICATION: Biography/History/
    International Relations
FORMAT: 198 × 128mm
EXTENT: 208pp
ILLUSTRATIONS: 6 photographs plus 4 maps
TERRITORY: world

Chronology of life in context, full index, bibliography innovative layout with sidebars

Woodrow Wilson: United States of America by Brian Morton
Friedrich Ebert: Germany by Harry Harmer
Georges Clemenceau: France by David Watson
David Lloyd George: Great Britain by Alan Sharp
Prince Saionji: Japan by Jonathan Clements
Wellington Koo: China by Jonathan Clements
Eleftherios Venizelos: Greece by Andrew Dalby
From the Sultan to Atatürk: Turkey by Andrew Mango
The Hashemites: The Dream of Arabia by Robert McNamara
Chaim Weizmann: The Dream of Zion by Tom Fraser
Piip, Meierovics & Voldemaras: Estonia, Latvia & Lithuania by Charlotte Alston
Ignacy Paderewski: Poland by Anita Prazmowska
Beneš, Masaryk: Czechoslovakia by Peter Neville
Károlyi & Bethlen: Hungary by Bryan Cartledge
Karl Renner: Austria by Jamie Bulloch
Vittorio Orlando: Italy by Spencer Di Scala
Pašić & Trumbić: The Kingdom of Serbs, Croats and Slovenes by Dejan Djokic
Aleksandŭr Stamboliĭski: Bulgaria by R J Crampton
Ion Bratianu: Romania by Keith Hitchin
Paul Hymans: Belgium by Sally Marks
General Smuts: South Africa by Antony Lentin
William Hughes: Australia by Carl Bridge
William Massey: New Zealand by James Watson
Sir Robert Borden: Canada by Martin Thornton
Maharajah of Bikaner: India by Hugh Purcell
Afonso Costa: Portugal by Filipe Ribeiro de Meneses
Epitácio Pessoa: Brazil by Michael Streeter
South America by Michael Streeter
Central America by Michael Streeter
South East Asia by Andrew Dalby
The League of Nations by Ruth Henig
Consequences of Peace: The Versailles Settlement – Aftermath and Legacy
    by Alan Sharp